“Reflections on Global Law”

"Reflections on Global Law"

Edited by

Shavana Musa
Eefje de Volder

BRILL

LEIDEN · BOSTON
2013

Also published as Volume 17, No. 2 (2013) of Brill's journal *Tilburg Law Review.*

This publication has been typeset in the multilingual "Brill" typeface. With over 5,100 characters covering Latin, IPA, Greek, and Cyrillic, this typeface is especially suitable for use in the humanities. For more information, please see www.brill.com/brill-typeface.

ISBN 978-90-04-26039-9 (hardback)
ISBN 978-90-04-26095-5 (e-book)

This book is printed on acid-free paper.

CONTENTS

A Short Foreword

Shavana Musa
Editor-in-Chief

The world has undoubtedly experienced some major changes within the last few decades – my inner historian would claim even earlier and beyond that – particularly, with respect to the workings of the State. The State, and all that makes it what it is, has certainly had a tumultuous life; a life, which does not intend to give up on its rebellious ways, in favour of an easy, calmer approach to all that it encounters. This is almost evidently a given when we think of how it has had to adapt to the ever-growing globalisation of the world in every facet of society and in particular, these facets' relationships to the law. Here is where a new friend – or foe, depending on how you view it – comes in: global law.

'Global law', which we have heard so much about recently, may be deemed as somewhat of an enigma. It is like the elderly hermit, living down the street from you. You know he's there, but what do you really know about him? Perhaps the bizarre rumours flying around the neighbourhood will provide some enlightenment; perhaps some newspaper archives shall have the answer. But what if you need definitive answers, what then?

Although the request for definitive answers on global law, may be a little idealistic – or perhaps even unattainable and rather a misconceived thought – it is time that an exploration of the relatively straightforward (at least at first glance) question of 'what is global law' occurred. This is even more so, in light of the fact that this year, and for many more years to come, the Tilburg Law School has been and will be responsible for many global law initiatives, including a new global law Bachelors degree and the signing of the Law Schools' Global League Constitution, with our very own Dean, Randall Lesaffer, as a founding Father.

In that spirit, what better way to celebrate the official birth of global law at Tilburg than to investigate this imperative subject matter and to act as a platform, where readers and writers alike can journey together in an attempt to discover global law's meaning; its utility as an approach to the changing nature of law in a globalising world; its connection to education and so on and so forth.

We have managed to obtain the involvement of many esteemed and excellent academics from various fields of law, including: methodology; international law; comparative law; private law; philosophy; economics; environmental; history, et cetera. This book is, without a doubt, a wonderfully diverse anthology of global law pieces, which will allow us to proceed one step closer to the crux of the enigma that is global law.

As a final word, I cannot end this foreword without paying tribute to those that made this book possible. Special thanks should first go to Morag Goodwin, who not only planted the source of inspiration for our involvement in the exciting global law initiatives taking place in Tilburg, but was a constant support throughout the whole process of putting this book together. Randall Lesaffer, Han Somsen and Machteld Geuskens were also excellent in their willingness to take the time to talk through ideas relating to global law and our involvement in the same.

Since this book was originally put together as part of a Tilburg Law Review summer publication, I must thank the TLR Executive and Editorial Board as well. All members of the Tilburg Law Review deserve the utmost recognition for their hard work, enthusiasm and initiative for making this book a success. I have to however, pay extra thanks to our Senior Article Editor, Eefje de Volder, whose determination and drive is one of the main reasons why this is out in print and, of whom, has gone beyond what is needed of an editor, making my job a lot easier.

Finally, many thanks must also be given to all the authors that have been kind enough to share their thoughts and knowledge on global law. I am positive that reading this book will surely illuminate our own views on the topic and bring us closer in answering that all important question: What is global law?

Interview with Professor Neil Walker*
Global Law: Another Case of the Emperor's Clothes?

Shavana Musa[a] & Eefje de Volder[b]
a) Editor-in-Chief of the Tilburg Law Review
PhD Researcher at the Public Law,
Jurisprudence and Legal History Department, Tilburg Law School
b) Executive Managing Editor of the Tilburg Law Review
PhD Researcher on the African Union's Collective Security System, Tilburg Law School

Abstract
Global law, in recent times, has seemed to have gained a life of its own: whether that be a new life or a new lease of life is certainly part of this exploration, but what is clear is that it appears to be at the forefront of the minds of many academics, especially within the legal field. This is in spite of the fact that there is still no definitive answer to what global law actually is. In this interview, Professor Neil Walker introduces us to his thoughts on the global law debate and concludes that global law is certainly more than just another case of the Emperor's clothes.

Keywords
global legal configuration; global law; constitutional pluralism; sovereignty; supranational law; transnational law; international law; law in development

What is the recent shift taking place within the nature of the state and how is it related to what you have previously described as a 'newly emerging global legal configuration'?

Probably the easiest way to begin to answer this from my perspective would be from my European perspective and then the global perspective. For years I worked in the European University Institute of Florence and there I was introduced to a really quite radically Europeanised version of law. The big debate when I was there was the debate about the collision between national constitutional courts and the European Court of Justice. To some

* Regius Professor of Public Law and the Law of Nature and Nations at Edinburgh University.

extent, the emphasis was on the German constitutional courts, but to some extent other constitutional courts too, such as Denmark, the House of Lords in the UK, the French Court, the Belgian Court etc. And the question was, what did sovereignty mean in the context of European integration? Did sovereignty still mean the idea that the national authority would have a monopoly on legal authority? Would it have the last word to all legal provisions relevant to the State? Or had we gone beyond that? Were we moving to a situation where authority had not only been delegated to transnational institutions like the UN (United Nations) or EU (European Union), but had actually been transferred irretrievably and irreversibly to these institutions?

Now of course the interesting thing was that there was no clear answer to that question. What was clear to me was that if you spoke to people in the national constitutional context, they tended to hang onto the old idea of national sovereignty, not just in Europe, but worldwide, which was very prevalent in the United States, but also in other continents as well. But if you talked to the new transnational centres of law, like the Court of Justice in Luxembourg or political organs of the EU and elsewhere, then they had a different perspective of the supremacy of their law. So, looking at this in a neutral way and trying to stand above that debate, as difficult as that is, what became clear was that there really was a genuine conflict of perspectives, where national authorities continued to think that they were sovereign, but supranationals were beginning to think they had a degree of sovereignty as well. So, there was no position above these that could necessarily resolve this debate.

To my understanding of this, and I coined the term 'late sovereignty' to describe this, was that late sovereignty was the situation where you could no longer talk about sites having exclusive and monopolistic legal authority, but what you could talk about was these sites having autonomous and independent legal authority. It would be overlapping legal authority and these overlaps would have to be resolved in a certain way, but we were now in a situation where previously, under the state based system, legal authorities were state based and therefore mutually exclusive, leaving aside imperialism where what you would have is hegemonic power. So you would either have hegemonic imperial power or you would have mutually exclusive power, but in the new legal order, what you had instead was overlapping authorities and all sorts of competitions at the margins.

One of my colleagues in Florence who was actually an Advocate General at the Court of Justice, Miguel Maduro, once described this very well by saying 'just imagine you're a Martian, looking down on Earth, and you look into national constitutional courts and you hear what they're saying and then you look into Luxembourg at the Court of Justice and you hear what they're saying ... you can't make any sense of it, you can't reconcile it. They all think they're sovereign, they all think they're supreme.' So, that's the world in which we live. Competing conceptions of sovereignty over overlapping areas of jurisdiction, so I think that is one major change that has taken place.

And is that embodied in your term of 'global legal configuration'? Is this what you mean when you use this term?

Yes, it is part of what I mean. It is a negative part of what I mean, in the sense that the old configuration was the state-based sovereignty, the one which is loosely and lazily called the Westphalian tradition, going back to the 17th century Peace of Westphalia, which was an attempt to say that religious authority had been overcome by secular authority and each king was a secular authority within his own state. There was a recognition of this between the states. Part of internal sovereignty was a mutual recognition between states. Now, when that begins to breakdown with new forms of globalisation, transnationalisation of economic, cultural processes, increasing interdependence, the development of supranational authority etc, you have this overlapping mosaic of authority and when I talk about the newly emerging global legal configuration that probably makes it sound more ordered than in fact it is.

In one of my papers, I actually talk about the 'disorder of orders'; the idea that what you have is not just all of these overlapping orders, but competing perspectives on the relationship between these orders. For example, international law has developed hugely in recent years. People have started talking about the constitutionalisation of international law. Why? Well, one of the reasons of doing that is that there is a recognition that there are more and more clashes between, say, international human rights law for example and state law. And peoples' sense of legal order compels them to try and find some kind of secondary principle that will resolve relationships between these different sorts of legal orders. So, they come up with new terms like global administrative law, international constitutional law: terms which presumptively try to resolve these relationships; often in favour of the higher order law, for example, some of the more pluralist approaches, which we will talk about later, also try to resolve the relationship between these, but not necessarily in favour of the higher order law.

For someone like me, who spends his life looking at this, there is a whole market of ideas for resolving the 'disorder of orders'. Some people talk about the universal code of legality. Patrick Glenn for example talks about the new common law, which is much different from the old English common law, but which is based on the idea that every positive legal system has a reversal set of common law principles behind it. Jeremy Waldron has talked about the new *ius gentium*; going back to the law of the peoples and saying that this is a new idea which is finding its time again in the new age of international human rights law etc. So what we have is a whole new vocabulary, which is trying to make sense of the 'newly emerging global legal configuration' and the very diversity of that vocabulary is one of the features of that emerging configuration.

How does global law differ from terms such as transnational, international, supranational et cetera?

Let us start by defining these terms.

Supranational has always been used for these very strong regional legal regimes, which somehow stand above the state and stand in a presumptively superior relationship to the state, so European law would be the paradigm case of that. But if you look at the African Union, if you look at NAFTA, the World Trade Organisation etc, you see at least, tentative movements towards some kind of supranational law there and what you need for supranational law is like a constitutional structure above the state, you probably need a court, you probably need some notion of supremacy of the law, you probably need some kind of legislative to generate the law, you probably need some kind of executive body with some degree of discretion. So, supranational law is not an exact term, but it is saying that you are looking at the relationship between law within the state and law beyond the state. And if the law beyond the state is able to dictate the relationship with the state then you are moving towards supranational law.

International law is the old fashioned term for the law between states/sovereigns, although there is an even older version of *ius gentium*, the law of peoples, where there is a putative sense of global law. Most people today would see international law as being the cousin to the notion of constitutional law: so within the Westphalian state-based system, internally of constitutional law, externally you have international law between these different constitutional states. One of the interesting things that is happening is that international law itself is being re-made, by both public international law and private international law. Traditionally though, international law is the old fashioned term for the law between states.

Transnational law is law that crosses states, where it is not necessarily mediated by the states. International law has to be mediated by the states. Supranational law has to be accepted by the states. Both these forms of law operate within the domain of public law. Transnational law doesn't. Transnational law could be the law of the internet, *lex mercatoria*, the various tentative efforts to having unified private law codes within Europe, law of football under FIFA – sports law. So, transnational law is impervious to boundaries, it is a different kind of term. It is based on an idea that is a vertical set of relationships, which are cutting across.

So, all of that is by way of introduction to what is global law and is it a different type of law? I think global law has two sets of meanings, which have an interesting relationship to each other. One is what you might call global-level law or planetary law, what I call 'globally extensive law': an idea of law that extends across the globe. And what is true in much of the post-national legal thinking is that there is an increasing attempt to think about global-level law, whether that be general principles of international law, *ius cogens*, whether there be the idea of peak institutions perhaps in the context of a reformed UN, whether it be attempts to re-think law in terms of a global imagination of *ius gentium* or a notion of some kind of universal common law or what Klaus Günther calls it, a 'universal code of legality'. He is a Habermasian scholar who believes that beneath every legal system there is a general code which allows all legal systems to communicate with each other. So, there is no end of these sorts of ideas.

There are also more concrete ideas, such as global constitutional law, global administrative law. Think of global administrative law for a second: what it says is that if you look at any administrative system, you will find that it will respect several general principles, such as: always listen to the other party; no-one should get judged on their own cause; the duty to give reasons and so on. And what global administrative law says is that why should these be rules that are confined to the state. There are many contexts where law emerges spontaneously in certain situations, say the law of the internet, where you have a system for regulating the registration of the names and numbers on the internet. What global administrative law is saying is that regardless of the political providence of these rules, surely that given that each of these rules has a user community and a producer community, the sorts of logic that says the duty to give reasons, the duty to hear that aside, also applies to these sorts of behaviours. Then you add the dramatic adjective 'global' to this and suddenly you have the notion of a globally administrative law, so administrative law is no longer something which is locked within the state, but is something that is globally effective aswell. So, even there what you have is a global dimension to it.

You also have global legal pluralism, which we will come back to, where the emphasis is on the interface of norms, the oil which keeps the chain of global legality together. It is more about connecting the parts than it is about having a hierarchy and looking all the way down. We also have the new hybrid law, where authors think that some of the old terminology, even like international law, is inappropriate. For example, Ruti Teitel is well known for her work on transnational justice and has recently written a book on the law of humanity. What she is saying is that there is a shift from security as a hard physical concept to a notion of human security. In the end, even with areas as diverse as international criminal law and humanitarian law, there is a new merging towards a new law of humanity.

Christine Bell is talking about a new law of peace, where there is a relationship between international law and constitutional law, backing each other up in a transitional justice context to developing new global rules of peace. So what you have there are not just different candidates for global law, but very different ways of thinking of how you even come up with an idea of global law to start with. The one thing they have in common though is a notion of there being some kind of global level to legal principles.

Now, alongside that is another notion where global law becomes a three dimensional, rather than two dimensional, concept, where it is not just the surface of the planet, but the idea that global law is something holistic, something which includes the whole. Now that is probably the other, more contentious use of the idea of global law. People can cope with thinking about global law as two dimensional, but when you say you have to look at law as something three dimensional, as something that takes in the entirety of the globe and relates to all different levels of global law together, I think people would be more concerned about it. They would say, where does this coherence come from? Is this a normative project? Is it a Western project? Is it a project of elites? Is it a project of the United Nations? What might this be? My sense is that in so far as we can think about it, it is something less than that. It is a new paradigm of thought. It is not a new concept. Global law isn't something we can find which will carve its way through everything else and shows how everything relates to each other. Its a good way of naming a new paradigm of thought, a new orientation, where there is partly reference to these global level laws, but also to the intricacies of relationships to other things. People increasingly think of the global whole as a global whole.

My lecture is called 'intimations of global law' and part of that is to try to suggest that this is something which is very unrealised. It is in a process of becoming and probably will always be in a process of becoming. But today, we live in a world, where just because of the interconnectedness that I mentioned earlier in the European context and elsewhere, we cannot pretend that national laws are mutually protected and compartmentalised. We know there is a global dimension to law. We know that global humanity and intervention, such as it may be, is a global issue. We know that the Arab Springs is a global issue. We know that the sovereign debt crisis is a global issue. We know that the solution to these things has global permutations. Someone talked about the fact that we live in an age of the global imaginary. We imagine ourselves not just as national subjects, but global ones. Many of the political movements of the last 40 years have been global movements: feminism; environmentalism. You cannot say that these started in one country, or even developed a lot of their resonance in one country. These are ideas that, almost by their nature, circulate globally. Also, many of the ideas that scare people in the modern age, such as global imperialism, global jihad, are ideas that people view as global. So there is a sense in which our mentality, our starting position, is one which is quite global. And this is a point which is quite underestimated.

The current generation takes this for granted. My generation has lived through it, probably more so. But if I think about what I think about law now, as someone who has been doing this on and off for 30 years, it is very different. I am a very different person from the guy that did a law degree in Scotland over 30 years ago, who studied Scots law, Scottish Constitutional law, English Constitutional law, who had a vague idea of something called Europe and something called international law, who then went to work in Florence and then discovered the intensity of European law, who then started thinking about global law. At the same time, the world was changing, the global polity was evolving in a much much more interconnected way. Just as if you grow old with people you don't see the changes, you grow old with yourself you don't see the changes, but there have been profound changes in my lifetime.

I know that Tilburg is going to start a new Bachelors degree in global law. This would have been unthinkable 30 years ago. Today, it seems interesting, innovative, certainly not ridiculous and very much part of the *zeitgeist*.

What are the challenges of the changes you have described and how can we overcome them?

One of the things that I would say there is the way that I think of globalisation and global law as not that they are a good thing or a bad thing, they're bigger than that, they're just things that are happening. Of course human agency is involved in all of these things. Lets face it, global law comes from so many different motives. It comes from the motive of transnational capital trying to facilitate itself. Many of the critiques at the WTO for example are that it's simply the hand maiden for a certain type of neo-liberal transnational order, which is a bit unfair. Of course the reality is that it is a political debate within the WTO about what it is. But many of the other transnational institutes that we talk about are precisely ways of trying to overcome or deal with or inhibit forms of private power, which would otherwise easily escape from public authority into transnational no-mans land.

So, global law stands at a very complex dialectical relationship with a whole range of global movements and that whole range of global movements is really something which you have to describe as the emergence of a kind of global polity, not state, but as a global polity, where the same kinds of huge fault-mine debates, which we've always had in the state, say between free markets, solidaristic re-distribution between right and left or identity debates between cosmopolitanism and communitarianism or the emphasis upon cultural particularity. These two major faultlines of modern politics are now replicated, complicated at a global level. So global law, globalisation, isn't a good thing or a bad thing, its a description of the way in which these things are taking place.

Now clearly there are challenges here, there is a huge challenge of democratic deficit. The only supranational organisation which even comes close to making any kind of democratic claim is probably the EU, except that we know that it is constantly criticised for its democratic deficit. One answer to that is that there is a huge democratic deficit within states: people don't vote; people aren't interested in politics; people realise that other states are deciding their fate, so the state itself isn't enough for your democratic voice to be vindicated. The fact that states themselves aren't the perfect situation doesn't mean that we shouldn't worry about the lack of transnational democracy, so that is one major issue.

Another major issue is cultural universalism versus cultural relativism. If you look at the debate over international human rights, there is a tremendous clash between those who see the universality of human rights as being a very good thing about global law and those who see it as being the hegemon of the West, imposing their idea on them. We are used to universality, particularity debates within states. Take France for example, it has a history of trying to impose some abstract universal notion of citizenship upon a multicultural community; the whole idea of the state being neutral. Now that has been very controversial, but you multiply that to the global level and it becomes all the more controversial. The stakes are much higher on all sides. So there are all sorts of issues there.

There is also the issue of the very idea of some kind of general authority and I don't mean a world government, but one of the features of our modern understanding of law is – and it is very much a modern understanding of law – coinciding it with the development of the nation state in the 17th, 18th and 19th century. It is a post-medieval understanding of law; an understanding which says that the world is something we can make over in our own terms. We are effectively in charge of our own destiny, which is a secular destiny. People might still have their religious faiths, but nevertheless, the game of politics is effectively people taking charge of their own destiny and deciding what that destiny might be.

Now under the Westphalian system, that worked for some people at least. There is a notion of mutually exclusive orders you get to make your world within its own space. Obviously, it doesn't work if you are in that part of the world where you are the victims of imperialism of the Westphalian order, which is always the dark side of the order. It was never about every state in the world, it tended to be about European states, but nevertheless, there is a notion there that for some people that modernist idea makes sense. The problem with globalism and globalisation is that no one writes the script anymore within the global legal order and there is no way therefore that we can imagine that we are collective writers of a single script. Thank god some people are of the secular equivalent, but the danger then is that it is seen as something that is out of control, that people are buffeted by all sorts of forces including legal forces which they are not necessarily controlled by. So, again one of the challenges of global law is how do we reconcile its diversity with some notion that law is still something that we are collective controllers of. So these are incredible challenges and they are not going away.

Could you describe the idea of constitutional pluralism and how it could benefit the debate on global law?

Constitutional pluralism is a notion which I have been associated with in my work and again it is one which originated in the European context and I think what is central to the notion of constitutional pluralism is a mixture of a recognition, on the one hand that states continue to have a high degree of investment in the control of their own law and the recognition on the other hand that they have to sometimes listen to external authorities, who may on certain subjects have a greater degree of legitimacy. The idea of constitutional pluralism isn't just about states, it is about any regime – it could be a state regime, it could be a transnational regime, it could be a global regime – and it is about them showing each other mutual respect, accepting the inevitability of an overlap between different legal systems and trying to find some kind of meta rules or rules in the margins which can resolve this.

So let's take an example, let's take the famous *Kadi* case. I will say something about it because your audience probably doesn't know about it. It has been a famous case over the last few years. It was a case which came before the European Court of Justice and what *Kadi* was about was what the relation should be between European law and United Nation resolutions when it came to confiscating assets of people who were on the lists as terrorist suspects after 9/11. So what we had were all these UN rules which were very strong about the confiscation of assets and which sought to impose these regulations upon both national and regional authorities for security purposes and the question was whether the EU had any autonomy simply to say that we are not going to accept the position of the UN rules here.

How it was resolved was by the EU saying that we are a polity in our own right, we believe in something called European values, we have our own notion of democracy, we have our own notion of integrity and we also have our own fundamental rules about freedom of property, freedom of information etc etc, so we do not accept this blanket resolution from the UN. So that is an example of what I would call constitutional pluralism, where the European Court did not disregard the global authority of the UN, they recognised that the UN was involved in some kind of global security situation, it did not say that it was pointless and nameless. But what they said was what we have to do as a European Court is not just think about what we want to do but think about the relationship between our constitutional values and other constitutional values and we may find ourselves in some kind of clash.

So what you are asking courts to do, I am trying to think of a way of describing this, what you are asking a court to do in that situation is somehow standing outside itself and say: 'I am not just a guardian of this legal order, I am also an interlocutor in a global legal order where we have to think about the relationship between what we do and what others do.'

Let's take another example, the German Constitutional Court, which over the last six months has had to resolve all sorts of cases about the authority of Germany to be involved in financial restructuring plans around Greece, Spain and so on. There are all sorts of quotations within the German constitution which safeguard the federal principle, the democratic principle. And the German Constitutional Court has said, in these sorts of situations that if the Executive is going to sign Germany up for arrangements, which will involve a significant transfer of fiscal resources of the state, then these things have to go through the national parliament: even though that might be politically impossible. What it has to do is it has to find some kind of balance between respecting that idea that is fundamental to the idea of German constitutional authority, is the democratic will of the German people with the notion that the European Union cannot survive unless there is some idea of fiscal solidarity between the states. So you are asking courts to be both custodians and mediators at the same time. And that might seem an impossible thing to do but I think increasingly this is what we do ask courts to do.

Let me take one final example. The Canadian Constitutional Court years ago had to look at the question of the secession of Quebec from Canada. The Constitutional Court in that case ruled - its job partly as a custodian of the constitution - under the constitutional rules that Quebec had no unilateral right to secede. Quebec's argument was partly the historical argument about the legality of the Canadian Constitution, but there was also an argument that said if you are the unhappy part of the Federation, and one of the things you might be unhappy about are the very rules of the breakup of the Federation. So if the people of Quebec unilaterally get to the situation to decide to be a part of another constitutional entity then surely you have to take that seriously, notwithstanding what the rules of the game actually are.

What the Canadian Constitutional Court said was, yes, we have to think of ourselves as the custodians of the Canadian Constitution, but we also have to think of ourselves as implicated in a plural situation, where this relation is between the Canadian people and some other category of people, putatively the Quebec people. So what we are introducing is a new expectation, a new duty, a new obligation on the part of the Canadian government, to negotiate in good faith the prospects and the possibility of independence. In other words, they should not set their stall against this, they should not use narrow legalistic objections against Quebec referendum etc. So that is a very good example of a court standing outside its role as custodian of a particular constitutional order, recognising the existing situation of constitutional overlap and constitutional plurality and taking on this additional mediating role.

So I have given you a few examples of how that might work, but to anticipate your next question of: 'how do you actually generalise what these principles should be?' Well, that is a very difficult thing to do because if there were another set of general principles above the constitutional rules then you would be getting globalism in that kind of top down way. What we are talking about here is just an openness of constitutional courts to the fact that there are other constitutional entities that there are other polities with their constitutional bodies as well and it is no longer the role of a supreme court within a legal order to have the last word, to batten down the hatches, to say it is this legal order against all other legal orders ('the world'). Increasingly, it is the role of the last and the top court to actually mediate the relationship between its legal order and other legal orders. That, in a nutshell, is what constitutional pluralism offers.

How are the developments that are taking place changing our legal education? How is it changing for our future students?

Big question! It changes all sorts of ways. If we go back to that distinction between global level and globally holistic: there is a difference between programmes which think about global law as a single entity - I'll come to that in a moment - but also what you might call global level, that is new global networks. So this week, think of this idea of the Global College of Law Schools, which has been launched at Tilburg. There are other network ideas, like old European ideas such as Erasmus, which were not global, but European. The idea of multi centred legal, either institutions of professional practice or institutions of education, so that is one way.

The more interesting question is the actual object of the education itself and in what sense that might be global. What I would say to that is that what you have to do in any legal education, I think, is somehow be aware of the fact that calling something global is not mutually exclusive with recognising that everyone still operates within a national jurisdiction.

So for example, one of the best global law journals is something called the German Law Journal, which is an online journal, run by a friend of mine, called Peer Zumbansen. It is a wonderful idea because it is not about German law; it is about how German law meets the world. It is about how law looks like from the perspective of Germany, which is a very different thing from German law. So what it says is that from a perspective of Germany, German domestic law is important, but just as if not more important is the relation between German domestic law and European law, German domestic law and ECHR law, German domestic law and WTO law. Also, no interested legal German could be uninterested in other relationships, say between British and Dutch constitutional law and EU law and ECHR law because that would impact upon them and this interconnected world aswell.

So there is a sense that globality is about deep interconnectedness, but it can still come from a particular perspective. In other words, what makes law global from that perspective is not that there is some view from nowhere - for instance a global view as opposed to a national view - it is that all of the national views and all of the regional views now incorporate the global dimension. So, I think that is very, very important.

Now that means, I think, that probably there is still going to be a better future or an easier future for global law programmes, which see themselves as looking both at domestic legal systems and looking from a perspective of that domestic legal system at the world (looking at things globally) than there would be for programmes which are purely global. I know that Tilburg, for example, is going to develop a global Bachelors degree and that global Bachelor will not qualify these people as Dutch lawyers. Now, that is alright; provided that there is a recognition that the totality of legal education will continue to incorporate both a domestic dimension and a global dimension. What I think probably, in a normal way, what is most likely to happen is that a larger percentage of people's legal education will, in the model of the German Law Journal, be looking at things beyond the state: international or transnational law; aspects of private law, whether it would be contract or tort, whatever which are more international in nature, often without even naming it as such because often these things are just kind of deeply implicated in the changing practice of these different sorts of subjects.

One other thing which I think is important here is that its probably linked to certain ways in which we are changing the way that we think about legal education. I think legal education, probably, increasingly, is not so much about people learning a canonical body of knowledge. When I was educated, you had to know 230 contract cases which were vital, 70 criminal law cases etc and obviously that remains important, but one of the reasons why you had to have such knowledge at your fingertips was because we did not live in a computerised age, so you actually did have to internalise knowledge in many ways because it wasn't right away accessible. Now I think one of the things that legal academics are most better at, including young legal academics, is simply knowing how to access information. So an awful lot about education is now about the combination of understanding general principles and understanding methodologies of accessing information. If you do that, if you shift legal education in that direction, I think it allows you to have a wider horizon, a wider perspective, on the sorts of subjects you can do because you don't have to spend all your time learning all the rules. That might be controversial to some people, but I think to some extent that is how it might change.

But once you still have national law as a starting point from which you look at other relevant fields of law, doesn't your national perspective then still limit you? Or would it be better then to have more knowledge about all kinds of systems, rather than the other way around? What would you say about that?

I am not against that. It is a complicated point. Part of the global awareness is an awareness of both transnationality and other systems, so it is both comparative and transnational. So if you look at online journals like global jurists, it still very much describes itself as a comparative law journal, interestingly, it doesn't describe itself as a transnational journal. And I think one of the reasons it does that, is that there is a recognition that in practice you are going to be a good lawyer than you actually have to go about national systems, it is not just about transnational law, but also there is a recognition that self-understanding comes from being able to situate yourself in a comparative continuum, in a comparative context. I understand an awful lot more about what it is to be a Scottish lawyer or even a UK lawyer through having had a lot of access, exposure, to continental legal systems. I understand the significance of common law precedent, custom, parliamentary sovereignty, far more, by seeing it in sharp relief against the alternatives. So I think it is important to understand our systems.

What I would insist upon, though, is that people are still primarily located within a particular system. That doesn't mean that they have to somehow unproblematically inhabit the worldview of that system. It just means that people are rooted somewhere. And it may well be that 80% of what you are doing as a contract lawyer in America is the same as 80% of what you are doing as a contract lawyer in Germany, but you are still rooted somewhere else, there is still a different set of perspectives there.

Related to that, I think maybe another implicit in your point, is that one of the features of the globalisation of law is the differentiation or segmentalisation; it becomes more important to be a contract lawyer than to be a German lawyer. And that is true to some extent. That is part of what the globalisation of legal education actually does. Edinburgh, for example, is very strong in intellectual property law and I see my intellectual property colleagues and they don't think of themselves as Scottish lawyers, they think of themselves as IP lawyers, particularly in the Internet age. An awful lot of their examples, their thinking is drawn from the transnational context. They don't show that; it is taken for granted, it is just done naturally. So there is that aspect as well and that is in recognition of the fact that probably more and more lawyers will be people who specialise in particular areas.

However, I think there is a balance there. I think both practically there will always be an awful lot of people who see themselves as general practitioners so to speak. So they need to have that holistic understanding of their own legal system. For them too, it becomes increasingly important that they understand how their system operates within the world. It is also important that you have people who understand the national system as a whole as well because at the end of the day law is also a political object, it is also a political product, of a national system. People should not see themselves as just happening to be locally situated lawyers of some sort of transnational practice.

A lot of my friends are criminal lawyers and many of them are very good transnational criminal lawyers. But the very best of them, I think, still have a very close understanding of what is distinctive about their national order, historically, but also in a contemporary way. How their national criminal law fits into, say, notions of fault, which you might find in civil law etc. So still an awful lot of legal understanding is nationally based as well. That is why I want to insist that a global lawyer is someone who sees it as a merger of a national perspective and a global perspective.

Do you think global law is a product of western thought and perspective?

Who am I to answer that question? Clearly, there is always a double bind, there is a paradox in these sorts of debates, both in the general global law debate, but also say in something like global human rights, which I have been writing about recently because either you treat these as western concepts, which may have the virtue of some kind of honesty, but also have a terrible arrogance; these western concepts nevertheless are treated as the master concepts, which define everything else. Or you genuinely put them forward as global concepts, which has the danger of being a fraud - something which is actually western, but dressed up as global - but has a virtue of at least aspiring to be global.

Now if you look at the global human rights debate, for example, you look at some of the different positions on the universality of human rights. Russia says for example, human rights is a genuine global discourse and the important thing is not to bang on about cultural differences, but to understand that if you are an Asian talking about this then it is incredibly important to pursue certain sorts of rights - economic and social rights - which have never been at the centre of the western canon, but which are compatible with and which have been at least contentious parts of the western canon: if you go back to 1948 and the USSR saying social and economic rights should come before first generation classic liberal freedom rights. Saying that any tradition is more open to struggle than you think it is. So rather say: 'give up on that tradition, it is an unreconstructed western tradition', see the tradition itself as being something very open, and something which can be participated in, added to, become genuinely globalised. That is one view.

There is another view. Someone like Upandra Baxi for example would say that some of these traditions are deeply hardwired, it is in their DNA that they put the individual first. There is a deep celebration of the global autonomous individual within this. It is not about changing human rights, it is about needing a new vocabulary.

Now my view is more the first view. I don't think that any of these concepts is so unreconstructable. I don't think that. I think we all have a moral duty to say what is the least worst way of proceeding. For me the least worst way of proceeding is always to start with the imaginable and the imaginable for me are the better more progressive discourses that we have transnationally, including discourses of global human rights but also discourses of say global parliamentarialism, in terms of the UN etc. I am not a huge advocate of a global parliament. I am just saying that for me the more constructive debates are the ones which are often inaugurated by the global south, which precisely try to come to terms with concepts which may know their history in the west. The point I would make is that often the western history is more a history of struggle, is more of an open history and is often conceded by those who are critical of western hegemony within these debates.

Can global law really be attained? Is it just another case of the Emperor's clothes?

Let me come back to some of the things I was saying at the beginning, this distinction between two dimensional global law and three dimensional global law. We cannot deny that today there is more globally extensive law, either at the hard level doctrine world order treaties etc or in terms of the way that people are thinking about it breaking ideas of global administrative law etc, which aren't just academic inventions. They are attempts to come to terms with hiatuses, certain gaps within global legality. So there is a global level. Now with the notion of a global law, what I am saying is that we should neither think that it is an aim to have a single global law or a single global legal system, nor should we think that it stands there as some kind of legislative ideal against which we can criticise actual practice. What I am saying though, is that increasingly in the world there is a paradigm shift: people are thinking, situating themselves as legal scholars, legal thinkers and even legal practitioners in a world which is globally connected. That idea is not going to go away.

The way in which that is contested, the way in which these matters are resolved and not resolved. For example, it is hard to imagine that anyone in my lifetime and your lifetime who is interested in human rights, for example, who will not have to constantly revisit the very subject that I just talked about there, which is what is the relationship between the universal and the particular, how seriously do we take group rights, how seriously do we take race hate law, how seriously do we take religious hate law, what is the relationship between dignity and the freedom of expression; questions about reproductive freedom? These questions are not going to go away and anytime that we will address these questions we are not just going to be asking ourselves moral questions about what is the right answer, we are going to ask ourselves meta-moral questions about who gets to decide what the right answer is. These questions are not going to go away, they are not easily going to resolve themselves, but these are questions which necessarily impose themselves upon us because of the new global horizons of law. That is all I mean by law having a global paradigm. You can't get away from these sorts of things and it is a good thing that people can't get away from that.

It comes back to some of the things that I was saying about constitutional pluralism. Lawyers have to see themselves increasingly as people who inhabit the in-between spaces between different systems, between different cultures. They don't just have to defend, they are not just custodians, they are also mediators. They are also people between these different sorts of orders. That may sound very big and it is, but I think that is the inevitability of the global horizon that people have to continuously situate themselves in. And there are some very positive things about that as well: the attempt, for example, to think about global administrative rules. So what you do there is you start with some ideas and say okay can we push the envelope? Can we actually get any agreement for the applicability of these rules at a global level? Maybe not. You have got to start from somewhere. You have to start with these sorts of ideas. And knowing that what you are doing is not simply evoking traditional authority anymore. It is more a form of a kind of entrepreneurship of ideas, you are pushing a set of ideas and seeing how successful they might be, how adaptable they might be to new global contexts.

Of course there is a downside to this as well. There is a whole rhetoric around globalism and global law and everyone jumps on the bandwagon. The well-known scholar John Alston once talked about what he called the 'civilising effect of hypocrisy'. What he meant by that was that often we have ideas imposed upon us because it becomes part of our culture. Take European law for example, here are two notions: European citizenship and subsidiarity; two notions which are central to European Law. At the time they were coined, no one really knew what they meant. What does subsidiarity mean? This is something that comes from church law, what does it mean? What is European citizenship? Seems like an oxymoron. We are national citizens, what does it mean?

Within that debate you would have people who would take it seriously, who genuinely were interested in these as coin breaking ideas. There were people that were saying that this is the rhetoric of the day, we have to deal with it. But all these people have to operate within a public debate. So if you are operating with new notions, then whatever your motivation might be, the very fact that you want to be a plausible contributor to the debate has a civilising effect.

So I am not one of these people who say, that the emperor has no clothes and that global law can't mean anything because people are just jumping on the bandwagon. They are not. They are jumping on the debate which has more or less cynical input from all sorts of different parties and if they want to be seen as participants of that debate, they have to participate in it at its highest level otherwise they will not be effective participants within that debate. So, if someone started a global law programme tomorrow, which was 95 % domestic law and 5% foreign law, then no one would think that that is what we mean with global law anymore. Or if someone would start a global law program, which simply was about the global transposition of western values, then there would be major objections because people are tuned to the sensitivities, the subtleties surrounding the subject that perhaps once they weren't.

So yes, global law is to some extent still a shot in the dark. It is about people entering a field, sometimes opportunistically, sometimes not; trying to make a fast buck; trying to make an intellectual reputation quickly, sometimes not. But I think many, many debates in law are like that and in a sense I think the debate has its own momentum and has its own development and I think many genuine positive things can be achieved through this.

The Lighthouse of Law*

Randall Lesaffer
Dean, Tilburg Law School; Professor of Legal History
Tilburg University and Katholieke Universiteit Leuven
r.c.h.lesaffer@tilburguniversity.edu

Abstract
The mere use of the terms 'globalization' and 'global law' is ripe with dangers, as if often causes the academic debate to slip towards the all too simple question of how much global law there really is. In fact, these are container terms which have become fashionable to indicate the historic and paradigmatic shift law is undergoing. Under it are caught three fundamental and interrelated evolutions which are dramatically changing the way we practice, teach and research law: the turn from systemic, disciplinary and methodological monism towards systemic, disciplinary and methodological pluralism. In this perspective and in the light of the challenges these shifts bring to the world of legal practice and academia, 'global law' becomes more than the sum of those legal rules and concepts which are truly global. It gains some of the function the *ius commune* of late-medieval Europe had: that of a lighthouse to which all the ships and boats of local law have to steer to.

Keywords
global law; legal history; ius commune; Roman law; international law; globalization

Since the end of the Cold War (1989), the interest of legal academia in globalization has vastly grown. The financial crisis of the West, which started in 2008, has put globalization center-stage and made it into one of the most fiercely debated issues in legal academia. In the debate, the term 'global law' is increasingly forwarded as shorthand to indicate the new or coming reality of law under the impact of globalization.

'Global law' is an umbrella term that covers many aspects of a process which is far from unequivocal and even farther from having attained any kind of conclusion.[1] It carries its dangers. One of these is that the sole use

---

* This paper is based on the introduction rendered at the First Annual Global Law Conference of the Law Schools Global League at Tilburg on 22 June 2012.

[1] In the Montesquieu Lecture, which he rendered at the occasion of the Global Law Conference at Tilburg on 21 June 2012, entitled 'Intimations of Global Law', Neil Walker indicated no less than seven dimensions of the term.

of it causes the debate to slip towards the all too simple question of how much global law there is and allows the opponents of the idea to reduce its relevance with the remark that ultimately there is little law which is truly global.

But that is not the heart of the matter. The relevant question is not how much law there is which is truly applied globally; the relevant question is how much impact globalization has and is going to have on the way we practice, teach and research law? Global law is not just a reality; it is also an ambition, a direction, maybe an end goal.

The heart of the matter is that law is a global phenomenon. This in itself is nothing new as this has been the case for all of recorded history, but it is a fact which has become far more relevant in our space in history. As we trade more, travel more, migrate more, intermarry more, communicate more across national borders and continents than ever before, we have more need for law that transcends national and cultural borders along with us. And as the great challenges of our age – such as climate change, energy shortage, security, nuclear proliferation, migration, sustainability of our financial system – have become global, we are forced to become global ourselves and develop a legal framework that allows us to address these problems in an adequate way.

At this point, a reference can be made to Sir Hersch Lauterpacht (1897-1960), one of the finest minds of the 20th century and of who applied himself to what was then the still fairly marginal subject of public international law. Lauterpacht, who was a student of Hans Kelsen (1881-1973),[2] asked himself what the 'fundamental rule' (*Grundnorm*) of international law was. His simple answer was that it was the mere existence of an international community.[3] When Lauterpacht wrote this in the 1930s, *that* international community was still very much thought of in terms of a community of States and the 'global law' that ruled it was a law solely applicable to States. But Lauterpacht was one of the earliest and staunchest proponents of the return of the individual on the scene of international law – mainly through the international protection of human rights – and thus the extension of the body of 'global law' outside the confines of public international law. Writing in the 1950s, Lauterpacht acknowledged that positive international law was still very much based on the fundaments of an international

2 Elihu Lauterpacht, *The Life of Hersch Lauterpacht, QC, FBA, LLD* (Cambridge University Press 2010) 22-27.

3 Hersch Lauterpacht, *The Function of Law in the International Community* (Oxford University Press 1933) 420-423.

society of States, but that this international society should, at the same time, be thought of as a community of human beings.[4]

Since the midst of the 20th century, the body of 'global law' in the narrow sense of rules that are globally applied has grown beyond the confines of traditional public international law, as we have seen the growth of an unprecedented mass of international law in relation to trade, business, environment or human rights. As globalization goes further, this will go further too. Nevertheless, for the foreseeable future, law will predominantly remain regional, national and even local. But the debate on the globalization of law is no less relevant in relation to these levels. As real life becomes more international, the global, local, national and regional law will have to adapt. The debate on the globalization of law goes much beyond the question of how much truly global law there is and moves into a debate on the need for the convergence of national and other legal systems, and on the need for a common legal language, common legal concepts and principles, common legal procedures, and common standards, values and ultimately ideals to guide that convergence. This function of global law as a common legal ideal or point of convergence is caught in the coining of global law as our age's new common law.[5]

To the European, the latter is reminiscent of the debate on a common law of Europe which has been waged in legal academia in the context of European integration.[6] To the European legal historian, it is reminiscent to the role the *ius commune* of Roman and canon law played in the Late Middle Ages. That role has been brilliantly captured in a metaphor by the Italian legal historian Manlio Bellomo. He compared the role of the *ius commune* to that of a lighthouse to which all the ships and boats of local law had to set their course.[7] One may of course argue, if one wants to substitute global law by Roman law, that there was a fixed body of Roman law laid

---

4 Hersch Lauterpacht, 'International Law – The General Part' in Elihu Lauterpacht ed, *International Law Being the Collected Papers van Hersch Lauterpacht, Q.C., LL.D., F.B.A.*, vol. 1 (Cambridge University Press 1970) 28-31. Also see Hersch Lauterpacht, *An International Bill of the Rights of Man* (Cambridge University Press 1947).

5 Patrick Glenn, *On Common Laws* (Oxford University Press 2005); Rafael Domingo, *The New Global Law* (Cambridge University Press 2010).

6 See eg Bruno de Witte and Caroline Forder eds, *The Common Law of Europe and the Future of Legal Education* (Deventer 1992); Reinhard Zimmermann, 'Civil Code and Civil Law: the "Europeanization" of Private Law within the European Community and the Re-emergence of a European Civil Science' (1995) Columbia Journal of European Law 1, 63.

7 I heard him say this at the Medieval Canon Law Conference organized at Catania in 2000. Manlio Bellomo, *The Common Legal Past of Europe 1000-1800* (Washington 1995).

down in the codification of Justinian, which served as a kind of Bible to the 'priests of justice' that the Roman law professors were,[8] and that there is therefore no such thing as global law. But in truth, the medieval 'Roman law' was as little a fixed body of applicable law as 'global law' is. The lighthouse of the *ius commune* was indeed vested on the foundational authority of the Justinian codification and built from the bricks and marble taken from it, but ultimately, it was built by generations of medieval and early-modern legal scholars who believed in the ideal of 'their' learned law and pragmatically framed it to the needs of their time.[9] Should we, with the global challenges we are facing, strive for less?

And whereas today's proponents of global law lack a fixed authoritative corpus of legal texts the medieval and early-modern lawyers had in the *Corpus Iuris Civilis* and *Corpus Iuris Canonici*, there is a source of authority to vest the new common law on. The recognition of our common humanity, while going far back in time, is, thanks to globalization, more widely spread and more deeply imbedded than ever. Moreover, over the last seven decades, our idea of common humanity has gradually become articulated into instruments of positive international and regional law as it has never before. A *Corpus Iuris Humani* is lurking in the collecting of the major multilateral instruments of public international law, human rights law, international trade law, international environmental law and transnational private law.

The debate on the globalization of law is also extremely relevant because under this flag we can catch some of the main challenges legal practice, legal education and legal scholarship face today.

First, we are going through a historic paradigmatic shift. The paradigm of law and legal teaching which most lawyers have been raised on is, while under challenge, still not defunct. It dates back to the great law school reforms of the latter decades of the 19th and the earliest decades of the 20th century, when Roman law had to abdicate its central position on law school curricula in favor of national law.[10] It is a paradigm which is premised on the sovereign State's claim to a monopoly on law making and law

---

[8] D. 1.1.1.1 (Ulpian) 'Cuius merito quis nos sacerdotes appellet: iustitiam namque colimus et boni et aequi notitiam profitemur (...).'

[9] On the *ius commune* and its role in the formation of law in Europe, Randall Lesaffer, *European Legal History: A Cultural and Political Perspective* (Cambridge University Press 2009) 265-75.

[10] See eg Reinhard Zimmermann, *Roman Law, Contemporary Law, European Law* (Oxford University Press 2001) 1-105.

enforcement. This paradigm has led to a triple monism in our approach to law and particularly legal education.

Primo, there is systemic monism. Since the early 20th century at the latest, in most systems of legal education, students do not study law; they study their own national law. Whereas the attention to international and comparative law has certainly grown, in most university programs, this remains an add-on. *Secundo,* there is disciplinary monism. The dominance of the sovereign State over law has caused, regardless of the rise of legal realism, traditional legal education, legal scholarship and, to a large extent, even legal practice to become self-contained realities where little room is left for reflection on the interaction between law and society. This does not mean that students are not taught to think critically about law, or even not taught to think *de lege ferenda,* but often this critical reflection is reduced to one about the consistency of the law, rather than its societal effects. *Tertio,* there is methodic monism. In most countries, traditional legal teaching and research are based on one method. Because this method is dominant and often goes unchallenged, it can largely remain implicit.[11] Of course, over the last decades this paradigm and this triple monism have been severely challenged, as the study of comparative law, transnational law as well as interdisciplinary approaches to law and methodological pluralism are on the rise. These trends are strong and will prove far more than just being fashionable. But what these also do is raise the question of a new paradigm, which has not been answered yet, but is the challenge of the generation to come. These three changes are not solely driven by globalization, but are closely intertwined with it and cannot be thought independently from it.

Second, there is the challenge of finding a new balance between the global and the local, a question which the sovereign State's claim to the monopoly of law had allowed us to dust under the carpet or to narrow down to a few formal questions, such as the status of international law in national jurisdictions. For the future, and in the context of convergence of legal systems, we will need to broaden the scope. If global law is to act as a standard for legal convergence, then the local, where most of the instruments and institutions of implementation and enforcement are situated, becomes ever more crucial to the global. It might be ironic, but the globalization of law will lead us to more in-depth studies about other people's local laws.

---

[11] Jan Vranken, *Exploring the Jurist's Frame of Mind* (Deventer 2006).

Third, there is the challenge of a multi-polar and multicultural world. As we gear up to answer the call of globalization as lawyers, we also need to embrace the – in some cases slowly dawning – understanding that we will have to do this in a world in which the civilization that was so instrumental in starting this process of globalization is no longer dominant. The old debate between universalists and relativists gains new traction, but also might become more productive if universalist and Western will no longer be, and be seen to be, one and the same.

Public International Law: A Forerunner in the Field of Global(ization of) Law

Willem van Genugten
Professor, International Law, Tilburg University
Dean, The Hague Institute for Global Justice
Visiting Professor, University of Minnesota, USA
Extraordinary Professor, International Law, North-West University, South Africa
w.j.m.vgenugten@tilburguniversity.edu

Abstract
Public international law has, in several ways, reached the status of global law. But take care: 'international' is not necessarily 'transnational' nor is it equal to 'universal'. In the article, the author draws attention to, *inter alia*, the limits to 'the consent to be bound' and to the role of General Principles of international law. Further to that, he discusses aspects of international lawmaking, while underlining that the emphasis should be more on processes of globalization than on global as such: in most cases there is a long way to go.

Keywords
international; global; globalization; consent to be bound; lawmaking

1. Introduction

Public international law is like an extended family with many children, nephews and nieces. They listen to names like 'WTO-law', 'peace and security law', 'human rights law', 'international humanitarian law', 'environmental law', and 'law of the sea'. Some can even be called grandchildren: a UN Specialized Agency like the International Labor Organization, established itself in 1919 in the context of the League of Nations and later on incorporated in the United Nations, gave birth to numerous treaties, for instance in the field of the rights of indigenous people(s), which developed into a separate field of expertise. All this is relevant in order to keep in mind that public international law as such is a broad field, with many subfields.

Despite this lack of internal homogeneity, the field is in many ways already 'global' and 'transnational' by its very nature, basically because large parts of it draw upon notions, which are shared by a variety of States worldwide.

2. The Consent to be Bound and Global Law

Before saying anything else, it is important to underline one overriding characteristic of public international law: *the consent to be bound.* International law is by its very nature not supranational - asking States to give up parts of their sovereignty - but based upon their will to participate. They join voluntarily. That at least is the starting point. However, there are many nuances to be added in this respect. Let me mention four of them, each relevant from the perspective of the theme of this article on global(ization of) law.

One is that 'some legal standards are more equal than others'. For instance, the duty to refrain from genocide - and something similar could be said about crimes against humanity and war crimes - is by all means binding, even if States are not party to the 1948 Genocide Convention or to the 1998 Statute of the International Criminal Court. The discussion on genocide is not anymore on the question whether States are bound by the duty to prevent and refrain from it, but about the application of and limits to the concept of genocide as expressed in judgments of, especially, international criminal courts. Also important is the question of who has jurisdiction to go after the crime of genocide, apart from the States concerned. That is the debate on universal jurisdiction, with its substantive side, of which we can say that the ban on genocide is qualified as a peremptory standard of international law and thus belongs to 'global law', and its jurisdictional side, of which we can observe that things are moving, but also that there is still a long way to go. The standard reasoning is that 'even' in cases of genocide, jurisdiction has to be established separately.

The International Court of Justice, for instance, struggled with the issue in the case of the *Democratic Republic of the Congo vs Rwanda* on 'Armed Activities on the Territory of the Congo'.[1] Despite some very interesting dissenting reflections, the Court came to the conclusion that the traditional

---

1 *Armed Activities on the Territory of the Congo (Democratic Republic of the Congo* v *Uganda)* [2005] (Application) ICJ Reports 168; ICJ *Armed Activities on the Territory of the Congo (Democratic Republic of the Congo* v *Rwanda)* [2006] (Jurisdiction and Admissibility) ICJ Reports 6.

system had to be applied: jurisdiction did not automatically follow from the *ius cogens* character of the genocide norm. The same dissenting opinions, however, might reflect future ways of dealing with the issue, thus developing a real global law path as to genocide, compulsory jurisdiction included.

Two: States are to some extent forced, by public pressure or by their peers, to become a party to a specific convention, while having an internal legal system that contradicts with some provisions of the convention concerned. In such cases, they have the escape of making reservations, as long as these do not relate to the object and purpose of the relevant convention (Article 19, Para. c, of the 969 Vienna Convention on the Law of Treaties).

In reality, however, many of such reservations are accepted by the other State parties, often because they want to have the State 'on board'. The fact that a convention has been ratified globally, therefore, does not mean automatically that all provisions can be seen as 'global law' because some might be 'undressed' by reservations. In addition, provisions are often openly formulated, thus leaving space to States to fill in and implement the norms in their own way, as long as they stay within the limits of the meaning of the convention, while using one of the methods of interpretation allowed by the Vienna Convention on the Law of Treaties (Articles 31-33), and/or the limits set by the relevant supervisory bodies. I will come back to that.

Three: sometimes an international organization is strongly in favor of introducing a specific norm while large groups of States are (still) against it. In the field of international law this is visible in many ways. The United Nations, for instance, or its Specialized Agencies often have an agenda which goes further than the common lowest denominator represented by their Member States. On each and every occasion, they keep pressuring their members to move ahead. A case in point is the policy of the World Health Organization on female circumcision or the policy of the UN on the death penalty. As to the latter: while the UN cannot enforce States to bow to its pressure and has to abide by the basic rule of the States' consent to be bound, in practice it can take action to make that norm more global than many States would want to have it.

Although the relevant convention, *i.e.* the 1989 Second Protocol to the 1966 International Covenant on Civil and Political Rights, has as of now (August 2012), been ratified by 75 States only, UN policy is to be against the death penalty in all its public statements and actions. One can think of the establishment by the UN Security Council of the International Criminal Tribunals for the former Yugoslavia and Rwanda, in 1992 and 1993 respectively, both not allowed to use the death penalty. The same goes for the treaty-based International Criminal Court. It makes the ban on the death penalty in a way more global law than the States against it would love to see it.

However, if States still want to exercise it, they have the legal space to do so, the core barrier being Article 6, Para. 2 of the International Covenant on Civil and Political Rights (ICCPR), which states that 'in countries which have not abolished the death penalty, sentence of death may be imposed only for the most serious crimes in accordance with the law in force at the time of the commission of the crime (...)'.

In addition, the death penalty 'can only be carried out pursuant to a final judgment rendered by a competent court'. States then have to be a Party to the ICCPR - as of now ratified by 167 States - while not having made a reservation to this particular Article, and while willing to live up to General Comment nr. 6 (1982) of the UN Human Rights Committee, in which it declares that the expression 'most serious crimes' 'must be read restrictively to mean that the death penalty should be a quite exceptional measure', that 'it can only be imposed in accordance with the law in force at the time of the commission of the crime (...)', and that procedural guarantees prescribed in the Article must be observed, 'including the right to a fair hearing by an independent tribunal, the presumption of innocence, the minimum guarantees for the defence, and the right to review by a higher tribunal'.[2] In addition, a State must be willing to listen to the Committee itself, if and when it discusses the death penalty policy and specific cases in the State concerned. In other words: there are many 'whiles' and 'ifs', but those who look through the mist can even, in the case of the abolishment of the death penalty, discover a small, mountainous way forward, in the direction of global law.

Fourth: General Principles of international law. Belonging to the core sources of international law, the General Principles also have 'something uneasy'. While many things can be found in conventions, General Principles are often not included. Nevertheless, they are the salt and pepper of many international law meals, needed to come to balanced judgments and views, where treaty law is not clear enough or leaves space otherwise. To the domain of recognized General Principles of international law do belong notions such as *Pacta sunt servanda*, the duty to notify in cases of disasters, the principle of estoppel and the principle of good faith. Such General Principles do no doubt qualify as 'global law', even if not in all cases put to

---

2 HRC Sixteenth Session April 1982 'General Comment no. 06: The Right to Life' (article 6) (30 April 1982) para 5-7.

the test before and thus approved of by, the International Court of Justice. There will be no (blocks of) States arguing to the contrary. But a professor would not be a professor if he would not add a warning: the Principles of international law have to be dealt with in more detail, from a philosophical as well as a more empirical perspective, in order to be sure whether or not and to what extent they really belong to the domain of transnational, global law.

To illustrate: while general international law is cautious in labeling issues as a General Principle, several subfields of international law are using the word 'principle' in a much broader sense and for many more issues. One such field is international environmental law, which is full of principles, the 'Precautionary Principle' being the most famous one. Parts of this 'duty to prevent harm', in this case to the environment, do already have equivalents in other fields of international general law. Think, for example, of the Responsibility to Protect (RtoP), as recognized in the 2005 UN Summit Document (Para. 138): 'Each individual State has the responsibility to protect its populations from genocide, war crimes, ethnic cleansing and crimes against humanity. This responsibility entails the prevention of such crimes, including their incitement, through appropriate and necessary means.'[3] These lines are followed by the promise that one will work on strengthening 'an early warning capability'. That sounds like 'precaution', but having observed that, it is clear that for such a principle to become global practice (and global law) there is a long way to go. Apart from 'RtoP crimes' to which the principle applies – genocide, war crimes, ethnic cleansing and crimes against humanity – one should for instance think of preventing gross conflicts about access to water and of structural poverty, but also of financial disputes about trading in derivatives leading to financial disasters all over the world, to mention but a few examples. The duty to prevent such problems touches upon views of political systems, economic interests, and shortcoming governmental and human capacities, which easily make the principle 'only' a principle. No less, no more.

3. International Lawmaking: Emphasis on 'Globalizing' rather than on 'Global'

Looking carefully at the foregoing, it will not come as a surprise that to my mind, in an article on global law, we have to look at what has already been

---

3 UNGA Res 60/1 (24 October 2005) UN Doc. A/RES/60/1.

reached, but even more at the way forward: processes of globalization of law, *i.e.* making law global. These words strongly emphasize the idea that reaching the stage of global law means adopting a process-like approach. This is all the more the case, in a world where civil society is gaining strength and influence, and is being recognized more and more by the UN as a co-constituent of the international legal order, alongside States and the business sector (see, amongst (many) other things, the 2004 UN report, *We the peoples: civil society, the United Nations and global governance* and the follow-up to that);[4] a world with manifold fragile and otherwise weakly governed States; a world where Brazil, the Russian Federation, India, China and South-Africa (the 'BRICS'), but also Mexico, Indonesia and many others do show growing self-confidence.

As to the latter: the BRICS and others are right in tackling Western dominance and in questioning to what extent international law as it is, is in conformity to their views and interests. To give a recent example: in the past the International Monetary Fund invested mainly in developing countries, but recently it had to act similarly in countries like Greece, while countries like China and India decided to invest in the Fund. For all these reasons, Belgium and The Netherlands decided to share in the near future their position in the Board of Governors of the IMF, as Poland and Switzerland did before.

Another example relates to the position of the African Union on international criminal law. While as of now a majority of African States have ratified the ICC Statute (33 out 54), and while the new Public Prosecutor, Fatou Bensouda, has an African background, her nomination and appointment being strongly supported by the AU Member States of the Assembly of States' Parties to the ICC Statute, the same AU is now discussing the adoption of a Protocol on adding a range of international crimes to the jurisdiction of the African Court of Justice and Human Rights. The reasons are so far not very clear, but one of them seems to be frustration about the first ten years of the ICC, with its focus on African situations and cases.

Raising the question to what extent international law reflects the existing worldviews does not mean that the answers are always negative or that such questions should not be raised. To my mind, there are many reasons to embrace diversity and regional differences. In international criminal law this might be called 'complementarity' ('you are allowed to do it your own way, as long as you do it'; see the terminology on unwillingness and inability

4 Panel of Eminent Persons on United Nations-Civil Society Relations, 'We the Peoples: Civil Society, the United Nations and Global Governance' (11 June 2005) UN Doc. A/58/817.

in Article 17 of the ICC Statute); in the field of human rights law this would be called the 'margin of appreciation' ('universality is not uniformity': the goals are by and large clear, but States can implement the standards their own way, within the frames set by the supervisory bodies). That diversity relates, amongst other things, to the views one has on the relation between individuals, communities/families, and States' governments.

To my mind, one should not overemphasize the individualistic character of the human rights concept, and ditto obligations of States, while neglecting the fact that community and family structures can also positively contribute to human dignity conditions, to begin with food, work, health care, shelter, security. However, stressing the role of the State and its negative as well as positive obligations in the human rights field, automatically leads to lowering the expectations one might have from families and other social entities, as we have seen in the recent history of human rights protection.

Right or wrong conceptually, it is a reality that in many African nations, and others alike, the State is not willing or able to provide the basic conditions within which human rights can flourish. So 'margins of appreciation' are in fact often much more than margins only. In addition, such margins of appreciation are not only relevant *between* States and the internationally acting supervisory bodies, but also *within* States. That relates to the space to be given to, amongst others, indigenous communities and their legal views and actions. That can and should be done more to my mind, as long as it is not romanticized and as long as individuals who do not want to be 'locked in' in the collective, or in the community-driven aspirations of the chief or other head(s) of the community, are effectively protected by law. The issue then of course is that some have an interest in keeping the law the way it is, while others are 'knocking on the door', often inspired by human rights based words and concepts. At that moment global (human rights) law aspirations again enter the scene.

Making parts of law more global, thus means first of all to discover and understand the local, national, and regional context, while using means that might have a realistic chance to be successful. Many such means relate to lawmaking and judiciary bodies and to the political domain, but also to economic notions and economic actors. In the past, economic interests have often been a driving force behind the globalization of law. Think for instance of the Law of the Sea, the development of which was at the beginning primarily driven by the economic interests of seafaring nations, later on followed by other nations conducting economic activities on open seas.

Recently, economic actors are getting new forms of recognition, for instance in the UN's Global Compact (2000), and even more recently by the adoption in 2011 of the 'Guiding Principles on Business and Human Rights', prepared by the UN Secretary-General Representative for Business and Human Rights John Ruggie and following his protect-respect-remedy framework.[5] Supported by all Member States of the Human Rights Council, the Guiding Principles reflect global law, weak as they are in the eyes of some and marking progress as they do in the eyes of others.

4. Concluding Remarks

Scholarship in the field of public international law misses many chances if its focus is too much on international law as it is. Clearly: all people working in parts of this large field of law, have to know what they talk about in terms of positive international law, avoiding the mistake of mixing the *lege lata* with the *lega ferenda* and thus reading their lawmaking wishes into law as it is according to the formal lawmakers and the judiciaries tasked with the role of supervisors. But each of us also have to look beyond handbook wisdom and needs to contextualize international law. Each of us also have to look with historical eyes in order to judge trends, and with empirical eyes - often qualitatively rather than quantitatively - in order to see how the gaps between norms and reality are (not) filled.

International law is about concepts and norms that in several ways have reached the status of global law, but even there one has to be aware that such norms are not necessarily a given 'for eternity' and do deserve constant critical reflection and adaptation to changing circumstances. In this article I mentioned, as examples, the self-confidence of the BRICS-States and others, and the frustration of African Union Member States as to the focus of the first ten years of the International Criminal Court. Both are issues to be aware of, with their impact on international law. Simultaneously, however, one does not necessarily have to look at these challenges with a defensive mindset. The first thing to do, is at least trying to understand where the frustration comes from. The next step might be to look at the legal consequences and to see to what extent the 'challengers' are right or can be convinced otherwise.

5 HRC, 'Report of the Special Representative of the Secretary-General on the issue of human rights and transnational corporations and other business enterprises, John Ruggie: Guiding Principles on Business and Human Rights: Implementing the United Nations "Protect, Respect and Remedy" Framework' (21 March 2011) UN Doc. A/HRC/17/31.

This article has offered some 'second thoughts' on several aspects of the relation between international law and transnational, global law. They are to be seen as knowledge-based warnings against oversimplified equations: even international law is only partly global law. Hence, the words 'Global' as well as 'Globalization' in the title of this article.

Legal Order and the 'Globality' of Global Law

Hans Lindahl
Professor, Legal Philosophy, Tilburg University; Research Fellow, Stellenbosch Institute for Advanced Study (South Africa)
h.k.lindahl@tilburguniversity.edu

Abstract
The aim of this paper is to develop a concept of legal order that is capable of accommodating several distinctive features of global law, as well as features which are traditionally associated to state law. To this effect, it sketches out the bold lines of a general concept of legal order, which draws on contemporary philosophical accounts of collective action. A legal order, it is argued, is an authoritatively mediated and upheld form of joint action. This general model of legal order explains (i) why global legal orders typically overlap or overlay each other; (ii) why these orders are organized as networks of places; and (iii) why they necessarily are organized as a spatial inside in contrast to an outside. That the inside/outside contrast remains constitutive for global legal orders suggests that globalization marks the emergence of new fault lines between legal orders, not the suppression of spatial boundaries.

Keywords
legal order; inside/outside; plural subjectivity; global law

1. Introduction

How are we to understand the 'globality' of global law? More generally, what concept of legal order is sufficiently capacious to account for the globality of global law, while also sufficiently flexible to accommodate state law and its distinctive features? In addressing this pair of questions, I will focus on three features that are widely held to be distinctive for the emergence of global law, and which stand in sharp contrast to distinctive features of states, or so it seems.

First, and in contrast to the claim of states to regulate all comportment within their territory, global legal orders typically overlap or overlay each other in crisscrossing patches of normativity. Second, and closely related to the former, the globalization of law by no means entails that place has ceased to be a distinctive feature of global legal orders; what we see emerging are webs or networks of places which are both sub-national and transnational. Third, whereas states have borders that separate the domestic legal order from foreign legal orders, this distinction is no longer meaningful for global law, which has no outside in the sense of a foreign legal order.

These three features by no means exhaust what might be defining characteristics of global law; but they do articulate quite well, I think, the preponderantly *spatial* dimension of 'global' law. In other words, although my claim is that although these spatial features do not fully capture the concept of global law, one does well to begin by making sense of them before moving on to consider its other distinctive characteristics.

This paper falls into four sections. The first briefly describes the three distinctive features of global law indicated above, contrasting them to the correlative features of state law. The second outlines the contours of a general concept of legal order. In the third section I show why this model of legal order allows for the explaining of each of the three features of global law, whilst also accommodating the correlative features of state law. Finally, the fourth section debunks a widely endorsed assumption about how global law might be different to state law.

2. The 'Globality' of Global Law

Although the concept of globalization remains highly contested, there is reasonable agreement among sociologists and legal theorists of globalization about the features that define the emergence of global law as a properly spatial transformation of law. The first of these concerns the concept of territoriality, which has traditionally been a distinctive feature of the state. According to the canonical definition, which is as empty as it is ubiquitous, a state is the kind of legal order in which sovereign power is exercised over a population in a given territory. On this reading, the state claims, on principle if not necessarily in fact, a monopoly on regulative power over its territory.

Certainly, this monopoly can be suspended or mitigated, as in the case of international human rights regimes. But defenders of state sovereignty will counter that the state commits itself to respecting human rights regimes and, to that extent, the validity of such regimes in its territories continues to presuppose that it exercises sovereign power over its territory. Be it as it may, global law seems to introduce a fundamental difference into this state of affairs. Indeed, *lex mercatoria*, cyberlaw, multinationals, international standards regimes, *lex sportiva*, and the like mark the emergence of *overlapping* legal orders.

On the one hand, each of these global legal orders claims to be narrow in scope, regulating only a particular kind of comportment; on the other, these orders claim to regulate comportment in the same physical space and time. This feature is the cornerstone of contemporary accounts of legal pluralism. As Twining puts it, legal pluralism entails that 'normative and legal orders co-exist *in the same time-space context*'.[1] Crucially, overlapping legal orders are inimical to state monism, which seeks to monopolize regulatory power over all comportment within 'the same time-space context.'

A second feature that merits attention is the shift whereby global law becomes both sub-national and transnational. Saskia Sassen, the well-known sociologist of globalization, has shown that the emergence of global normative orders remains strongly anchored in localities or places. Whereas 'the global is generally conceptualized as overriding or neutralizing place and as operating on a self-evidently global scale,' Sassen argues, drawing on a wide range of rich empirical material, that global normative orders bypass national states by giving rise to 'particular cross-border circuits connecting specific localities,' such that 'the vague notion of the global' acquires concretion when viewed as 'networks of places'.[2]

This insight amounts to a critique of the notion of the 'glocal,' to the extent that this neologism articulates the global and the local. Sassen effectively shows that *global law is itself a form of the local*, of localization, rather than something that is added or superimposed onto the local. Accordingly, locality and place are not distinctive features of state law nor of global law; what is distinctive of the latter is that global law locates itself in a way that is both subnational and transnational.

Let me conclude this section by pointing to a third and decisive feature of the 'globality' of global law. Indeed, classical international law is predicated on the existence of borders which allow each of the states to distinguish between its internal affairs and its external relations. In other words, the distinction between inside and outside, interpreted as the distinction between domestic and foreign legal orders, is the indispensable presupposition absent which no sense could be made of *inter*national law, even—and especially—in those situations in which international law allows for intervention in the internal affairs of a state. By contrast, it makes no sense to understand the spatiality of global legal orders by appealing to the

[1] William Twining, *General Jurisprudence: Understanding Law from a Global Perspective* (Cambridge University Press, 2009) 70 (emphasis added).

[2] Saskia Sassen, *A Sociology of Globalization* (WW Norton & Co 2007) 11, 13. See also Boaventura de Sousa Santos' discussion of 'localized globalisms', in his *Toward a New Legal Common Sense*, (2nd edn, Butterworths 2002) 179.

inside/outside distinction, at least when interpreted as the domestic/foreign divide. After all, its geographical scale is *global*.

Although *lex mercatoria*, cyberlaw and the other modes of global law we see emerging before our eyes are limited in the scope of comportment they seek to regulate, theirs is a claim to global validity. And while there is of course always the latent possibility of conflicts of jurisdiction between these manifestations of global law, such conflicts are not unleashed by the violation of borders that differentiate between domestic and foreign places.

3. Law in the First-Person Plural

What concept of legal order would allow us to make sense of the spatial transformations leading from state law to global law, while also revealing the continuities between the two? My hunch is that a theory of legal order that draws on analytical studies of collective action and on a phenomenology of strangeness can do the trick. Borrowing an expression coined by my colleague, Bert van Roermund, let me call this a theory of 'law in the first-person plural'.[3]

To get a hang of what I mean by this, compare the following two situations. Here is the first: several persons who happen to be in the same place, see a stork fly by. This is rather unusual in that place, say Tilburg, and so all follow the majestic bird in its flight till it moves beyond their visual domain. And now the second: a group of birdwatchers are out on an expedition and they happen to chance on a stork. The birdwatchers happily point it out to each other, and make notes about the bird in their logbooks. Suppose that someone were to ask 'what are you doing?' in each of the situations. In each case, the answer might run, 'we are looking at a bird fly by.' But the use of the word 'we' is quite different in each scenario.

In the first, 'we' functions as an *aggregative* term: each of a number of individuals happens to be watching the stork fly by, independently of what the others are doing. Margaret Gilbert deftly characterizes this use of the term 'we' as 'we, each'. In the second, 'we' functions as an *integrative* term:

---

[3] Van Roermund has taken decisive steps to develop such a theory in the following papers: Bert van Roermund, 'First-Person Plural Legislature: Political Reflexivity and Representation' (2003) 6 Philosophical Explorations 235; Bert van Roermund, 'Kelsen under the Low Skies. Recognition Theory Revisited and Revised' in Robert Walter, Clemens Jabloner and Klaus Zeleny (eds), *Hans Kelsen anderswo. Hans Kelsen Abroad* (Manz Verlag 2010) 259-279; and Bert van Roermund, 'Objectifying Legal Norm Claims: Validity and Self-Reference' in John Gardner, Leslie Green & Luis Duarte de Almeida, (eds), *The Pure Theory of Law Revisited: The Jurisprudence of Hans Kelsen* (forthcoming, Oxford University Press 2012).

a manifold of individuals functions as a group of bird-watchers; they act together, such that, for example, one of the members, who was distracted, hadn't noticed the bird, and another group member points it out to her, 'look, there goes a stork!' In such cases, notes Gilbert, 'we' functions as in 'we, together'.[4] When acting together, the members of a group take up a first-person plural perspective: it is we who act as a *unit*, even though there can be no act by a group, absent a set of interlocking acts by its members or participant agents.

To see the difference between the two, imagine that, in the first case, one of the persons who happened to be at the place where the bird was spotted hadn't noted that the stork was flying by; no one alerted her to the bird, and she simply remained absorbed in what she was doing. As things have it, she had been hoping for many years to see a stork and would surely be hugely disappointed at having let the opportunity to see one slip by. But she would have no standing to rebuke the other persons who had looked at the stork fly by; they had no *obligation* to alert her to the bird. In the second situation, the bird-watcher would certainly be entitled to rebuke her fellow bird-watchers. After all, looking for birds is something they were doing *together*; what was the point of going out to look at birds together unless they were prepared to help each other out to realize their joint aim? See here the elementary structure of entitlements between members which attaches to collective action.[5]

Now, my claim is that legal orders are a species of collective actions, as described above. In other words, legal orders take on the form of collectives whereby a manifold of individuals act together over time. By the same token, legal obligations and sanctions are a species of the entitlements and rebukes which emerge between participant agents in the course of collective action. The nature and scope of legal comportment, namely what we ought to do together, is internally related to the normative point of joint action: that which our joint act ought to be *about*.

Significantly, what it is that we ought to do together—the normative point of joint action under law—may itself be open to discussion and transformation over time. However, and in contrast to other modes of collective action, legal orders involve second-level authorities which, acting on behalf of the group, monitor and uphold participant agency with a view to realizing the (transformable) normative point of joint action. Notice, to conclude, that this is an extremely capacious concept of legal order, which

4 Margaret Gilbert, *On Social Facts* (2nd edn, Princeton University Press 1992) 168.
5 Margaret Gilbert, *A Theory of Political Obligation* (Oxford University Press 2006) 189ff.

easily accommodates not only state law but also all and sundry varieties of global law, such as *lex mercatoria*, cyberlaw, and *lex sportiva*, as well as other forms of law, including indigenous law, religious law, and the like.

Let me take a further and final step in fleshing out the concept of law in the first person. Indeed, modern legal theory, particularly legal positivism and normative theories of law, have taken for granted that a legal order is a (putative) unity of a specific kind of norms of action. This is, however, an extremely reductive understanding of legal orders and their (putative) unity. For what legal orders do is to regulate four dimensions of human comportment: its material dimension, indicating *what* comportment is called for; its subjective dimension, indicating *who* ought to engage in certain forms of comportment; its temporal dimension, establishing *when* certain comportment ought to take place; its spatial dimension, laying down *where* certain comportment ought to come about. Here, ought can mean comportment which is demanded, prohibited or permitted. In short, legal orders establish who ought to do what, where, and when with a view to realizing the normative point of joint action. This entails that legal orders are never only (putative) unities of legal norms; this abstracts from the concreteness of legal collectives, which order themselves as a four-dimensional (putative) unity of ought-places, ought-times, ought-subjects and ought-contents of comportment. Again, this four-dimensional (putative) unity of legal orders holds for state law no less than for global law, in all its forms, as well as for other forms of law.[6]

4. The 'Globality' of Global Law Revisited

How can this general, albeit highly abridged, account of legal order help us to make sense of the three features which, on the reading I have defended, determine the 'globality' of global law? More generally, in what way does a theory of law in the first-person plural explain both the deeper unity of and the difference between state law and global law?

Let us first turn to the notion of global law as comprising overlapping legal orders. The upshot of our foregoing analyses is that the unity of ought-places that comprises the legal space of a collective is never only a geographical surface, never only the material support of one or more legal systems, but rather a concrete articulation of normative and physical dimensions. As a result, the metaphor of overlapping legal orders tends to

---

[6] See my paper: Hans Lindahl, 'Boundaries and the Concept of Legal Order' (2011) 2 Jurisprudence 73.

conceal that even if two distinct legal orders cover precisely the same geographical extension, human comportment that is relevant to one of these orders, in terms of its normative point, might be entirely immaterial to the other.

The spatial unity of a legal order is subject-relative, such that different collectives with different normative points can organize themselves as spatial unities in different ways, while sharing all or part of a geographical extension. Accordingly, the mutually exclusive territoriality of states is but a *limiting case* of a far broader spectrum of possibilities available to law.[7] Overlapping legal orders have always been the rule, rather than the exception—even when state law was at its acme.

Consider, now, the second of the defining features of the globality of law. As noted, the emergent globalization of law does not mean that law ceases to be anchored in concrete places; what happens is that global law takes on the form of what Sassen calls a 'network of places' that is both subnational and transnational. The abridged theory of law in the first-person plural outlined heretofore easily accounts for this feature of global law, too. In effect, all law, to be law, must regulate the *where* of comportment, and it does so by setting up *ought-places* in which certain kinds of comportment by certain kinds of individual (and at certain times) are permitted, prohibited or demanded.

To the extent that the normative point of collective action requires a variety of interlocking acts, it follows that different kinds of ought-places will be required to realize this normative point, and that these ought-places appear as a *unity* in light of their normative point. It is precisely for this reason that global law has the structure of a 'network of ought-places', to slightly modify Sassen's apt expression. This need not mean, of course, that a global legal order must paper over, as it were, the entire globe with ought-places; while the scale of the 'networks of ought-places' of *lex mercatoria, cyberlaw* or *lex sportiva* is global, they may be quite selective in the number and kinds of ought-places which they require to realize their normative point.

Lex constructionis, as a form of *lex mercatoria*, is a case in point, to the extent that it largely focuses on the sites for international (often turn-key) construction projects, such as airports, hydroelectric dams, bridges, etc., as well as the places in which arbitration commissions are located, such as the International Chamber of Commerce. While this spatial configuration of

---

[7] See Hans Lindahl, 'A-Legality: Postnationalism and the Question of Legal Boundaries' (2010) 73 Modern Law Review 30, 36-37.

global law differs in important ways from the territoriality of state law, nonetheless it shares with the latter the basic characterization of law as a (putative) unity of ought-places. By these lights, also state law has the structure of a 'network of ought-places'.

There is, finally, what many commentators take to be the decisive difference between global law and state law. Whereas the latter is organized according to the spatial distinction between inside and outside, the former no longer is bounded in space because the distinction between domestic and foreign legal orders ceases to apply. A case in point is Teubner's systems-theoretical approach to global law, which he defines as a 'self-reproducing, worldwide legal discourse which closes its meaning boundaries by the use of the legal/illegal binary code and reproduces itself by processing a symbol of global (not national) validity'.[8]

We can easily concede that the domestic/foreign distinction, as a specification of the inside/outside distinction, is historically contingent. We would reify the modern nation state, making of its peculiar features an a-historical constant, if we took for granted that legal orders must be bounded in space according to the distinction between domestic and foreign spaces. Here again, the model of legal order I have developed can account for state law, organized according to the divide between domestic/foreign spaces, and global law, in which its spatial configuration as a (putative) unity of ought-places in no way requires that divide.

5. Fault Lines of Globalization

But we need to take a step further. Granting that the domestic/foreign distinction is historically contingent, need we also grant that the emergence of global legal orders marks the end of the inside/outside distinction? In other words, need we accept that the state form of territoriality, hence the domestic/foreign distinction, exhausts how a legal collective closes itself into an inside vis-à-vis an outside? Or would the emergence of a global legal order only be possible on the basis of a self-closure, whereby a legal collective organizes itself as an inside that stands in contrast to an outside?

Consider the hypothetical case of a world polity, as an extreme case of global law. Whatever else might be required, its officials would need to posit a distribution of places determining where comportment ought or ought

---

[8] Gunther Teubner, '"Global Bukowina": Legal Pluralism in the World Society' in Gunther Teubner (ed), *Global Law Without a State* (Dartmouth 1997) 14.

not to take place. Although a world polity would have no outside in the sense of foreign places, or at least not initially, the inclusion and exclusion of interests articulated by the spatial boundaries that give shape to its normative point entail that the polity's foundation would give rise, at least latently, to *strange* places—places that do not fit in the distribution of ought-places deemed to be the collective's *own* legal space. Strange places are, in the twofold sense of the term, 'outlandish'.

What a world polity could not avoid is to posit boundaries that close it off as an inside—as a *familiar* distribution of places—in contrast to an indeterminate outside. This outside manifests itself through comportment and situations that, contesting the claim to commonality raised on behalf of a global distribution of ought-places, intimate ought-places that have no place within that (putative) unity of global ought-places. Accordingly, the emergence of global legal orders reveals that the inside/outside distinction, when construed as the distinction between domestic/foreign territories, is historically contingent; legal orders are certainly conceivable that do not require fixed territorial borders like those of a nation-state. But to the extent that a world polity, if it is to be a legal order, must in some way organize the face of the earth as a common distribution of ought-places, any of the boundaries that mark off a *single* ought-place from other ought-places in the world polity also appears, when contested, as marking off the *whole* distribution of ought-places as an inside vis-à-vis a strange outside.

The model of legal order I have developed entails that no legal order, global or otherwise, is possible absent the divide between an own legal space inside, and strange places outside. Call this divide a *fault line*, in contrast to borders or boundaries. Succinctly, and as contemporary developments show all too clearly, the emergence of globalization goes hand in hand with the emergence of fault lines: in its fundamental significance for our times, the inside/outside distinction speaks to the *fault lines of globalization*. It would take us too far afield to discuss the normative implications of this insight.[9] It may suffice to note, in conclusion, that, contrary to Jürgen Habermas' assumption that postnationalism introduces the possibility of a *Weltinnenpolitik*, i.e. a world internal politics, the emergence of global law marks the genesis of a *Weltaußenpolitik*—a world external politics.

---

[9] The empirical, conceptual and normative dimensions of this insight are developed at length in my forthcoming monograph: Hans Lindahl, *Fault Lines of Globalization: Legal Order and the Politics of A-Legality* (forthcoming, Oxford University Press 2013).

The Structural Characteristics of Global Law for the 21st Century: Fracture, Fluidity, Permeability, and Polycentricity

Larry Catá Backer*
W Richard and Mary Eshelman Faculty Scholar & Professor of Law, Professor of International Affairs, Pennsylvania State University, State College, Pennsylvania; Director Coalition for Peace & Ethics, Washington, D.C.
lcb911@gmail.com

Abstract
Global law can be understood as the systematization of anarchy, as the management of a loosely intertwined universe of autonomous governance frameworks operating dynamically across borders and grounded in functional differentiation among governance communities. More conventionally, global law can be defined as the law of non-state governance systems. Global law posits a stable universe of objects of regulation around which governance systems multiply, the inverse of the traditional approach to law grounded on the presumption of a dynamic population bound to static and stable systems. The essay considers the structure of global law in this context, understood as an amalgamation of four fundamental characteristics that together define a new order in form that is, in some respects, the antithesis of the orderliness and unity of the law-state system it will displace (though not erase). These four fundamental characteristics—fracture, fluidity, permeability, and polycentricity—comprise the fundamental structure of global law. These also serve as the structural foundations of its constitutional element, its substantive element, and its process element. The essay considers each in turn in the construction of global law.

Keywords
global law; fracture; permeability; polycentricity; fluidity; sovereignty; international law; governance; anarchy; public law; law beyond the state

* My thanks to Jan Broekman for his excellent comments and suggestions and to my research assistant, Nabih Haddad (Penn State MIA School of International Affairs 2012 expected) for his excellent work on the essay. Special thanks to the staff of the Tilburg Law Review, and in particular Shavana Musa (Tilburg), for the invitation to participate and more importantly, for their excellent work and support.

1. Introduction: Not Global Law, but Governance Systems Beyond the State

Global law is coming.[1] In some respects it has already made an appearance in efforts to govern the behavior of states.[2] But it steals into the global village in darkness,[3] a village once populated by a relatively homogenous collection of states gathered together behind thick walls of protective ideology.[4] Its form and purpose are shrouded,[5] and the hands that wield it are only partly visible.[6] Global law, to the extent it is not the law of states, is threatening to the political order that reached its high point in the second half of the 20th century.[7] For traditionalists, the question of its form revolves around the parameters of a dominant ideology that posits primacy of place to the state,[8] to law,[9] and to order.[10] For others, global law can be seen in the shadow of the law[11] and the state[12]—in social norms, for

---

1 Phillip Allott, *Eunomia: New Order for the World* (Oxford University Press, 1990); Martin Shapiro, 'The Globalization of Law,'(1993) 1 Indiana Journal of Global Legal Studies 37.

2 Ruti G Teitel, 'Humanity's Law: Rule of Law for the New Global Politics,' (2001-2002) 35 Cornell International Law Journal 355.

3 'The current world order is ending, but there is no clear replacement for it.' Keith Suter, *Global Order and Global Disorder: Globalization and the Nation-State* (Praeger Publishers 2003) 1.

4 John Griffiths, 'What is Legal Pluralism?' (1986) 24 Journal of Legal Pluralism And Unofficial Law 1, 3; Larry Catá Backer, 'Governance Without Government: An Overview, in Günther Handl, Joachim Zekoll, Peer Zumbansen (eds), *beyond territoriality: transnational Legal Authority in an Age of Globalization* (Brill Academic Publishers, forthcoming 2012).

5 gralf-peter calliess and peer zumbansen, *rough consensus and Running Code: A Theory of Transnational Private Law* (Hart 2010).

6 See Larry Catá Backer, 'Economic Globalization and the Rise of Efficient Systems of Global Private Law Making: Wal-Mart as Global Legislator,' (2007) 39(4) University of Connecticut Law Review 1739.

7 Ralf Michaels, 'The Re-State-ment of Non-State Law: The State, Choice of Law, and the Challenge From Global Legal Pluralism', (2005) 51 Wayne Law Review 1209, 1227-37.

8 Mireille Delmas-Marty, *Global Law: A Triple Challenge* (Martinus Nijhoff 2003).

9 Pierrick LeGoff, 'Global Law: A Legal Phenomenon Emerging From the Process of Globalization' (2007) 14 Indiana Journal of Global Legal Studies 119.

10 Giuliana Ziccardi Capaldo, *The Pillars of Global Law* (Ashgate 2008); Anne Marie Slaughter, *A New World Order* (Princeton University Press 2005).

11 Günther Teubner, *'Global Bukowina': Legal Pluralism in the World Society, in Global Law Without a State* (Ashgate 1997).

12 William Twining, 'Normative and Legal Pluralism: A Global Perspective' (2010) 20 Duke Journal of Comparative and International Law 473; Simon Chesterman, 'Globalization Rules: Accountability, Power, and the Prospects for Global Administrative Law' (2008) 14 Global Governance 39.

example.[13] It is left to those with a taste for such things to begin to suggest both its form and its structure as a singular construct producing a unified world order,[14] or as something else, as something plural but still law, still strongly attached to the state and the ordering structures it represents.[15] But the examination of global law in its own right tends to be occluded by the ideology of the state system that itself has contributed to the difficulty of engaging in these changes that effectively threaten the fundamental ordering presumptions inherent in the law-state ideological framework.[16]

I have been asked to explore the concept of 'global law', to provide insights into what global law means to me, and in so doing, to help the reader see global law through my eyes. I start with the Mexican poet, Octavio Paz's insight from an engagement with the socio-cultural and political upheavals of the 1960s.

> [M]odern time—linear time, the homologue of the ideas of progress and history, ever propelled into the future, the time of the sign *non-body*, of the fierce will to dominate nature and tame instincts, the time of sublimation, aggression and self-mutilation—is coming to an end. I believe that we are entering another time, a time that has not yet revealed its form and about which we can say nothing except that it will be neither linear time nor cyclical time. Neither history nor myth. The time that is coming, if we really are living a change at times, a general revolt and not a linear revolution, will be neither a future nor a past, but a present.[17]

Octavio Paz could have been speaking to the emergence of global law. Global law does not represent an extension of past patterns of governance, nor can it be understood as a barnyard full of tame animals with utility to

---

13 John G Ruggie, 'International Regimes, Transactions, and Change: Embedded Liberalism in the Postwar Economic System' (1982) 36(2) International Organization 379-415.

14 Richard Falk and Andrew L Strauss, *A Global Parliament: Essays and Articles* (Committee for a Democratic UN, 2011); Benedict Kingsbury, Nico Krisch and Richard B Stewart, 'The Emergence of Global Administrative Law' (2004-2005) 68 Law & Contemporary Problems 15; Sabino Cassese, 'Is There a Global Administrative Law? in Armin von Bogdandy and others, *The Exercise of Public Authority by International Institutions: Advancing International Institutional Law* (Springer 2010) 761-776.

15 Eg Neil Walker, 'Constitutionalism and Pluralism in Global Context, in Matej Avbelj and Jan Komárek(eds) *Constitutional Pluralism in the European Union and Beyond* (Hart 2012).

16 Larry Catá Backer, 'On the Tension between Public and Private Governance in the Emerging Transnational Legal Order: State Ideology and Corporation in Polycentric Asymmetric Global Orders' (2012) Working Paper 4/2012, 16 <http://ssrn.com/abstract=2038103> accessed 25 June 2012.

17 Octavio Paz, *Conjunctions and Disjunctions* (First published 1969 as *Conjunciones y Disyunciones,* Helen R Lane, trans, Arcade Publishing 1982) 138.

the state and deployed for the consumption of the state system.[18] Nor can it be understood as the project of lawyers in the construction of juridico-bureaucratic enterprises that provide a rule of law based systematization of institutionalized politics.[19] Global law does not exist per se; the focus is on action—formalism is alien to the foundation of global law (though central to the ideology of the law-state). Regulatory power is not inherent in the law construct or the entities from which it emanates, but is instead something like the offal of governance activity—one grasps global law when it speaks through its actions, objects and constituent parts.

Global law, then, can be better understood, to the extent it is capable at this early stage of being understood, as the *systematization of anarchy*.[20] I speak here not of chaos[21] but of the converse of *archê*,[22] and away from notions of command grounded in the central reality of the state as the primary authoritative and legitimate expression of order.[23]

Global law is a way of pointing to an emerging universe of systems that share characteristics and whose interactions lend them to organization. Globalization, as such, embodies the inverse of *archê*, in its sense as

---

[18] For a critique of that view that also embraces a broader reading of law, Boaventura de Sousa Santos, *Toward a Nee Legal Common Sense* (2nd ed, Reed Elsevier 2002) 21-99.

[19] For an excellent description of this vision, eg Ran Hirschl, *Towards Juristocracy: The Origins and Consequences of the New Constitutionalism* (Harvard University Press 2007).

[20] With a nod to Edward Sandford Martin, 'Systematized Anarchy,' *Harpers* (February 1933).

[21] Here also is rejection of the utility of traditional anarchism that speaks to anarchy as order without power. Rather I am suggesting order and power without a controlling superstructure in the state system. Eg Pierre-Joseph Proudhon, *Confessions d'un révolutionnaire pour server a l'histoire de la revolution de février* (first published 1850, Adamant Media 2002) <http://gallica.bnf.fr/ark:/12148/bpt6k551822od/f8.image.r=proudhon.langFR> accessed 29 July 2012; Mickhail Bakunin, *Stateless Socialism: Anarchism, in The Political Philosophy of Bakhunin* (GP Maximoff ed, The Free Press 1953) 'We hasten to add here that we vigorously reject any attempt at social organization which would not admit the fullest liberty of individuals and organizations, or which would require the setting up of any regimenting power whatever.' In that respect state minimalists also fail to understand the revolutionary challenges of global law to what had been the contained universe of the state and its problems. Eg Robert D Kaplan, *The Coming Anarchy: Shattering the Dreams of the Post Cold War* 3-58 (Random House 2001).

[22] This suggests the idea of international relations theory of *archê* as hierarchy and ordering under a common government. Philip G Cerney, 'Globalization, Governance and Complexity, in Globalization and Governance' in Aseem Prakash and Jeffrey A Hart (eds), *Globalization and Governance* (Taylor & Francis, Routledge 1999) But it also touches on older anarchist notions. Sam Dolgoff (ed), *The Anarchist Collectives: Workers' Self-Management in the Spanish Revolution 1936-1939* (Black Rose Books 1990).

[23] For an example of the traditional approach, eg Robert Noziak, *Anarchy, State and Utopia* (Basic Books 1974).

sovereignty, domination and first causes, that structure the hierarchically and self-contained system of states and their international organizations, the ends of which, its *telos*, is the structure and maintenance of the law-state system itself.[24] Global law posits a system uncomfortable with first causes and without singular objective, a system grounded in an-*archê* and dispersion of purpose; "Nothing has any meaning",[25] the essence of the market.[26]

More conventionally, global law can be defined as the law of non-state governance systems. The definition suggests both commonalities and differences between "global law" as a distinct legal field and conventional legal fields derived from the legal orders of nation-states. Unlike domestic legal orders, global law covers a wide number of distinct governance communities existing simultaneously and organized beyond the rule imposing power of states. Moreover, these governance communities are not necessarily organized in the same way as states—with a population and a defined geographic territory and an institutional framework exercising plenary authority. Rather, global law communities may be understood as functionally differentiated societies organized for mutual benefit for specific objectives. They can include groups, institutions, and networks.

The structure of global law can be understood as an amalgamation of four fundamental characteristics that together define a new order in form that is, in some respects, the antithesis of the orderliness and unity of the law-state system it will displace (though not erase). These four fundamental characteristics—fracture,[27] fluidity,[28] permeability,[29] and

---

[24] Jan M Broekman and Larry Catá Backer, *Lawyers Making Meaning: The Semiotics of Law in Legal Education II* (Springer forthcoming 2012).

[25] Freidrich Nietzsche, *The Will to Power* (Walter Kaufmann and RJ Hollingdale trans., Walter Kaufmann, ed., first published in German in 1901, Vintage Books 1968) Book 3, ¶ 660 ('This melancholic sentence means "All meaning lies in intention, and if intention is altogether lacking, then meaning is altogether lacking, too."' ibid.).

[26] milton Friedman, *Capitalism and Freedom* (University of Chicago Press 1962).

[27] Andreas Fischer-Lescano and Günther Teubner, 'Regime-Collisions: The Vain Search for Legal Unity in the Fragmentation of Global Law,' (2003) 25 Michigan Journal of International Law 999.

[28] Larry Catá Backer, 'Inter-Systemic Harmonization and Its Challenges for the Legal-State,' in Sam Muller, Stavros Zouridis, Morly Frishman and Laura Kistemaker (eds), *The Law of the Future and the Future of the Law* (Torkel Opsahl Academic EPublisher 2011); Günther Teubner, 'A Constitutional Moment? The Logistics of 'Hitting the Bottom', in Poul F Kjaer and Günther Teubner (eds), *After the Catastrophe: Economy, Law and Politics in Times of Crisis* (forthcoming 2011).

[29] Hans Lindahl, 'A-Legality: Postnationalism and the Question of Legal Boundaries,' in Ronald Tinnevelt and Helder de Schutter, (eds) *Global Democracy And Exclusion* (Wiley Blackwell 2010) 117.

polycentricity[30]—reveal both the end time of the modernity at the heart of the law-state system and posit a new form of governance organization that is neither a unified history nor myth (determinism or instrumentalism) but a collective present. These characteristics speak to a dynamic system in which order is dependent on the ability of actors to form and deploy a large number of governance structures simultaneously, where the state continues to assert a substantial power, but in which it can no longer claim pride of place.

To find global law, one must look outside the state. To understand its character one must focus on commodification within markets for governance. To frame global law, one must abandon the study of a system for the study of governance systematization, of the process and substantive boundaries of markets for governance, something with a legal, political, economic, social and cultural dimension. To apply global law one must learn the language of governance beyond territory,[31] and beyond the state.

2. Fracture

Global law is fundamentally the law of fracture, of self-constitution,[32] of a leveling of governance power hierarchies among states, non-state actors, religion, and other collectives[33] that come together for the purpose of organizing a group whose functions and structures are a reflection of the group's will.[34] The essence of global law follows from the reality of deterritorialization of governance power that is at the foundation of globalization.[35]

---

30 Günther Teubner, 'The King's Many Bodies: The Self-Deconstruction of Law's Hierarchy,' (1997) 31(4) Law & Society Review 763; William Twining, *Globalisation And Legal Theory* (Cambridge University Press 2000).

31 Jan Arte Scholte, *Globalization: A Critical Introduction* (MacMillan 2000); Naoki Yoshihara, *Fluidity of Place: Globalization and the Transformation of Urban Space* (Trans-Pacific Press 2010).

32 Günther Teubner, *Constitutional Fragments: Societal Constitutions and Globalization* (Oxford University Press 2012).

33 Adelle Blakett, 'Global Governance, Legal Pluralism and the Decentered State: A Labor Law Critique of Codes of Corporate Conduct,' (2000-2001) 8 Indiana Journal of Global Legal Studies 401.

34 Hans Lindahl, 'Constituent Power and Reflexive Identity: Towards an Ontology of Collective Selfhood,' in Martin Loughlin & Neil Walker (eds), *The Paradox of Constitutionalism* (Oxford University Press 2007) 9-24.

35 Eg John G Ruggie, 'Territoriality and Beyond: Problematising Modernity in International Relations,' (1993) 47 International Organization 139; Stuart Elden, 'Missing the Point: Globalization, deterritorialization and the Space of the World,' (2005) 30(1)

With it, the emergence of governance spaces beyond the reach of the state - which until recently could with substantial confidence assert itself as the holder (and collectively as members of the community of states) of a (at least theoretical) monopoly of governance effectuated through the institution of government as the embodiment of the highest form of political, social and economic authority operated through law.

Global law posits the de-centralization of non-governmental organizations from states.[36] No longer are they mere secondary derivative collectives that owe their existence solely to the states that recognize them, these entities now acquire a self-constituting autonomy, and the governance power that flows therefrom. These entities can mimic the state in organization form; principal among them is the emerging class of self-governing multinational corporations that in many ways has begun to exercise governance authority within its own supply or value chains[37] that resemble the legislative authority of states.[38] But they can also assume other forms—they can manifest themselves as product or process certification organizations,[39] as standard setting organs, as assessment entities, or as a *volk*-like group evolving customs and shared practices (e.g. cyber-communities).[40]

Transactions of the Institute of British Geographers 8; Scholte (n 31) 89-109. Deterritorialization is used here broadly, to refer both to the diminishing of the power of political borders to enclose, that is a weakening of ties between political organization and place, as well as its re-territorialization within other or different spaces. Cf. Gilles Deleuze and Félix Guattari, *Anti-Œdipus: Capitalism and Schizophrenia* (Robert Hurley, Mark Seem and Helen R Lane trans (First published 1972 as *Capitalisme et schizophrénie: L'anti-Œdipe*, Penguin Classics 2009); Saskia Sassen, *Cities in a World Economy* (Sage 1993).

36 Robert D Cooter, 'Structural Adjudication and the New Law Merchant: A Model of Decentralized Law' (1994) 14 International Review of Law and Economics 215.

37 Li-Wen Lin, 'Corporate Social Accountability Standards In The Global Supply Chain: Resistance, Reconsideration, And Resolution In China,' (2007) 15 Cardozo Journal of International & Competition Law 321; Larry Catá Backer, 'Multinational Corporations as Objects and Sources of Transnational Regulation,' 14 ILSA Journal of International & Comparative Law 499.

38 Jennifer A Zerk, *Multinationals And Corporate Social Responsibility: Limitations And Opportunities In International Law* (Cambridge University Press 2006).

39 Errol E Meidinger, 'Multi-Interest Self-Governance through Global Product Certification Programs' in Olaf Dilling, Martin Herberg, and Gerd Winter (eds), *Responsible Business? Self-Governance in Transnational Economic Transactions* (Hart 2008).

40 Günther Teubner, 'Societal Constitutionalism: Alternatives to State Centered Constitutional Theory,' in Christian Joerges, Inger-Johanne Sand, and Günther Teubner (eds), *Transnational Governance and Constitutionalism: International Studies in the Theory of Private Law* (Hart 2004).

Fracture is not the end of order but merely its re-ordering. Where once only the state could claim a definitive role in the development of webs of rules and commands for the management of behavior, now other entities, social entities, have claimed that power to constitute themselves as well.[41] Global law also posits the emergence of private governance from out of the shadow of the state, and of law. 'This suggests a fundamental reorientation of governance, a movement away from the law-state binary to one grounded in the law-norm binary (within which the state is not necessarily present).'[42] Law, no longer a monopoly of the state,[43] becomes a *relational* concept; what falls beyond the jurisdiction or structural norms of a governance collective may fall within another, and both may understand what falls outside the norms and structures of their respective legal orders differently.[44] This applies not just between states (and their domestic legal orders) but between states and other governance collectives.

Law fractures its form; it gives way to the disciplinary technologies of an administrative bureaucracy available to governance organs of all kinds,[45] but to contract as well, which is transformed from bilateral arrangements between parties for a specific objective to an instrument of managing behavior.[46] The focus is on function rather than form, on norms.[47] What serves to compel behavior serves as law; the rest is mere field boundary

---

[41] David Sciulli, *Theory of Societal Constitutionalism: Foundations of a Non-Marxist Critical Theory* (Cambridge University Press 1992).

[42] Larry Catá Backer, 'Inter-Systemic Harmonization and Its Challenges for the Legal-State,' in Sam Muller and others (eds), *The Law of the Future and the Future of the Law* (Torkel Opsahl Academic EPublisher 2011).

[43] Kenneth W Abbott and others, 'The Concept of Legalization,' in Robert O Keohane (ed) *Power and Governance in a Partially Globalized World* (Routledge 2002) 132–48.

[44] See Hans Lindahl, 'Presentation: We and Cyberlaw: Constitutionalism and the Inclusion/Exclusion Difference' (International Conference, Transnational Societal Constitutionalism, Torino, 17 May 2012) <http://www.youtube.com/watch?v=IHv8-RecXEw> accessed 29 July 2012.

[45] See, eg Michel Foucault, *Discipline and Punish: The Birth of the Prison* (Alan Sheridan trans, Allen Lane 1979); Michel Foucault, *Security, Territory, Population, Lectures at the Collège de France 1977-1978* (Graham Burchell trans, Picador Palgrove Macmillan 2007) 87-110; 115-120. Cf., eg Bart Simon, 'The Return of Panopticism: Supervision, Subjection and the New Surveillance' (2005) 3(1) Surveillance and Society 1; David Lyon, *The Electronic Eye: The Rise of Surveillance Society* (University of Minnesota Press 1994) 57-80.

[46] Peer Zumbansen, 'The Law of Society: Governance Through Contract,' (2007) 14 Indiana Journal of Global Legal Studies 191; Marc Amstutz, Adreas Abegg & Vaios Karavas, 'Civil Society Constitutionalism: The Power of Contract Law' (2007) 14 Indiana Journal of Global Legal Studies 235, 236.

[47] Robert C Ellickson, 'Law and Economics Discovers Social Norms,' (1998) 27 Journal of Legal Studies 537.

protection by those seeking to retain the privilege of peculiar forms of behavior management. To the extent that these arguments rest on the classic distinction between the legitimating power of democratically enacted commands and the democratic deficit of other forms of rule making, the essence of the old *Rechtsstaat* ideal suffused with the normative power of Post-War *Sozialstaat* notions, is undercut by the move toward disciplinary techniques in the operations of nation-states.[48]

Fracture also re-orders the mechanics of societal cohesion and legitimacy. Just as fractures in territorial integrity that flows from the logic of globalization created spaces for non-state governance organizations to emerge, so the fractures in democratic accountability created spaces within which alternative methods of accountability could arise and be legitimated. Global law in this sense is about the law of system legitimacy in a heterodox world of governance organizations.[49] It posits consent, not as a historical fact from which successors may not withdraw and which is managed through the formal mechanics of voting, to a more dynamic and functional action-consent,[50] in which the mechanics of and linkages between democracy, legitimacy and law/governance will have to be re-thought within contextually distinct governance spaces.[51]

States understand fracture in a very distinct way. As between public organs, the notion of fracture is understood as a species of federation, or of extraterritoriality.[52] The principle object is the routinization of channels

---

48 The arguments about the democratic deficit in the European Union capture the spirit of this notion. Andreas Follesdal, and Simon Hix, 'Why There is a Democratic Deficit in the EU: A Response to Majone and Moravcsik,' (2006) 44(3) Journal of Common Market Studies 533. But it is an insight with wider application. All systems in which there are substantial separations between the centers of the origination of rules and the parties that are meant to hold rule makers to account face the same issue of legitimacy, of democratic deficit. Larry Catá Backer, 'Democracy Part XXVI: Democratic Accountability—From Voter to Managed Mob,'(*Law at the End of the Day*, June 2 2012) <http://lcbackerblog.blogspot.com/2012/06/democracy-part-xxvi-democratic.html> accessed 25 June 2012.

49 Ian Clark, 'Legitimacy in a Global Order,' (2003) 29 Review of International Studies 75.

50 Peer Zumbansen, 'Law After the Welfare State: Formalism, Functionalism, and the Ironic Turn of Reflexive Law' [2008] American Journal of Comparative Law 769; cf. Jonathon W Moses, 'Exit, Vote and Sovereignty: Migration, States and Globalization' (2005) 12(1) Review of International Political Economy 53.

51 Amanda Coe, Gilles Paquet and Jeffrey Roy, 'E-Governance and Smart Communities: A Social Learning Challenge' (2001) 19(1) Social Science Computer Review 80. Cf. Thomas S Franck, 'Democracy, Legitimacy, and the Rule of Law: Linkages' in Norman Dorsen & Prosser Gifford (eds), *Democracy and the Rule of Law*, (CQ Press 2001).

52 Eg Daniel Augenstein, 'Study of the Legal Framework on Human Rights and the Environment applicable to European Enterprises operating outside the European Union' Study for the European Commission ENTR/09/045 (2010).

for the division of authority, hierarchically arranged among a number of public bodies organized as government,[53] either as a form of devolution of state power or as a means of managing power through privatization.[54] Devolution posits the possibility of non-state governance only when it is borrowed, but also suggests an essential role for the state in the organization and enforcement of non-state governance systems.[55] Management fracture takes this notion one step further, positing the state at the center of a system in which sets the rules and objectives that it has privatized but still controls.[56] The object was to transform government from an entity that performed tasks to one that managed others in the performance of tasks—leveraged governance.[57]

The state has been overtaken by global law in the sense of a set of presumptions that exist beyond the state but that posit that the state is one but not the only organ for the institutionalization of power within a global system in which territory is no longer demarked by physical borders alone, but in which territory has become a three dimensional construct. Groups can come together to constitute themselves along functionally differentiated lines which are demarcated by function rather than by physicality. The scope of the authority of such groups may be small indeed, but to the extent that they proceed from the group autonomously, they suggest a space for governance separate from that of other groups, including the state.

Governance, then, is dependent not on meeting the requirements for legitimacy as a state under international law,[58] but rather of a self-constituting character marked by boundaries functionally differentiated

---

[53] Larry Catá Backer, 'Forging Federal Systems Within a Matrix of Contained Conflict: The Example of the European Union,' (1998) 12 Emory International Law Review 1331.

[54] Kenneth W Abbott & Duncan Snidal, 'Strengthening International Regulation through Transnational New Governance: Overcoming the Orchestration Deficit' (2009) 42 Vanderbilt Journal of Transnational Law 501.

[55] See Rod AW Rhodes, 'The Hollowing Out of the State' (1994 65 Political Quarterly 138.

[56] B Guy Peters, 'Managing the Hollow State' in Kjell A Eliassen and Jan Kooiman (eds), *Managing Public Organizations: Lessons fron Contemporary European Experience*, (SAGE Publications 1993).

[57] Allen Schick, OECD 50th Anniversary—Leveraged Governance: Avoiding Fracture and Getting Results 20-28 (OECD 2011); Peter G. Drucker, *The Age of Discontinuity: Guidelines to Our Changing Society* (Harper & Row 1992).

[58] Eg Malcolm N Shaw, *International Law*, (6th edn, Cambridge University Press 2008) 198-99; Ian Brownlie, *Principles of Public International Law* (7th edn, Oxford University Press 2008) 70.

from those of other groups.[59] Beyond a defined 'territory', the self-constituted group must manifest itself through government—an institutionalization of its cohesion with the power to manifest the normative objectives of the group. The government of governance groups can be as democratic as the Internet or as hierarchical as the multi-national corporation. That government must be able to manifest the group will, to make rules derived from and subject to the foundational rules (the constitution) of the group. The group must be able to discipline its members, enforce it rules and determine membership. The foundational premise rests on acceptance of the existence - independent of the control or authority of any one state or of the community of states - of a system of non-national, supranational or multi-national principles and rules applicable, in accordance with its own terms and logic, to public and private actors, natural and juridical persons.

Global law then can be understood as those norms that structure and organize fracture in a world order populated by an aggregate of a large variety of governance organs with territorial boundaries that vary with the variation in the character of the governance organization. Its constitution is 'form-recognizing'—the elements of this form-recognition include self-constitution, institutional autonomy, regulatory authority, and dispute resolution mechanisms. Its normative element is grounded in the customary expectations of the members of the organization:[60] citizens and residents in states; investors and customers in corporations; party members in state-party systems; believers in good standing in religious organization and so on.

These norms are all around us—from those derived from the *grundnorms* of religions and ideological systems, to the *jus cogens* notions of

[59] Ulrich Pruess, 'Disconnecting Constitutions from Statehood: Is Global Constitutionalism a Viable Concept?,' in Petra Dobner and Martin Laughlin (eds), *The Twilight of Constitutionalism?* (Oxford University Press 2010) 23-46.

[60] Custom and law understood here in its Aristotelian sense as both grounded in the internalized beliefs of those governed (Book II, cp. VIII) and requiring substantial effort to change functionally (Book IV, ch. V) even though easily changed in form. Aristotle, *A Treatise on Government* William Ellis trans, (JM Dent 1912). Cf. See The Paquete Habana, 175 US 677 (1900). The tension between the communal nature of rules and the instrumental application of rules remains a feature of governance now extended from the state to other governance organs. Eg John Ruggie, 'UN Special Representative of the Secretary General, Protect, Respect and Remedy: A Framework for Business and Human Rights: Rep. of the Special Representative of the Secretary-General on the Issue of Human Rights and Transnational Corporations and Other Business Enterprises' (2008) Delivered to the Human Rights Council, UN Doc A/HRC/8/5.

international law.[61] But fracture suggests that while there are many places from which to draw these process, structural and substantive norms, there is no system for arranging them in any definitive hierarchy other than those that follow the logic of the customs of the organizers of groups. Global law, then, posits not just fracture, but struggle among and within governance organs with respect to the arrangement and content of *grundnorms*.[62]

3. Fluidity

The great object of the state system was the preservation of states. The United Nations system was meant to serve as a culmination of this drive to preserve the state, its territorial integrity and the primacy of the state (and law) as the paramount systems for asserting governance power in a context in which there were no governance gaps between states.[63] The system was meant to produce stability and equilibrium, where, freed of substantial worry about their preservation, states could turn their attention to the management of their populations within a global governance framework that would be self binding on each state as a reflection of consensus of the community of nations memorialized through international conventional and customary law.[64]

The great object of global law is to permit fluidity - it is based on the assumption that governance organizations are impermanent and that there is no need to organize a meta-system around the premise that once established, self-constituted organizations ought to be preserved. It provides structure within which dynamic governance interaction is possible - as well as a space beyond the organization of governance - within which multiple governance units operate.[65] Global law, then, speaks to

---

[61] Kamrul Hossain, 'The Concept of Jus Gogens and the Obligation Under the U.N. Charter,' (2005) 3 Santa Clara Journal of International Law 72; Rafael Nieto-Navia, International Peremptory Norms (Jus Cogens) and International Humanitarian Law (2001) <www.iccnow.org/documents/WritingColombiaEng.pdf.> accessed 29 July 2012.

[62] Ironically this state of affairs reproduces the anarchy of the grundnorm in international public law. See eg Stefan AG Talmon, 'Jus Cogens After Germany v Italy: Substantive and Procedural Rules Distinguished,' [2012] Leiden Journal of International Law 25 <http://papers.ssrn.com/sol3/papers.cfm?abstract_id=2085271> accessed 29 July 2012.

[63] Larry Catá Backer, 'The Fuhrer Principle of International Law: Individual Responsibility and Collective Punishment,' (2003) 21(3) Pennsylvania State International Law Review 509.

[64] Harold Hongju Koh, 'Review Essay: Why Do Nations Obey International Law?' (1997) 106 Yale Law Journal 2599.

[65] Cf. Joseph A Camilleri and George Myconos, 'WTO: The Competitive Dynamic of Globalization at Work' (2004) 12(1) Law in Context 21.

temporality of border, objectives, organization, and structure as an organizational principle, and to uncertainty. A self-constituted organization exists as long as its members wish it or can preserve it within the context of its ability to satisfy the needs of its constituent bodies and its outside stakeholders. 'Consumer choice, civic activism and public engagement are also indicative of this altering environment, albeit in a manner that may well lack cohesion due to both the differing behaviour of new governance processes and the resistance fostered by traditional ones.'[66] Here, the principles of the market but not the law of the jungle are applicable;[67] not chaos, but anarchy in the sense of a willingness to allow self-constitution to come and go.

Global law provides structure to the fluidity of a governance order made up of a large variety of actors who have little but the basic structures of their organization and operation in common. Global law can be understood as the set of customary (generally accepted) rules within which organizations may come and go, grow and shrink, project power and defend territory (understood in its three dimensional functional differentiating sense). Anarchy, the possibility of emergence and disappearance, is thus systematized through a focus on constituting elements and away from the intrinsic permanence of the institutions themselves. The logic of mass movements (sometimes as mass democracy)[68] on which politics is now founded, and from which law proceeds, thus comes to its limiting principle. Law proceeds from the masses, but the masses are not constrained by the institutions they may create from time to time (states, corporations, religions, and the like). Global law turns its gaze to the masses; it serves as the fundamental charter of mass action and societal constitutionalism in which the masses remain constant and its institutional manifestations become fluid.

Yet fluidity also can be understood in another sense, one that is also central to the idea of global law as a distinct field of study: global law is the aggregate of a set of self-reflexive and closed rules that structures and contains movements of people, goods, information, services and capital, as a

---

66 Jeffrey Roy, 'E-Government, Good Government and Knowledge Management' (2005) 6(1) Journal of Electronic Commerce Research 44, 47.

67 This vision was meant to scare people back into the arms of a stable system of stable states. Thomas Hobbes, *Leviathan* (first published 1651, Penguin 1985) (though it need not be limited to the social construction of states, and where so limited, it appears that sometimes the cure was worse than the disease; eg Daniel Jonah Goldhagen, *Hitler's Willing Executioners: Ordinary Germans an the Holocaust* (Vintage Books 1997) 27-130.

68 Edward Hallett Carr, *Nationalism and After* (MacMillan 1945). Internationalism, like nationalism, must become social, ibid 63.

space of.[69] But this 'space of' is dynamic - as John Urry suggests, it is fluid, capturing trends toward heterogeneity in governance.[70] Fluidity suggests that self-constituting organizations - states, international public and private organizations, corporations, and religious communities - are moving targets. What is fluid in global law can 'represent the de-territorialized movement of people, information, objects, money, images, and risks across regions in undirected and non-linear fashion and at variable speeds'.[71] This touches also on the idea of permeability, discussed below, but here focuses on its consequence: the constitutional character of organizational borders (space) within which it flows (the substantive character of movements) develop in accordance with their own logic.

Fluidity, then, suggests the dynamic nature of communities constituting substructures, which when aggregated, provide a glimpse of the normative framework of global law. 'Indeed, from this perspective it is the legal system itself, and not external political, administrative, or corporate economic actors, that determines what the law is.'[72] Institutions are not tombs within which the customs and practices of a governance community are mummified, buried and worshipped from afar. Fluidity also suggests the customary nature of global law, in the sense that the patterns of flows tend to produce habit and expectation that in turn is understood and utilized as norms; instrumentalism is here more difficult.[73] The logic of globalization suggests that customs and practices have emerged from their tomb, whether that tomb is understood as the conventional static oriented state or a similar governance organ (in religion, economics or otherwise), and now embrace and are embraced by the flows of people, goods, capital, services, and information to form and reform a community. Resistance challenges the relevance of the community and ultimately may doom it. Communities group

---

69 Manuel Castells, 'An Introduction to the Information Age, in Frank Webster and others (eds), *The Information Society Reader* (Routledge 2004); Saskia Sassen, *The Global City: New York, London, Tokyo* (Princeton University Press 2001); Manuel Castells, *The Informational City: Information Technology, Economic Restructuring, and the Urban-Regional Process* (Wiley Blackwell, 1989).

70 John Urry, 'Mobile sociology' (2000) 51(1) British Journal of Sociology 185.

71 John Hannigan, 'Culture, Globalisation, and Social Cohesion: Towards a De-Territorialized, Global Fluids Model' (2002) 27(2) Canadian Journal of Communications 277, 278.

72 Jean L Cohen, 'Whose Sovereignty? Empire Versus International Law' (2004) 18(3) Ethics & International Affairs 1, 9.

73 Poul F Kjear, 'The Metamorphosis of the Functional Synthesis: A Continental European Perspective on Governance, Law and the Political in the Transnational' [2010] Wisconsion Law Review 489, 523.

and regroup within and between old communities and create their own.[74] Even states now disappear when suffocated by the contradictions of their inertia; corporations disappear with greater facility, religions with less grace. Global law can be understood as a legitimation of these movements and a presumption that the loss of a governance actor does not doom the aggregate system of governance—from the old something else will spring and over again.

4. Permeability

This world of heterogeneous systems of limited jurisdictions that exist without expectation of permanence and in accordance with the desires of their constituents and that can simultaneously affect actors that cross into their jurisdiction cannot exist in isolation. These systems communicate with each other - across and within borders to adjust internal structures in response to other systems' operations; discursive space permits the coupling of these systems as they learn to live among each other.[75] But structural coupling is not necessarily bounded by borders, and system closure does not suggest impermeability except, like Japan during the Shogunate, through designated trade portals. These systems also project themselves *into and through* each other. Global law can also then be understood as a set of rules of permeability,[76] one that posits the operational closure of systems,[77] but also the porous nature of boundaries that distinguish between system and non-system space but that do not impede the flows into and out of systems. Global law posits the permeability of all governance systems, though, of course to varying degrees.

Permeability does not suggest mere passive penetration, but instead suggests communication and reaction grounded in the fracture and fluidity of governance units operating, as will be discussed in the next section, within

---

[74] Matthew A Zook, 'Underground globalization: mapping the space of flows of the Internet adult industry' (2003) 35 Environment and Planning A 1261 (on the governance structures of the Internet adult industry).

[75] Günther Teubner, 'Global Bukowina: Legal Pluralism in the World-Society,' in Günther Teubner (ed) *Global Law Without a State* (Dartmouth Publishing Group 1997) 3–15.

[76] Louis Henkin, *International Law: Politics and Values* (Martinus Nijhoff 1995) ('while impermeability is still a general characteristic of statehood, it is no longer absolute. That ceased to be wholly true half a century ago and is increasingly less true').

[77] Niklas Luhmann, 'Operational Closure and Structural Coupling: The Differentiation of the Legal System' (1992) 13 Cardozo Law Review 1419.

a polycentric construct that makes communication, and intervention, a natural part of governance unit operation.[78] Permeability follows from the porosity of governance systems that overlap in a global order the territories of which are not measured simply by physical geography. Governance porosity follows the permeability of physical borders that have made it difficult for a single actor, traditionally a state, to exercise control of flows of ideas, capital, goods, culture, information, and people. Actions by any one actor has significant effect on other actors connected with the flows affected by governance actions (e.g., corporate policy over wages in their supply chain can affect the labor policy and law enforcement of host states, and both can be affected by investor tastes).[79] Systems that can simultaneously affect an actor tend also to speak to each other; their actions tend to affect the manner and extent to which other simultaneously applicable systems can manifest themselves. This structural (and structuring) communication produces a symbiosis of systems that sometimes manifests itself as a new form of private international law;[80] governance not only serves as a signifier of a space that exists outside of the state-government master construct, but also in intimate connection with it.[81]

Gunther Teubner speaks of systemic irritants, both internal and external to a societally constituted organization,[82] 'to indicate that legal transfers do not automatically displace pre-existing legal meanings and practices,

[78] Sol Picciotto, 'Constitutionalizing Multi-Level Governance?,' (2008) 6(3&4) International Journal of Constitutional Law 457. But in the state system, that communication has tended to be vertically arranged, a state of things made more complex in discerning hierarchy outside the state system. Eg Nigel White, 'Hierarchy in Organizations: Regional Bodies and the United Nations,' in Nicholas Tsagourias (ed) *Transnational Constitutionalism: International and European Models* (Cambridge University Press 2007) 135.

[79] James N Rosenau, 'Global Governance as Disaggregated Complexity,' in Alice D Ba and Matthew J Hoffman (eds) *Contending Perspectives on Global Governance* (Routledge 2005) 131-153.

[80] Gralf-Peter Calliess and Peer Zumbansen, *Rough Consensus and Running Code: A Theory of Transnational Private Law* (Hart 2010) 109.

[81] Larry Catá Backer, 'Governance Without Government: An Overview, in Günther Handl, Joachim Zekoll, Peer Zumbansen, (eds), *Beyond Territoriality: Transnational Legal Authority In An Age Of Globalization* (Brill Academic Publishers, forthcoming 2012) (citing, James N Rosenau, 'Governance, Order, and Change in World Politics' in Ernst Otto Czempiel ed, *Governance without Government: Order and Change in World Politics* (Cambridge University Press 1992); Edgar Grande & LW Pauly (eds), *Complex Sovereignty: Reconstructing Political Authority in the Twenty-first Century* (University of Toronto Press 2005) and Anne Wagner & Jan Broekman eds, *Prospects of Legal Semiotics* (Springer 2010).

[82] Günther Teubner, 'Legal Irritants: Good Faith in British Law or How Unifying Law Ends Up in New Divergences' (1998) 61(1) The Modern Law Review 11-32.

but instead trigger a new set of unpredictable choices and outcomes.'[83] The implications extend well beyond the internal operations of national law.[84] Dan Wielsch speaks to permeability in the governance of knowledge sharing.[85] Just as territory has become porous, the integrity of governance systems is no longer measured by their imperviousness to influence by or projections from other systems. A corporation with worldwide operations will likely harmonize practices across national borders in ways that may affect local legal cultures that may affect legal interpretation of indigenous law; 'convergence of form suggests a functional convergence of governance - the private corporation with public obligations, and the regulatory state that participates in markets. Public and private corporate bodies, once divided by an insurmountable conceptual barrier, now become mirrors of one another.'[86] But these are mirrors grounded in double reflexivity.[87] Porousness is also inherent in the three dimensional nature of borders. Multiple governance regimes may apply simultaneously on a single actor - that will likely have a penetrative effect on that actor, and by that actor's actions affect, in turn the governance systems simultaneously internalized. The logic of global law facilitates the constant interplay - the constant irritation - of systems operating simultaneously on a common set of actors. Global law can be understood both as the normative framework that legitimates permeability as well as the condition of permeability itself.

5. Polycentricity

If law is no longer the only authentic and legitimate means of effectuating governance systems, and if states are no longer necessarily the principal

---

[83] John Gillespie, 'Towards a Discursive Analysis of Legal Transfers Into Developing East Asia,' (2008) 40 International Law and Politics 657, 665.

[84] Michael W Dowdle, 'Completing Teubner: Foreign Irritants in China's Clinical Legal Education System and the 'Convergence' of Imaginations', in Penelope (Pip) Nicholson and Sarah Biddulph (eds), *Examining Practice, Interrogating Theory: Comparative Legal Studies in Asia* (Martinus Nijhoff 2008) 169; Günther Teubner, 'A Constitutional Moment? The Logistics of 'Hit the Bottom' in Poul F Kjaer and Günther Teubner (eds), *After the Catastrophe: Economy, Law and Politics in Times of Crisis* (forthcoming 2012).

[85] Dan Wielsch, 'Private Governance of Knowledge: Societally Crafted Intellectual Properties Regimes' [forthcoming 2013] 20 Indiana Journal of Global Legal Studies.

[86] Larry Catá Backer, 'Private Actors and Public Governance Beyond the State: The Multinational Corporation, the Financial Stbility Board, and the Global Governance Order' (2011) 18 Indiana Journal of Global Legal Studies 751, 759.

[87] Günther Teubner, 'Self-Constitutionalising TNCs? On the Linkage of "Private" and "Public" Codes of Conduct,' (2011) 18 Indiana Journal of Global Legal Studies 617, 624-28.

and superior organization for the management of behavior, it may also follow that governance can exist in multiple locations simultaneously. In a world in which states govern through law and administrative apparatus, using law, regulation and non-state groups govern through contract, standards and internally generated rules, and both invoke disciplinary techniques, it is possible to posit the autonomy of these systems and their existence simultaneously in the same governance space.[88] Governance systems, no longer arranged in vertically ordered power stacks, now collide with increasing frequency and with greater consequence.[89]

People, organizations, and states are now simultaneously governed by multiple systems of rules, rule systems that are produced by states and organizations and that may not be consistent, deriving their authority and character from autonomous sources. Polycentricity is the foundation of global law.[90] States are subject to the logic of their constitutions, but are simultaneously bounded by the rule systems imposed by the community of nations. States that reject the move from state centered to transnational constitutionalism[91] act at their peril - lessons learned recently from the constitutional crisis in Honduras,[92] and the discrediting of the long standing governments in Syria and Libya.[93]

Non-state actors provide a better view of the polycentric character of global law.[94] Corporations may be subject to the laws of the states in which

---

88 Ralf Michaels, 'True Lex Mercatoria: Law beyond the State' (2007) 14 Indiana Journal of Global Legal Studies 447.

89 On collisions, see eg Larry Catá Backer, 'Collisions of Societal Constitutions: Hierarchical Power Arrangements and Horizontal Effects in the Management of Human Rights Regimes' [forthcoming 2013] 20 Indiana Journal of Global Legal Studies.

90 Fischer-Lescano (n 27); Michael D McGinnis, 'Legal Pluralism, Polycentricity, and Faith-Based Organizations in Global Governance,' in Mark Sproule-Jones, Barbara Allen, and Filippo Sabetti eds, *The Struggle to Constitute and Sustain Productive Orders* (Lexington Books 2008) 45-64. And as neo-medievalism, eg Hedley Bull, *The Anarchical Society: A Study of Order in World Politics* (Columbia University Press 1977).

91 Wen Chen Chang and Jiun-rong Yeh, 'The Emergence of Transnational Constitutionalism: Its Features, Challenges and Solutions' (2008) 27 Pennsylvania State International Law Journal 89.

92 Larry Catá Backer 'Democracy Part XX: Democracy With or Without Elections in Honduras,' (*Law at the End of the Day*, Dec. 4, 2009, <http://lcbackerblog.blogspot.com/2009/12/democracy-part-xx-democracy-without.html.> accessed 25 June 2012.

93 Larry Catá Backer, 'On Intervention in Libya: The Emerging Nature of Supra-National Legal Framework/Norms for Disciplining States and Their Leaders by Others,' (*Law at the End of the Day*, July 13, 20911, <http://lcbackerblog.blogspot.com/2011/07/on-intervention-in-libya-emerging.html> accessed 25 June 2012.

94 Alice De Jonge, *Transnational Corporations and International Law: Accountability in the Global Business Environment* (Edward Elgar 2011).

they operate and are chartered, they may be subject to the laws of the states in which their subsidiaries are chartered and operate, they may be subject to international law in conflict zones, and to international soft law standards administered through states,[95] the U.N. system,[96] and private entities,[97] to the rules of listing entities,[98] and to its own internal governance systems.[99] The systems to which the entity may owe an obligation may not be compatible and they may not form parts of the same system, (emphasizing the fracture aspect in global law), but they may have an effect on the operations of the entity nonetheless, even if one system does not recognize the legitimacy of the rules of the others.

Polycentricity in its emerging form was at the center of recent efforts to develop an international framework for the management of businesses and human rights. These efforts focus on the simultaneous obligations of states and corporations, separate, simultaneous and separately founded.[100] It is well evidenced in the operations of the system of soft law regulation administered through the Organization for Economic

---

95 OECD Guidelines for Multinational Enterprises (2011).

96 John Ruggie, Report of the Special Representative of the Secretary-General on the issue of human rights and transnational corporations and other business enterprises, John Ruggie Guiding Principles on Business and Human Rights: Implementing the United Nations 'Protect, Respect and Remedy' Framework (2011) A/HRC/17/31.

97 Fair Labor Association Launches Independent Investigation of Foxconn <www.fairlabor.org/blog/entry/fair-labor-association-launches-independent-investigation-foxconn> accessed 28 July 2012.

98 See Sustainable Stock Exchange Initiative, 2012 Sustainable Stock Exchanges Report: A Report on Progress <www.responsibleresearch.com/Sustainable_Stock_Exchanges_2012__Online.pdf.> accessed 28 July 2012.

99 See Nike Inc Corporate Sustainability Report 2012 <www.nikebiz.com/crreport/> accessed 20 July 2012; Walmart 2012 Global Responsibility Report <www.walmartstores.com/sites/responsibility-report/2012/pdf/WMT_2012_GRR.pdf.> accessed 28 July 2012.

100 John Ruggie, Opening Remarks (Consultation on operationalizing the framework for business and human rights presented by the Special Representative of the Secretary-General on the issue of human rights and transnational corporations and other business enterprises, Palais des Nations, Geneva, Swirzerland, 5-6 October 2009), at 5 <www.business-humanrights.org/Documents/Ruggie-speech-to-Geneva-consultation-Oct-2009.pdf.> accessed 25 July 2012. What is described, effectively, is polycentric norm making among multiple systems of functionally differentiated governance communities that are required to interact with each other in complex and dynamic ways. Incompatible systems, law and norm – must effectively find a way to communicate and to harmonize values and relevance for their constituting communities, whether these are citizens, consumer, employees, or investors. Larry Catá Backer, 'On Challenges to Operationalizing a Transnational Framework for Business and Human Rights-the View From Geneva,' (*Law at the End of the Day*, Oct. 13, 2009) <http://lcbackerblog.blogspot.com/2009/10/on-challenges-to-operationalizing.html> accessed 28 July 2012.

Cooperation and Development (OECD) under the Guidelines for Multinational Enterprises.[101] It suggests the structures of what some have called 'open source anarchy.'[102]

A joint venture co-owned by a subsidiary of Vedanta was challenged in its efforts to develop aluminum mining on indigenous land in the Orissa Province in India. The Indian Supreme Court determined that the joint venture had complied with all national law. A non-governmental organization unrelated to any of the parties in India brought a complaint in the U.K. alleging violation of the OECD Guidelines for Multinational Enterprises on the part of the parent corporation. Vedanta challenged the standing of Survival International to bring the complaint and the compatibility of the proceedings in light of the actions of the Indian Supreme Court approving the project. The U.K. National Contact point determined that the law of standing applicable in the U.K. was not applicable in the U.K. by an instrumentality of the government of the U.K. when acting under the governance system of the Guidelines.[103] The U.K. National Contact Point then determined that the action by the Supreme Court of India was irrelevant to the obligations of the parent corporation under international law and the Guidelines themselves.[104] Though the complaints under the OECD Guidelines were dismissed as 'soft law' and unenforceable as 'law' in the U.K. or India, the action eventually produced an Indian Parliamentary Commission investigation and further action on the claims of the indigenous people.

The polycentricity at the heart of global law reframes the traditional approach to law that posits a dynamic population and a static and stable system into its inverse. The 'psychology of the masses'[105] has been

---

[101] OECD Guidelines for Multinational Enterprises (2011) <www.oecd.org/dataoecd/43/29/48004323.pdf.> accessed 27 July 2012.

[102] David P Fidler, 'Architecture amidst Anarchy: Global Health's Quest for Governance' (2007) 1(1) Global Health Governance 1.

[103] Initial Assessment by the UK National Contact Point for the OECD Guidelines for Multinational Enterprises: Complaint from Survival International against Vedanta Resources plc, 27 March 2009 <www.business-humanrights.org/Links/Repository/266990/jump> accessed 27 July 2012.

[104] Final Statement by the UK National Contact Point for the OECD Guidelines for Multinational Enterprises: Complaint from Survival International against Vedanta Resources plc, 25 September 2009 <www.business-humanrights.org/Links/Repository/266990/jump> accessed 28 July 2012.

[105] This is a term usefully derived from Robert Musil's work worth quoting here and then recasting in globalized terms: 'So far as it applies to the masses, it makes very good sense to me. The masses are moved only by impulses, and of course that means by the impulses that most individuals have in common, that's only logical. That's to say, of course, it's illogical.

recast - where once law was understood as an instrument for their management, now it has assumed more the character of a commodity that must sell itself for mass consumption; and the masses are free to buy several products at once. The state has been decentered, but the masses are now even more central - and less passive in the sense of an empowerment to choose among distinct governance frameworks.[106] It is in this sense of global law's fracture, fluidity, permeability and polycentricity, and of the choices made possible, that one can understand both the dynamics of the Iranian constitutional crisis of 2010 and the contests between soft law and legal frameworks for consumer and investor loyalty.

6. Conclusion

I have sought to offer something of a counter-vision to more conventional ideas of the structure and character of global law. Global law is best understood as the management of anarchy, of the systematization of a loosely intertwined universe of autonomous governance frameworks operating dynamically across borders grounded in functional differentiation among governance communities. Global law can be understood as focused on the study of the system of principles and rules applied in lieu of or in addition to the domestically germane law of a state, or of the community of states, to the relationships among persons and institutions—public and private, natural and legal, grounded in fundamental principles of fracture, fluidity, permeability and polycentricity.

Fracture, fluidity, permeability and polycentricity are the basic characteristics of global law, the systematization of which marks its field boundaries. These also serve as the structural foundations of its constitutional element (a basic set of presumptive and supreme organizing principles

---

The masses are illogical, they make use of logical ideas only as trappings. What they're really guided by is simply and solely *suggestion*.' Robert Musil, *The Man Without Qualities* III:420 (first published 1933 as *Der Mann ohne Eigenschaften,* Eithene Wilkins & Ernst Kaiser trans, Secker & Warburg 1960).

106 Where the state held something closer to a monopoly of power within a territory, legal instrumentalism was possible and management was straightforward. 'If you give me the newspapers, the wireless, the cinema industry, and perhaps a few other means of influencing public opinion, I undertake inside a few years (...) to turn everyone into cannibals.' Musil, *The Man Without Qualities,* ibid, III:420. For global law, management in the context of fracture, fluidity, permeability and polycentricity now turns the methods of legal instrumentalism into the battlefields for allegiance and legitimacy.

and rules),[107] its substantive element (implementing the constituted system),[108] and its process element (rules for the development of substantive rules and dispute resolution).[109]

From that systematization one can derive a method of theorizing the emerging framework of the unity of disunity in governance, in which law and governance systems multiply within a discernable internal logic, while the objects of regulation remain constant. While traditional law starts with the state and traces its relationship with the governed; global law starts with the governed and traces their relationship with and effects on governance organs.

Global law thus embraces the nature of governance as commodity. The rest follows. I have posited in place of *archê* and *telos*, an ordering framework in the fundamental character of which embraces an-archê and nihilism, the former in its anti-hierarchical sense, and the latter in its sense of lack of objective.

> Nihilism as a psychological state has yet a *third* and *last* form. Given these two insights, that becoming has no goal and that underneath all becoming there is a no grand unity in which the individual could immerse himself completely as in an element of supreme value, an escape remains: to pass sentence on this whole world of becoming as a deception and to invent a world beyond it, a *true* world.[110]

Global law has no order to it; it has no object, it has no law about it. Global law amalgamates orders, objectives and governance. It is less a model derived from the ideology of the law-state and hierarchies of law than a *system of systems*, teeming with sub-systems, each autonomous, fluid, and permeable, existing side by side and stacked in a constantly changing governance universe, the parameters of which are discernable only in the wake

---

107 Usually described as its societally constitutive element, and bound up in the jurisdictional rules of fracture. See eg in addition to source cited above, Gavin W Anderson, *Constitutional Rights After Globalization* (Hart 2005) 99-140.

108 Eg William E Scheueman, 'Reflexive Law and the Challenges of Globalization' (2001) 9 Journal of Political Philosophy 81; Claire Cutler, 'The Privatization of Global Governance and the Modern Law Merchant' in Adrienne H Zritier (ed), *Common Goods: Reinventing European and International Governance* (Rowman & Littlefield Publishers Inc 2002) 127-158.

109 Eg Harm Schepel, *The Constitution of Private Governance: Product Standards in the Regulation of Integrating Markets* (Hart 2005) (substance and process of standardization).

110 Freidrich Nietzsche, *The Will to Power* (Walter Kaufmann and RJ Hollingdale trans, eds Vintage Books 1968) Book I ¶ 12. Better put, perhaps, a world that is true because it is embraced as such and remains true for the time that people consent to belief in its truth. During that time, but only during that time, its truth is eternal.

of the actions taken by them.[111] Yet the future is not inevitably written in favor of a global order; nor is the state and its ideology, of great utility to powerful actors and an important element in security likely to disappear. There is a choice, and thus the caveat to the global law project: 'If contemporary rebellion (...) is not dissipated in a succession of raucous cries and does not degenerate into closed, authoritarian systems.'[112] The failure of global law could lead not back to the democratic, but instead to the authoritarian state[113] or anarchy with an authoritarian streak.[114]

---

111 Jan-Hendrik Passoth and Nicholas Rowland, 'Actor-Network State: Integrating Actor-Network Theory and State Theory,'(2010) International Sociology 818 ('ANT accounts treat markets, bodies and states as socio-technical assemblages that come into being as concrete actors are enrolled: price-calculation devices, traders trained in economic theory and Reuters terminals in the case of markets; (...) land, borders, measurement and counting procedures and ideological treatises in the case of states.' ibid 828).

112 Octavio Paz, *Conjunctions and Disjunctions* (Helen R Lane, trans, AP 1982) 139.

113 Eg Azar Gat, 'The Return of Authoritarian Great Powers' (2007) 86 Foreign Affairs 59.

114 Eg Robert Altmeyer, *The Authoritarian Specter* (Harvard University Press 1996).

Global Law for Private Law

Eric Tjong Tjin Tai
Professor of Private Law, Tilburg University, The Netherlands
t.f.e.tjongtjintai@tilburguniversity.edu

Abstract
The standard concept of law, consisting of legislation and case law, provides authority and legitimacy to law, as well as a methodology. Transnationalisation of law has necessitated the recognition of non-state influences. Although this should lead to an updated concept of law, authority and legitimacy are not actually problematic as these are in practice derived from the authority and legitimacy of national courts which decide most cases, albeit using new sources of law. The main problem of global law is methodology.

Keywords
transnational law; global law; legal knowledge; methodology; authority; legitimacy

1. Introduction

The debate on global law or transnational law[1] turns effectively on the question of what law actually is. Somewhat surprisingly, this question is rarely touched upon in the extensive literature on global law.[2] I will try to provide an answer to the question of 'what is global law' from a private law perspective. Given the limited space available, this answer cannot be but sketchy.

2. The Concept of Law

The need for a concept of law derives primarily from the need to distinguish law from non-law, in particular from morality and natural law. Hence the notion of positive law: law which is institutionalised, in particular in

[1] I will use both terms as synonyms.

[2] Exceptions are in particular D von Daniels, *The Concept of Law from a Transnational Perspective* (Ashgate 2010) and P Zumbansen and GP Callies, *Rough Consensus And Running Code* (Hart Publishing 2010).

statutes and case law. This concept explains two functions of law, namely to provide decisive arguments regarding the applicable rules (hence we need no longer rethink these)[3] and thereby provide coordination (because we know the state of the law). However, this concept is limited as it does not encompass what actually occurs in legal practice.

In a broader view of legal practice, law is anything we use to decide legal issues.[4] This means that we should possibly not speak of law but rather of *legal knowledge*. This is broader than law in the classic positivistic sense: knowledge may lack 'hard' authority, but may still have argumentative force or 'normal' legal authority. This is, in effect, the route along which precedential force has come to be accepted in most countries. It also involves the debate between judges, which may be informed by doctrine and case law even if in their official pronouncements the courts refer only to the code.[5] In private law in particular we have effectively always used a broader notion of 'soft' legal authority.[6]

This does not mean that the notion of binding, 'hard' authority is useless. Complying with official authority serves the purpose of providing a clear *methodology*, in which statute stands above case law, after which doctrine and other sources may play their role. Without a core of more or less binding authority, law would lose its basis. Furthermore, this methodology provides *legitimation* of legal practice, as formally we respect the decisions of the democratic legislator and the independent courts. This legitimation is in effect based on state sovereignty.

3. The Decline of Sovereignty

The root causes of the receding prominence of sovereignty are twofold. First, the rise of supranational law (European Union, fundamental rights – particularly the ECHR –, and treaties such as CISG and WIPO) and the growing recognition of what is called 'soft law'.[7]

---

[3] The service conception of law (Raz).

[4] Very provisionally I would define law as a system to allow rational discussion of our basic intuitions on justice, guided by our sense of justice. But the following argument does not turn on this definition.

[5] Cf. M Lasser, *Judicial Deliberations* (Oxford University Press 2004) regarding French courts.

[6] Eg N Jansen, *The Making of Legal Authority* (Oxford University Press 2010). Also PAJ van den Berg, *The Politics of European Codification* (European Law Publishing 2007) and other publications.

[7] In particular, norms created (and possibly enforced) by non-state actors; a broader definition might include state norms that are not enforced.

Supranational law has come about by a voluntary partial transference of sovereignty. Although the general idea was that this would not diminish the actual prominence of national sovereignty, in fact these supranational organisations and their courts have gradually encroached upon the national domain to such an extent and so regularly that they become part of the picture of what law actually is in practice. No longer can we view supranational influence on national law as a temporary imbalance that is quickly absorbed in the national system; nowadays we have a system of multi-level regulation.

Soft law in itself is not new and has always been recognised as an influence on the operation of law, be it in the form of local, customary law, business practices, professional ethics, state of the art, general conditions and the like. It has come to the fore partly by regulators who see it as an alternative to government-proclaimed rules, partly by a renewed interest in what previously was called sociology of law. Soft law rules influence behaviour and are recognised in court decisions, even if they are not law in the traditional positivistic sense of the word. Furthermore, soft law is not limited to state boundaries: soft law appears to have a decided advantage to state law in regulating new areas where international uniformity is paramount.[8]

Strictly speaking neither of these developments falsifies national sovereignty, as that involves the *normative* (instead of empirical) claim that nation states supremely decide what they recognise as legally relevant materials.[9] However, the incursions into national sovereignty appear to be growing, whereby the appeal of this ideal diminishes. Within quite a lot of areas of legal practice – in particular in specialist areas, 'functional' domains of law – lawyers need to consult and apply a large number of sources of law[10] that are not all state-proclaimed, where various courts have jurisdiction, and where the ideal of a coherent legal system[11] does not provide much help in solving inconsistencies and uncertainties. This naturally leads to a state that may be called legal pluralism.[12] An encompassing theoretical framework would be 'general jurisprudence',[13] which however appears to lack sufficient solid guidelines for legal argumentation.

---

[8] See for example PP Polanski, *Customary law of the Internet: In Search for a Supranational Cyberspace Law* (Asser Press 2007).

[9] Secondary rules (Hart) or Grundnorm (Kelsen).

[10] Used more loosely, not in the strict positivistic sense of the word.

[11] Exemplified in the Dworkinian model of Hercules.

[12] See P Zumbansen in particular.

[13] Cf. BZ Tamanaha, *A General Jurisprudence of Law and Society* (Oxford University Press 2001) W Twining, *General Jurisprudence: Understanding Law from a Global Perspective* (Cambridge University Press 2009).

4. Towards Global Law?

A 'pluralistic' conception of global law has the decided disadvantage that it lacks unity. It is in danger of becoming a bundle of disconnected facts. From a private law perspective, some degree of coherence, consistency, and system is necessary in order for law to be more than a mere bag of tricks. That does not mean that we have to stick with the traditional positivistic conception: as discussed, that conception never reflected actual practice.

A proper concept of global law should, to my mind, take into account the practice of dispute resolution (the available courts and their practices), as these to a large part set the standard as to what is formally and informally accepted as legal authority. A distinction between legal authority and non-legal authority is unavoidable as otherwise we would be unable to distinguish law from other kinds of rules, such as morality, and cultural or social rules.[14] State-sanctioned dispute resolution is unquestionably authoritative, and thereby provides a basic bench-mark for what is law. Indeed, we do have to look beyond the formal pronouncements and also take actual practice into account.

If we investigate actual practices of courts, we see that law to a large extent is still national law, and that supranational and soft law norms are irregularly taken into account where applicable. There is not really much discussion on the theory that would systematise such a practice, nonetheless the courts appear to manage. More importantly, laymen seem to be completely oblivious to the legal discussions around global law, with the possible exception of ECHR case law.

This suggests that global law is primarily a problem for lawyers. We cannot use our old concept, and have to develop a new one. The problem is one wherein we lack our old, familiar system, and have to operate without one or develop one anew. The puzzle of how to conceptualise a multi-level system of regulation has up to now eluded the sharpest minds of our generation, possibly there is no actual solution. Global law cannot be a system in the traditional sense of the word, and is at present primarily a practice of law wherein lawyers are more aware of global developments, at the expense of detailed knowledge of national law. Global law is an approach, a community and an ideal.

For the future it is not impossible that more systematic tendencies will prevail. A rise of doctrine regarding issues of global law would provide

---

14 Cf. The critique of R Cotterrell, *Law & Social Inquiry* 2012 (37/2), 500–514.

additional supports in the absence of the traditional pillars of statute and case law. Although these do exist in global law, they are first of all too diverse and inconsistent, and secondly little developed.

5. The Theory of Global Law

So what does this tell us at the level of legal theory?

Authority in itself is not a problem: lawyers have always juggled sources of varying authority. However, there is to my mind – which I cannot develop here – a certain ambivalence in the kind of authority that supranational law and courts provide, which differs from national courts. Supranational courts are unable to provide the same systematising, unifying role that national courts have been able to in the past: this is due to the sheer volume of questions that could arise. National courts furthermore were only able to do so by resting on loyal lower courts that had the same unifying aim, often with support of a national code. All this is absent in the global arena. Supranational courts explicitly rely on national courts to apply their interpretations of supranational law, but as they cannot rule on the context of national law, they are thereby singularly handicapped in actually providing the proper development of law.

Regarding *legitimacy*: the legitimacy of such varying sources and courts of global law actually appear hardly to be questioned, as far as private law goes.[15] Only supranational law is viewed with distrust as it breaches the national systematic unity. However, this appears due more to the lack of integration of supranational law with national law. A proper developed legal practice of global law in itself supports legitimacy. This does not turn solely on the judge's authority or manner of proceeding, but also in the surrounding institutions. Hence law is not only the set of applicable rules, but also the practice of the law, the legal system, including judges, lawyers who provide advice, and the dissemination of law into general society and culture.

Finally, on the *methodology* of global law. The current diversity of approaches, legal sources and literature is bewildering and makes it impossible for anyone to take into account all possibly relevant materials. The traditional anchors of national sovereignty and hierarchy are now unavailable. I would provisionally suggest that a viable methodology should throw

[15] It appears to be more of an obstacle for public law.

off the ideal of sovereignty and instead assume a model of distributed legal supervision, through a plurality of rules and dispute resolution fora.

The ideal should not solely be consistency or coherence of a system of rules, but rather a balance or equilibrium between the competing ideals or principles that are alive in the network of global law. If we critically examine earlier national practices in the era of codification we see that the legal system always assumed a distributed responsibility for unification and promulgation of the law, through the system of appeal and cassation, and supported by publication of case law, case notes, and doctrine. In order to allow such development in a multi-level legal system, supranational law should not be viewed as being intrinsically sovereign over national law, but instead as part of a larger system of global law, in which it is balanced against systematic considerations of national law. Only in that way can national and supranational courts together work towards greater coherence and consistency.

Once we recognise that actual practice was always more messy than the clean outlines of theory, we may fruitfully revise theory on the existing basis.

A Vision of Global Legal Scholarship

Pierre Larouche*
Professor of Competition Law, Tilburg Law and Economics Center (TILEC)
Department of European and International Public Law, Tilburg Law School (TLS)
pierre.larouche@tilburguniversity.edu

Abstract
Global legal scholarship should aim to be both post-national and inter-disciplinary. By post-national, we imply that it should rise above national legal systems and cover a more abstract corpus of knowledge about law, of which national legal systems would be an application. By inter-disciplinary, we mean that legal scholarship is enhanced by a deeper understanding of other sciences, without merging with any of them. This places global legal scholarship in a 'sweet spot', between traditional national legal scholarship and other social sciences. In order to retain its strong link with reality, global legal scholarship should also espouse empirical research methods.

Keywords
legal scholarship; global law; comparative law; inter-disciplinarity; empirical legal research

What is the future of legal scholarship? This question is on the mind of many a legal scholar, as the traditional ways of legal scholarship are being challenged. These challenges come not just from long-term socio-economic trends (globalisation, technological advances, climate change). They also result from factors closer to home, such as the scarcity of means generally available for research. As a consequence, legal research needs to present a compelling and competitive case for access to resources, as against rival claimants.

Over the past 20 years, research faculties, including Tilburg Law School (TLS), have sought to rise to these challenges. Often taking US legal scholarship as a benchmark, European and other non-US scholars have by

---

* Research available at <http://ssrn.com/author=537158>. Thanks to my colleagues at TLS who commented on a previous version of this paper, and in particular to Randall Lesaffer and Willem Witteveen.

all accounts improved their research performance, in both quantitative and qualitative terms. Yet, US legal scholarship also suffers from its shortcomings. We are coming to the point where a new standard for legal scholarship might emerge from the continuing efforts of researchers across the world.

What should such scholarship look like? This short paper seeks to sketch an answer to this question. Legal scholarship should become *global*,[1] a term whose understanding is articulated around three characteristics. First of all, global legal scholarship should be *post-national*,[2] in that it rises above national or other legal orders in order to address law as a common, global phenomenon. Secondly, it should be *inter-disciplinary*, in that it puts law in relation with other disciplines and concerns itself with the interface between law and these disciplines. Thirdly, it should be *empirical*, in that it strives to retain a strong bond with reality, albeit perhaps a different one than before.

None of these characteristics are new, and yet – or perhaps therefore – each of them are construed in various ways in the literature. The following passages aim to go beyond received wisdom and propose a more concrete understanding of each.

1. Post-National Scholarship

This first characteristic – which is difficult to express in a single term – refers to the relationship between legal scholarship and its traditional object of study, i.e. positive law, seen as the law of a particular jurisdiction. In a nutshell, with the rise of the nation State, borders were also drawn within legal scholarship. By the end of the 19th century, within each national

---

[1] For lack of a better term. It should become apparent to the reader that there are few appropriate labels left that have not already been loaded with meaning in the literature. Accordingly, what matters here is not so much the label used, as the definition given to it.

[2] Here as well, there are plenty of terms to choose from to try to reflect how global legal scholarship is meant to stand in a different relationship to national legal orders than the traditional understanding of the past two centuries. 'International' or 'Multi-national' simply do not match the underlying concept. 'Transnational' is already quite widespread and has acquired a specific meaning, referring to private ordering next to, or bypassing, State ordering. 'Supranational' has a specific meaning in EU law. In the end, 'post-national' was chosen, even if it is also already in use, on the basis that it does suggest a dynamic phenomenon, and that it also implies that nationally-bound legal scholarship might have been a historical contingency.

legal order, legal scholarship was concerned first and foremost with the study of that given order. Even then, this one-to-one relationship loosened up over time with the growth of international law and – for EU Member States – of EU law, both of which expanded the scope of inquiry of legal scholarship. At this point in time, there is widespread agreement that this one-to-one relationship might have outlived any usefulness it ever had.

Next to that, there has always been an effort, through comparative law, to break the bond between legal scholarship and the positive law of a specific regime. It is interesting to see how comparative law itself evolved over time. When it began, modern comparative law was carried out from a given national regime: it was the study of 'foreign law', aiming at enriching the understanding of one's own law. In short, comparative law took place from the inside looking out.

Progressively, comparative law scholars began to form an international community, which led them to take some distance from national legal communities. The perspective of comparative law then evolved, from the study of foreign law, towards the study of the various legal orders set next to one another, i.e. a proper comparison of legal orders.

It is conceivable to go one step beyond and anchor legal scholarship, not within national law, nor at the level of the various national legal orders, but above these systems. The latter are then viewed, not so much as objects of comparison, but as concrete applications of a higher, more abstract corpus of knowledge about law. The object of study of legal scholarship then becomes not a specific legal order, or even a comparison of legal orders (or *Rechtsvergleichung*, as the Germans put it), but that abstract corpus of knowledge which manifests itself in the various national legal orders. For instance, knowing what options and choices are available in the design of liability law (including the degree of relevance of conduct, various conceptions of wrongfulness – if needed – and illegality, devices to limit the ambit of liability etc.), one can study how different legal orders have made similar or different design choices and how this affects the quality of liability law.[3] Of course, the options and choices are not known *a priori*; they are identified either as a result of a comparative study of the type described in the previous paragraph or otherwise through inter-disciplinary inquiries (using economic analysis, for instance).

[3] Quality can be measured according to many parameters, be it efficiency, effectiveness, satisfaction of the parties, etc. For the purposes of the present discussion, it is immaterial how quality is defined.

Moving to a post-national scholarship changes the position of the legal scholar. In a sense, the legal scholar is freed from the shackles of national law (or more generally of a relationship to a single legal order) and of law-producing institutions such as the *trias politica*. Even if scholarship – legal or otherwise – has always been conceived as an independent venture, it cannot be denied that a close relationship to a specific legal order creates some dependency, even if only as a matter of supplying the scholar with sources to work with and issues to research. By turning specific legal orders into applications, the legal scholar regains control over his or her research agenda, and over his or her materials. Legal scholarship regains more autonomy.

Of course, with freedom always comes responsibility. In the absence of a reference point in positive law to provide structure, it is up to the legal scholar to organise his or her research work and defend his or her choices as to how to approach, organise and select legal issues. Without wanting to explore this in detail,[4] it can be ventured that comparative law can serve as inspiration, with its functionalist methodology. The shortcomings of functionalism can be addressed with a more elaborate policy dimension and with more dynamism, so that the resulting approach can provide a sound basis for the legal scholar.

In the longer term, post-national scholarship has significant theoretical implications as well. First of all, it is pushing the whole of legal scholarship in a more abstract and more theoretical direction. Post-national scholarship, in and of itself, tackles law at a more general or fundamental level since it takes place at a level above national legal orders; requiring a measure of abstraction from the details of these orders. The more traditional scholarship that relates to a specific legal order can then be reframed as applied research. Even if it is seen as applied, traditional scholarship would benefit from taking into account the fundamental, post-national research.[5] By the same token, traditional scholarship is also drawn towards a more abstract level.

Secondly, the greater autonomy of legal scholarship affects its authority and its legitimacy. As long as legal scholarship relates to a specific positive law regime, it can derive some authority and legitimacy from that regime,

[4] This is the object of a longer piece: see Pierre Larouche, 'Legal Emulation between Regulatory Competition and Comparative Law', TILEC Discussion Paper 2012-17, available at <http://papers.ssrn.com/sol3/papers.cfm?abstract_id=2044679> accessed 31 July 2012.

[5] For instance, by way of literature review in introduction.

in the sense that legal scholarship enables a better understanding of that regime (whether through synthesis or critical examination) and therefore contributes to its improvement (or at least to its sustainability). We can leave open the precise shape of that line of argument, since what matters here is that post-national scholarship stands on its own and must earn its own authority and legitimacy.

I would suggest that the answer to this issue lies in a greater emphasis on the scientific nature of legal scholarship. Here, science should not be defined too narrowly as something akin to natural sciences, but rather more broadly as a rational endeavour in pursuit of knowledge.[6] The authority and legitimacy of legal scholars would then rest on the strength of their method and their independence.

At the same time, there are some obstacles in the way of enhancing the scientific nature of legal scholarship. One of the main ones is the lack of a clear theoretical foundation. It never ceases to amaze colleagues from other disciplines that there is no agreed definition (nor even an agreed upon set of alternative definitions) for such central concepts such as justice, fairness or legitimacy. This is not to say that these concepts are meaningless or useless, quite to the contrary. They will remain at the heart of legal thought and scholarship.

One can doubt, however, whether these concepts can be defined endogenously, from within legal scholarship. This would imply that the legal scholar would have to look outside of the law for guidance on how to fill in or construe a number of concepts which play a central role in high-level legal scholarship. In other words, input from other disciplines is needed to elaborate the normative content of legal scholarship (and by extension, of law itself), hence the significance of the second characteristic, inter-disciplinarity.

2. Inter-Disciplinarity

Even if it may sound somewhat counter-intuitive, 'inter-disciplinarity' is more appropriate than related concepts such as 'multi-disciplinarity' or 'pluri-disciplinarity'. Indeed global legal scholarship is not about

[6] For all intents and purposes, the Popperian view is widely accepted, whereby falsifiability is the central pillar of science. Unfortunately, it is not clear that legal scholarship can meet that standard.

combining legal scholarship with another discipline, let alone integrating it with another discipline. Rather, it should develop an interface between law and other disciplines, which would be broader than a one-on-one relationship with a single other discipline, but at the same not so deep that it would encompass entirely the other discipline.

For that purpose, it might be useful to conceive of inter-disciplinarity as a progression along a number of stages. The following model of figure 1 is based on the experience at TILEC over the past 10 years.

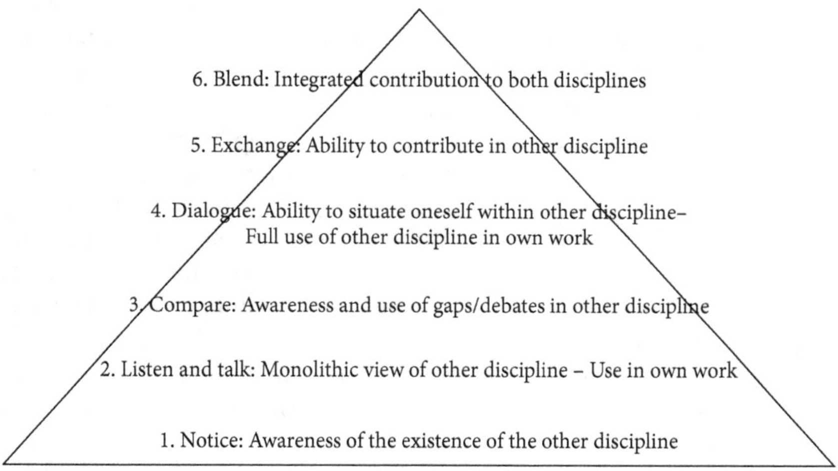

Figure 1

Stage 1 (Notice) is the minimum requirement to engage into any inter-disciplinary enterprise.

At Stage 2 (Listen and talk), scholars hold a monolithic view of the other discipline, i.e. the other discipline is there to provide answers to questions, as a mere input for work in one's own discipline. That input, however, does not do full justice to the other discipline.

With time, the scholar moves to Stage 3 (Compare). He or she gains a richer and fuller understanding of the other discipline. He or she understands that, much like his or her own discipline, the other discipline also has competing theories, gaps and unresolved issues. That richer understanding, however, does not yet fully feed back into the work in the own discipline.

At Stage 4 (Dialogue), the scholar goes one step further. He or she is able to situate his or her work in perspective with, and in relation to, the discussion in the other discipline. He or she connects the competing theories, gaps and unresolved issues across the disciplines. He or she uses the richer and fuller understanding of the other discipline gained at Stage 3 to sharpen and enhance his or her analysis of the open issues in his or her own discipline. Meaningful dialogue between disciplines begins. Stage 4 is probably the furthest one can go when working as a single researcher with a mono-disciplinary background and training.

The step to the further stages is large, in our experience, and it marks a departure from inter-disciplinarity towards a more multi-disciplinary model. In other words, while it is possible to bring a number of disciplines into the analysis at Stage 4, the level of integration reached at Stages 5 and 6 is hard to sustain outside of a single pairing of disciplines (e.g. law and economics, law and psychology, etc.). In order to reach Stages 5 and 6, a multi-disciplinary research team or a multi-disciplinary training (dual degree) seems required. At Stage 5, the flow of information is reversed: in addition to using knowledge of the second discipline to improve the quality of work in the first discipline, that improvement is such that in return the second discipline can be enriched: this can be achieved when two scientists from the respective disciplines work together on a joint product. Finally, at Stage 6 (Blend), the two disciplines are integrated into a larger whole.

Indeed, legal scholars should be aware of over-ambition when it comes to inter-disciplinarity. In Europe, for sure, few legal scholars are trained in another discipline in addition to law. European scholars may not be able to contribute significantly to other disciplines, at least not without working in teams of colleagues from these other disciplines. At the same time, European legal scholars are usually trained more intensively in law, since a Ph.D. in law tends to be a pre-requisite for academic positions in Europe. This opens up a window of opportunity for European legal scholarship: it could seek to build on its deeper legal expertise, while enriching it by emulating state-of-the-art inter-disciplinarity from US scholarship, thereby pushing the frontier of scholarship.

The main challenge – and the main opportunity – is to position legal scholarship in the middle of the other disciplines, without tying it too tightly to one or the other discipline in particular.[7] By way of metaphor, the legal scholar could be assimilated to a general practitioner (GP) of medicine. General medicine connects with all specialities, without going into depth in any given speciality. However, it is concerned with the day-to-day

[7] Which can lead to insularity or a loss of relevance.

care of patients. It deals with patients in their entirety and in their specific context. In comparison, specialists typically deal with a subset of the human body, seen with a certain measure of abstraction. Legal scholars would then be general practitioners in social sciences, able to understand specialists, call upon them, communicate with them and learn from them. At the same time, the metaphor allows some room for legal scholarship to have its own domain and function: legal scholars are ultimately being best placed to oversee the general operation of law in society. They are the ones who have the best overview and the best knowledge of what could work, or not, in a real, practical setting.

Continuing with the metaphor, with respect to any other discipline, legal scholarship will therefore be more applied. Legal scholars should not shy away from that, even if it implies that their work will be perceived as less 'scientific' by other disciplines (all the while aspiring to be more scientific than heretofore). Being more applied than pure economics or pure sociology means being more concerned with how the output from these sciences could actually work out in the practical context of our societies, in particular given institutional and procedural (transactional) constraints.

Herein lies a massive challenge for legal scholarship: we are not yet equipped to deal with the normative consequences of the findings of other social sciences. Not only are those findings analytical in nature, but they are also made under a set of assumptions and a research hypothesis which typically narrows the focus of inquiry to make it more manageable. A premium is put on the strength of the findings at the expense of complexity. In contrast, when it comes to investigating which normative content the law should take, lawyers are bound to take a broader perspective: the law must be such that it achieves the objectives it is meant to achieve (as they might have been agreed in the polity) while remaining coherent. A legal norm which would achieve efficiency while completely ignoring competing values, such as social justice, personal integrity or the coherency of the legal order, might conform to the findings of economic research, but it would not be acceptable from a legal perspective. Law must be operational within the broad context of the polity, with any and all goals and objectives which the polity might decide upon (even if these goals and objectives are not 'pure' from the analytical perspective of a given social science).

In the end, when the relationships between global legal scholarship and legal orders - on the one hand, post-national, and between global legal scholarship and other social sciences on the other hand (inter-disciplinary), are put together, one can picture a 'sweet spot' for global scholarship, at the intersection between the specificities of legal orders and those of each neighbouring discipline.

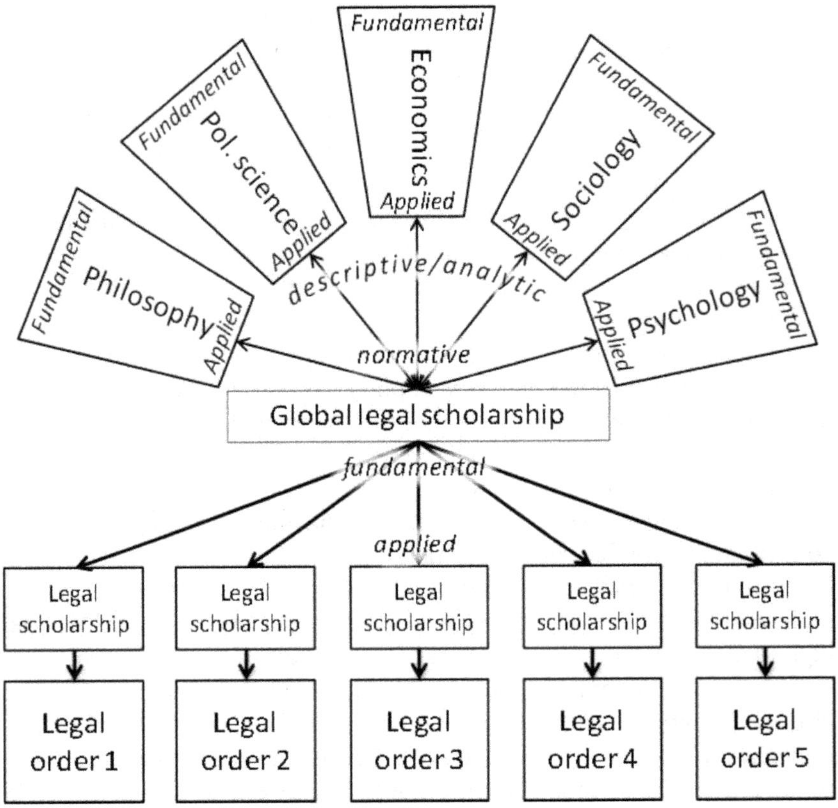

Figure 2

Even if legal scholarship remains more applied than mono-disciplinary scholarship from other social sciences, the emphasis on inter-disciplinarity nevertheless risks compounding the trend towards abstraction and generality, which was noted above in the discussion of trans-national scholarship. Legal scholarship could then cut loose from its moorings and lose a lot of its social relevance. US scholarship has already been affected by this, as evidenced by the on-going discussion on the relevance of legal scholarship (and even of the current model of legal education). In order to avert that risk, a third characteristic should be added to global legal scholarship, namely reliance on empirical research methods.

3. Empirical Research

Whereas the first two characteristics of global legal scholarship have been discussed for some time, the third one corresponds to a more recent development. At this point in time, it should be considered as an aspiration more so than a benchmark.

Empirical legal studies are rapidly expanding in the US and they are already taking root in the EU as well. Of course, it could be argued that it is a logical consequence of inter-disciplinarity: if legal research is to open up to other social sciences, then it should also open up to the methods of these sciences. Yet, this would sell both other sciences and empirical legal studies short. On the one hand, inter-disciplinary legal scholarship does not need to be empirical: many works seek to incorporate some of the more theoretical aspects of other social sciences into law,[8] while some social sciences offer non-empirical methods which have been useful to inter-disciplinary legal scholarship.[9]

On the other hand, it could be argued that empirical research is more than just a methodology. It safeguards the close link with reality, which has always been the hallmark of legal scholarship. However, that link is recast. Traditionally, legal scholarship is anchored in reality through a relatively close link with legal practice: the research agenda is often driven by problems arising out of practice, the object of study is often practical situations arising out of court cases or otherwise, and the research output is meant to be relevant to legal practice.

Legal practice, however, does not necessarily offer a representative view of reality: it is often concerned with difficult or major issues, where some intervention is needed. To continue with the medical metaphor, the influence of legal practice can draw legal scholarship towards a pathology of sorts, where troublesome instances are thoroughly investigated.

The use of empirical methods to bolster legal scholarship offers another way of connecting with reality, this time via the study of empirical data. Instead of seeing a slice of reality through the prism of legal practice, the legal scholar investigates it directly and more comprehensively via empirical methods. In so doing, the legal scholar can step out of a 'pathological' approach into a broader perspective. Furthermore, he or she can take some

---

[8] Not to mention legal philosophy, which is by nature theoretical.

[9] Economics being the prime example: many of the mainstays of law and economics literature use economic models – as opposed to econometrics or experiments – to analyse the law.

critical distance from legal practice. By following an empirical approach, a scholar can afford not to be content with simply taking at face value the issues identified in legal practice. Rather, he or she can weigh them properly by investigating basic questions such as: How often does this problem arise? What are the consequences?

The current surge in empirical legal research remains strongly influenced by social science methodology. While empirical legal research is already enriching legal scholarship, at the same time its full potential still has to be developed. More specifically, other social sciences often want to match the scientific model of natural sciences.[10] As a consequence, their empirical methods emphasise replicability and falsifiability. When investigating law, other social sciences therefore focus on measurable and quantifiable factors, for instance the characteristics of the judge or the jury in a case, the political affiliation or geographical origin of members of parliament voting on a bill etc. Often, the actual content of the law is left outside of the investigation, since it is subject to the vagaries of interpretation (including the interpretation made by the researcher him - or herself). The most sophisticated empirical research uses computer tools to apprehend content, via word counts etc.

Nonetheless, we are still far away from having developed empirical research methods that can account for the content of law, while maintaining a satisfactory level of scientific rigour. That is one of the main challenges awaiting legal scholarship in the coming years.

4. Conclusion

In the previous paragraphs, I sought to provide new insights into the three main characteristics of global legal scholarship, i.e. that it is post-national, inter-disciplinary and empirical. These characteristics are also applicable, by extension, to global legal education, which feeds from such legal scholarship.

If global legal scholarship can develop along the lines outlined above, law schools will become one of the most vibrant places on campus and in society at large, a place where social (and other) sciences meet around global legal scholarship and where the most exciting, relevant and consequential research is conducted.

---

[10] We can leave aside whether this is a desirable aim or not.

Jurisprudence for Global Law?

Willem J. Witteveen
Professor, Tilburg Law School, The Netherlands
w.j.witteveen@tilburguniversity.edu

Abstract
In developing a jurisprudence for global law, we have to move beyond the paradigms of the Western legal tradition. A crucial issue is how legal professionals will be able to deal with complex interdependencies involving cultural notions from a non-western legal tradition. A dialogue is then called for, as the example of Amartya Sen's analysis of the Indian concepts of niti (somewhat like organizational propriety) and nyaya (somewhat like living law) demonstrates. Accordingly, global legal scholarship must not only become post-national, inter-disciplinary and empirical (as Pierre Larouche argues elsewhere in this issue) but it must also concern itself with cultural issues of justice and injustice.

Keywords
global law; legal traditions; injustice

The challenges the shift towards global law poses for jurisprudence have been extensively discussed by William Twining, in two books: *General Jurisprudence* and *Globalisation and Legal Scholarship*. He gives a splendid overview of the many developments that urgently call for a re-orientation of my field of study, jurisprudence. I agree with almost all of his conclusions, summarized in the second book in a list of 7 propositions that I will summarize in my turn. Transnational fields of study deserve a lot of attention; traditional topics of domestic law acquire a transnational dimension; within a national context there will be more awareness of pluralism and multiculturalism; the interrelationship between various fields will have to be re-thought; we must pay attention to forgotten jurists in the Western canon and we must inquire which jurists and schools of thought from other legal traditions demand our attention as we try to cope with the problems of an increasingly interdependent world. His last conclusion is:

We cannot but work largely within our received tradition and law is a practical subject that on the whole requires particular detailed local knowledge. We should not abandon our heritage, but rather set our scholarship in a global context and have at least a general working knowledge of other traditions.[1]

The traditions referred to in this passage are those of analytical jurisprudence. This is a branch of knowledge developed mostly within the common law world. Bentham, Austin, and Hart are its household names. While I agree it is prudent to work within the tradition you know, I think more is needed in relation to other significant traditions. Within the broad stream of Western traditions relating to law there is more on offer than analytical jurisprudence, much more. But we should also find a response to other legal traditions that are non-Western ones and it is here where the greatest challenge lies. So my emphasis here is a little different, but in the same line of thinking as that developed by Twining who in his other book shows himself to be an informed and empathetic observer of what goes on in a number of other legal traditions.[2]

It is not easy to develop as a scholar the kind of informed and empathetic attitude Twining exhibits towards the diverse phenomena loosely described as affecting the globalization of law. And maybe the inherited traditional ways of viewing law in the world are making this even harder. Let us as a thought experiment – if only for a moment - step out of the boundaries of the tradition of analytical jurisprudence itself.

This tradition is very sophisticated in its classification of kinds of law and its investigation of the institutions that create, shape and apply law in Western societies. But it does not seem to be quite adequate in channeling the information coming at it which does not fit the Western definitions and theories of law. How can we get the facts of the new global reality right? What is globalism and how does it affect law? There is bound to be an uneasy feeling.

Interdependence must be the key word, but it appears to offer opportunities while it also bodes dangers. The cause of unease is – for me, anyway - captured in a terrible jargon word, *glocalization.* The term suggests that globalization starts at home, in one's immediate environment. Rather than use the g-word I will paraphrase some perceptive remarks by the German philosopher Rüdiger Safranski (*How much globalization can a person handle?*) on what it does to one's perception of one's position in relation to what happens out there in the world:

---

[1] William Twining, 'Globalisation and Legal Scholarship, Montesquieu Seminars' in *Montesquieu Seminars* (Wolf Legal Publisher 2011).

[2] William Twining, *General Jurisprudence* (Cambridge University Press 2009).

In the globalism of today, politics and economics function as reductions of the perception of the whole. Small wonder today you can only think about the global order with a feeling of constriction and nausea. Economism produces a view of a monotonous universe, consisting of the workplace, the market, money streams and traffic of goods. Politicization narrows thinking to the dimension of strategy and counter-strategy. The global order is reduced to an object of calculation in terms of power and powerlessness. Thought turns in circles around the basic questions: how can you control or manage the global? Some ask. How can you save it? Others ask.

Our imagination is caught in the same trap, remaining stuck in the television images that have been watched over and over a thousand times of terrible poverty and embarrassing riches, violence and entertainment, deserts and megacities. For the global consciousness that rests on media images the spaces become too cramped, there is no feeling of open space. Everything looks familiar and yet you do not know it. It is surprising and also frightening. There is the strange sensation that everything on a global scale is diminishing. Even the bad news is a familiar presence. There are imperative calls to action from all parts of the globe. In the flood of information, the sense of helplessness and powerlessness is delivered right away. Globalization appears as one vast systematic interrelationship that functions so powerfully and so much without acting subjects that it is almost obscene to point at the meaning of the individual as a conscious agent.[3]

For the individual, read: the person trained in law. Safranski eloquently raises an issue that we can rework into this question: how to deal as a legal professional or a scholar or a student of law with all those situations where it is brought to your attention that what you are doing in the setting in which you work has ramifications far away and beyond your control and how to respond to developments coming from far away that transform the actual setting in which you find yourself? How to grab the chances and achieve some aim, how to avoid the danger of powerlessness or of being in some sense involved and responsible for events beyond your reach?

In fact, this is a very old issue. In the *Digest* we find the famous maxim about the duties of the jurist and his art, his unique qualification as a priest of the law: *Ars aequi et boni*. To give everyone their due and to contribute to the good life are still the aspirations of jurists, and the condition of global law is yet another challenging one that requires adaptation from legal

[3] Rüdiger Safranski, *Hoeveel globalisering verdraagt de mens?* (Atlas 2003) 77,78,84.

professionals in order to do useful and meaningful work.[4] We may also refer further back in time still to Socrates who in a number of Platonic dialogues defends the thesis that it is better to suffer an injustice than to commit one and that an ethical life carries the duty of acting in such a way as not to commit an injustice. That ethical way of life is complicated considerably under conditions of global law.

As legally trained people participating in the practices that occupy our attention, we are even confronted with this twice over. We have to deal with the balancing act between empowerment and helplessness that regards us and with that undergone or experienced by our clients or the people affected by our actions. Jurists are becoming mediators and translators and their art of justice as translation becomes more difficult and urgent under global conditions but it remains still an identifiable concern.[5] Already this early in our elementary thought experiment we can reach the conclusion that instead of focusing too intensely on the myriad forms of regulation under conditions of globalization, we should ask what the people of the law can or cannot do and what they must or must not do in the new predicament we are all in, from trained lawyers to untrained civilians.

Fortunately, there is a lot of material in the Western legal and political tradition that becomes relevant again in the context of global law. But there is another resource as well, and that derives from the insight offered by Patrick Glenn in his great study of the legal traditions of the world. His thesis is that other legal traditions have developed meaningful ways of reasoning to deal with their problems that are increasingly becoming relevant for the adherents of the Western legal traditions as well. Dialogues within traditions extend outwardly to engage the dialogues going on in other traditions. In the global world, these traditions will meet more often and out of these meetings and interactions the Western style law person may enrich her repertoire.[6]

A good example of this is found in Amartya Sen's seminal book on *The Idea of Justice*, where he makes use of concepts from Indian jurisprudence in order to highlight the limitations that he finds in Rawlsian political philosophy, such as the distinction between *niti* and *nyaya.* (With *niti* relating to organizational propriety and behavioral correctness and *nyaya* being

---

[4] The locus classicus of this view of the ethics of the legal profession, as well as of the office of politicians, is still Marcus Tullius Cicero, *On obligations* (PG Walsh tran, ed, Oxford University Press 2000).

[5] James Boyd White, *Justice as Translation* (Chicago University Press 1990).

[6] Patrick Glenn, *Legal Traditions of the World* (Oxford University Press 2010).

concerned with what emerges from the lives people are actually able to lead.) Institutional design and practice of established ways falls under *niti*, empirical openness to the problems as actually experienced under *nyaya*, and while these concepts are richer than I manage to suggest in summary, Sen strikes a familiar note in this conclusion:

In the inclusive perspective of *nyaya*, we can never simply hand over the task of justice to some niti of social institutions and social rules that we see as exactly right, and then rest there, and be free from further social assessment. To ask how things are going and whether they can be improved is a constant and inescapable part of the pursuit of justice.[7]

Pierre Larouche argues, elsewhere in this issue, that global legal scholarship has to satisfy three conditions. It must be post-national, inter-disciplinary and empirical, on top of all it already was. I add the ancient and actual concern with justice and injustice to the list. In closing, I wonder what the effects of global law as a development that is already taking place will have on the concept of law itself (noting that I am then returning, once more, to one of the perennial questions of the tradition of Western jurisprudence).

During the historical period of the sovereign states which is perhaps ending, the bounded fields of law, the division of labor on the basis of recognized fields of law, in short the heyday of legal positivism, the law took a number of standard forms that were duly studied, such as the contract, the treaty, the statute et cetera. These standard forms, of which we know a lot thanks to their ancient lineage and the rich heritage of the Western legal tradition, will surely not disappear. But new and hybrid kinds of regulation such as soft law have been added to them, as a result of social processes which have made law more instrumental than value-oriented.

Under the regimes of the new global law I expect there to appear large variations in legal forms, and no doubt also bastard forms and new mutations that we might find strange at first. Cultural, religious and political differences and the discursive weight of other legal traditions will also make themselves manifest in the forms of law. Thus I can only underscore the appeal towards inter-disciplinarity and an empirical orientation, since we will have to approach these phenomena with an open mind.

---

7 Amartya Sen, *The Idea of Justice* (Allen Lane 2009) 86.

Global Environmental Law

Jonathan Verschuuren
Professor, international and European environmental law, Tilburg Sustainability Center
Tilburg University
j.m.verschuuren@tilburguniversity.edu

Abstract
Globalization is profoundly changing environmental law. As a consequence, environmental legal scholarship and the teaching of environmental law are changing as well. This article shows that these changes, in general, have to be evaluated as promising and exciting.

Keywords
environmental legal scholarship; teaching environmental law; globalization; self-regulation

I am writing this contribution while attending a conference for environmental law professors from around the world in Baltimore, entitled 'Global Environmental Law at a Crossroad'.[1] While this fact does not deliver a whole lot of empirical proof, it is at least an indication that the 'global' is very much present in the work of environmental law scholarship. Why is that so?

To make that clear, I am afraid I have to start by conveying some bad news. We have run against the limits of environmental law. Environmental law, in its traditional sense of domestic law instruments - mainly command-and-control and financial instruments, applied by public authorities to improve and protect the natural environment, partly orchestrated, or at least influenced by international and regional law - works pretty well with regard to localised or regional environmental issues, but does not seem to be effective in addressing the global environmental problems that we face today. Global climate change, the global loss of biodiversity and the pollution and over-harvesting of the oceans are environmental problems of

[1] IUCN Academy of Environmental Law 2012 Colloquium, see <http://www.iucnael.org/en/iucnaelorg-academy-events/220-the-10th-annual-colloquium-of-the-iucn-academy-of-environmental-law.html> accessed 30 July 2012.

an alarming magnitude. There is no doubt about the existence of these environmental problems, and even no disagreement about the fact that they indeed are very serious.

At the international level, all of these issues were already recognised more than 20 years ago (with such conventions as the 1992 UN Framework Convention on Climate Change, the 1992 Convention on Biological Diversity and the 1982 UN Convention on the Law of the Sea). Unfortunately, now, there are no signs of improvement whatsoever. On the contrary, loss of biodiversity is increasing at an alarming rate and global greenhouse gas emissions have risen by 36% between 1992 and 2008.[2]

The reasons for the ineffectiveness of environmental law in addressing these global issues are manifold and diverse. There are the more legal issues, such as fragmentation of the law. International biodiversity law, for example, not only has been codified in the Convention on Biological Diversity, but also in such conventions as the Ramsar Convention (on wetlands), the Convention on Migratory Species, the European Wildlife Convention, the World Heritage Convention, the Convention on Trade in Endangered Species, and more. Command-and-control instruments, in general, have their limitations, as they require much government intervention and monitoring which, in times of a call for deregulation and a smaller public service, is not available. Much of the legal wording in these conventions is very weak, leaving plenty of room for manoeuvre for states at the domestic level. This indicates, probably, the main reason for the ineffectiveness of international environmental law: a lack of political will to really do something about global environmental problems. The examples are well-known.

Eventhough, since the drafting of the Kyoto Protocol to the UN Framework Convention on Climate Change in 2007, everybody knew that the Protocol would expire in 2012, the international community was not able to come up with a successor. During a Conference of the Parties in Durban in 2011, it was only agreed that there should be new rules in place as of 2020. The Rio+20 conference on sustainable development and the green economy that took place in 2012 in Rio de Janeiro, with more than 100 world leaders and many more government delegates from nearly all countries in the world present,

2 Secretariat CBD, Global Biodiversity Outlook 3, Montreal (2010) http://www.cbd.int/gbo accessed 14 August 2012; UNEP, Keeping Track of Our Changing Environment. From Rio to Rio+20 (1992-2012), Nairobi (2011) 21 <http://www.unep.org/geo/pdfs/keeping_track.pdf>. accessed 14 August 2012

only produced a 49 page document that did not do anything else, but to reaffirm the agreements that had been reached in a similar conference in 1992.

Such a standstill on the major issues that the world has been facing for the past decades basically means that developments are driven by the world economy. Having regard to environmental impacts is not automatically done in economic processes (to put it mildly). Increasing globalization of the world economy makes it even more difficult for states to act upon environmental degradation. Although production and consumption chains run across the globe, domestic law usually only applies to activities within the borders of a specific nation.

Interestingly, however, globalization also offers opportunities for environmental protection. The Rio+20 conference makes that very clear. Whereas the official governmental talks did not amount to much, the real action took place in all these other meetings during the conference: meetings of NGOs, business organizations, large multinationals, and other stakeholders. Of the 40,000 delegates at the conference, only a small number was involved in the unsuccessful negotiations among states. The vast majority was involved in these other meetings, achieving remarkable results.

Just a few examples. A group of multinational corporations agreed to ensure that by 2020 there would be no net loss of forests for the production of soy, palm oil, beef and paper, involving such major global players such as Unilever and Walmart. 39 internationally operating banks, investors and insurers committed to integrating 'natural capital considerations', i.e., the value that is connected to ecosystem services such as clean water, clean air, biological resources etc., into their assessments of bonds and equities and into their credit and insurance policies. NGOs, like the WWF, and international governmental organizations, such as UNEP and the World Health Organization, turned to such initiatives by private actors, rather than to governments because they knew that these business corporations could be powerful drivers of global change.

It is precisely because of globalization and the associated interconnectedness within the world economy that actions of a few big companies can make a difference. First and foremost, they are concerned about their reputation. Reputations can be squashed within weeks through the use of Facebook, Twitter and Youtube, as Unilever, for instance, experienced when Greenpeace published a report on the company's use of unsustainable palm oil, together with an impressive 80 second video targeting Dove products. Unilever immediately used its power within a business led growers and supply chain certification scheme, which involved all major global traders and processors of palm oil, to strengthen the rules of that scheme. They also suspended trade with a number of suppliers, which then led to significant changes among these and other suppliers because suppliers did not want to miss out on major buyers. Companies increasingly impose supply chain requirements on the actors within their supply chains because they want to be certain that their end-product cannot harm their reputation. Since supply chains, more often than not, are global, the impact of such measures is global as well.

Self-regulatory systems, usually centred around a certification scheme, obviously have the huge benefit of not being bound by any domestic legal system, neither by WTO-rules that hamper national legislatures in extraterritorial application of environmental protection laws. That does not mean, however, that these systems, from a legal point of view, are simple. They require a lot of law: rules on the substantive requirements that have to be met, rules on the certification process, rules on monitoring and enforcement, rules on dispute settlement.

It gets even more interesting for the legal scholar when states or international governmental organizations step in. The EU, for instance, applies a similar approach to the import of wood and wood products into the EU. An example is the so called FLEGT Regulation.[3] FLEGT stands for 'Forest Law Enforcement, Governance and Trade'. The FLEGT Regulation establishes a licensing scheme for imports of timber into the EU in order to combat illegal logging, through halting the import of illegally and unsustainably logged timber into the EU. The licensing scheme under the FLEGT Regulation is a binding scheme: no timber can be imported in the EU without a FLEGT license. The licensing scheme, however, only applies to imports from countries with which the EU has concluded a Voluntary Partnership Agreement (VPA). Such agreements have been concluded with three African countries (Ghana, Cameroon, Republic of Congo), while negotiations are underway with seven others, including big exporters of timber like Malaysia and Indonesia. The substantive criteria that have to be met for a shipment to obtain a FLEGT license are laid down in these agreements.

Taking the Cameroon agreement as an example, it is obvious that much of these criteria are aimed at sustainable forest management in general and at protecting biodiversity in particular.[4] The 122 page long agreement

---

[3] Regulation 2173/2005/EC, [2005] OJ L 347/1 and implementing regulation 1024/2008, [2008] OJ 277/23. In the areas of fisheries, the EU also follows an extraterritorial approach with the Regulation 2005/2008/EC on Illegal, Unreported and Unregulated Fishing, [2008] OJ L 286/1.

[4] Voluntary Partnership Agreement between the European Union and the Republic of Cameroon on forest law enforcement, governance and trade in timber and derived products to the European Union (FLEGT), [2011] OJ L 92/4.

regulates the species of trees from which wood and wood products can and cannot be imported into the EU. It sets up a very comprehensive certification scheme in Cameroon; it applies a series of national laws aimed at sustainable forest management, as well as the rules laid down in the Convention on Biological Diversity and in the Convention of International Trade in Endangered Species and it sets criteria aimed, not only at environmental protection and biodiversity preservation, but at the protection of human rights as well. One of these criteria, for instance, reads as follows:

> The forestry entity has made the necessary arrangements to prohibit the involvement of its staff in poaching, commercial hunting and the transportation or trade in hunting equipment and means. It encourages, supports and/or initiates all campaigns seeking to ensure application of the regulations in relation to hunting and to the protection of the fauna on its sites.[5]

This example shows how far the arm of the EU is stretching. Through its external trade in tropical timber, the EU even tries to combat poaching in Cameroon's forests.

Under the EU's policy, aimed at concluding bilateral agreements with each specific country involved, the EU does influence national biodiversity policy and law in the targeted country quite substantially, as the Cameroon example shows. Interestingly enough, the same goes the other way around: the norms that are agreed upon have to be applied in the licensing process in the EU. So an EU Member State cannot impose other norms than those that have been put into place in the exporting country, in the above example, norms laid down in Cameroon legislation.

The EU provides another very interesting example of how globalization helps to protect the global environment. The centerpiece of the chemicals legislation in the EU is the REACH Regulation.[6] There are numerous law journal articles that show that the impact of this regulation is felt throughout the world.[7] Sachs states:

---

[5] Ibid, Annex II, criterion 5 [Dick Kraaij says:

[6] Regulation 1907/2006 concerning the Registration, Evaluation, Authorisation and Restriction of Chemicals, [2006] OJ L 396/1.

[7] For instance, NM Sachs, 'Jumping the Pond: Transnational Law and the Future of Chemical Regulation' (2009) 62(6) Vanderbilt Law Review 1817; DA Wirth, 'The EU's New Impact on U.S. Environmental Regulation' (2007) Boston College Law School Research Paper No. 144 <http://papers.ssrn.com/sol3/papers.cfm?abstract_id=1028733> accessed 30 July 2012; LE Kersey, 'Trans-Atlantic Reach: the Potential Impact of the European Union's New Chemical Regulations on Proof of Causation in U.S. Federal Courts' (2009) 36(2) Boston College Environmental Affairs Law Review 535.

> The extraterritorial impact of REACH is just one example of a larger trend in which the EU is increasingly setting de facto global standards through its internal environmental legislation. The EU is the world's largest economy, and decisions in Brussels, applicable throughout the twenty-seven Member States of the EU, are affecting how products are designed and manufactured from Boston to Beijing. Since 2000, the EU has embarked on ambitious environmental lawmaking in areas such as chemical regulation, energy efficiency, hazardous waste, and climate change. Europe has in many cases supplanted the United States as the leading originator and exporter of environmental law innovation.[8]

Since the EU's norms in the field of the environment are the strictest, manufacturers prefer to follow these, so that they can sell their products anywhere. Globalization, therefore, does not necessarily lead to a race to the bottom, as was often predicted. Instead, globalization might very well lead to a race to the top.

All of the above developments show the huge impact of globalization on environmental law. They are changing environmental law altogether and making environmental legal scholarship and the teaching of environmental law much more exciting and interesting. They require us to have a much wider view on the law than the simple domestic perspective. To understand what is going on in the field of environmental law, a transnational approach is required, focusing on the interplay between domestic, regional and international law, as well as on the interplay between state and non-state law. Polycentric governance raises complex questions on legitimacy, as the normal rule of law and democratic principles no longer (fully) apply. Multiple nodes of government are involved, applying multiple legal norm systems, multiple courts, tribunals and dispute resolution bodies are involved. Although, as a consequence, the legal situation gets somewhat blurred and messy, the legal approaches through which Earth can be protected are multiplied as well, with much greater chances of success.

[8] Sachs, ibid 1819-1820.

International Criminal Law as Global Law: An Assessment of the Hybrid Tribunals

Mathias Holvoet[a] **& Paul de Hert**[b]

a) PhD-Candidate, Institute for European Studies, Vrije Universiteit Brussel
Member Research Group 'Fundamental Rights and Constitutionalism' (FRC)
Senior Analyst, Global Justice Section, Global Governance Institute (GGI)
Mathias.Holvoet@vub.ac.be

b) Professor of Law and Technology, Tilburg Institute for Law and Technology (TILT)
Faculty of Law and Criminology, Vrije Universiteit Brussel
paul.de.hert@uvt.nl

Abstract

This contribution will focus on the facet of International Criminal Justice where the influence of global law is the most apparent, namely the hybrid or internationalized criminal tribunals. Since many of these tribunals have closed their doors or are in the advanced stage of the proceedings, the time is ripe for a preliminary evaluation. Furthermore, the future necessity and viability of hybrid tribunals will be assessed, both for crimes that fall within and without the jurisdictional regime established by the International Criminal Court (ICC).

Keywords

hybrid tribunals; International Criminal Court; domestic tribunals; complementarity; impunity gap; fairness

1. Introduction

In our view, global law is an approach to law that encompasses not just international law. Instead, global law is more hybrid in nature, taking into account domestic laws of different countries and aiming to understand domestic regimes within the broader context of international laws, instruments and institutions. In a sense, the whole project of International Criminal Justice can be seen as a legal hybrid. International criminal procedure, for example, does not originate from a uniform body of law. It substantially results from an amalgamation of two different legal systems, obtained in common-law countries and the system prevailing in countries of civil-law.[1]

During the late 1990s and 2000s a 'third-generation' of international criminal tribunals emerged, drawing on the heritage of the first generation tribunals at Nuremberg and Tokyo and the second generation of *ad hoc* tribunals: the International Criminal Tribunal for the Former Yugoslavia (ICTY) and the International Criminal Tribunal for Rwanda (ICTR). These third generation tribunals, alternatively called 'hybrid'[2] or 'internationalized'[3] tribunals, blend the international and the domestic as a product of judicial accountability-sharing between the states in which they function and international entities.[4] As such, hybrid tribunals are the most apparent manifestations of the influence of the concept of global law on the field of International Criminal Justice.

The Oxford Companion on International Criminal Justice, considered as a kind of encyclopedia of International Criminal Justice,[5] classifies the following tribunals under the category of hybrid tribunals: the Special Court for Sierra Leone (hereinafter: SCSL), the Serious Crimes Panels in the District Court of Dili in East Timor (hereinafter: the East Timor Panels), the Regulation 64 Panels in the courts of Kosovo (hereinafter: the Regulation 64 Panels), the Extraordinary Chambers in the courts of Cambodia (hereinafter: the ECCC) and the Special Tribunal for Lebanon (hereinafter: the STL).[6] In other publications, the Bosnian War Crimes Chamber is also discussed as being part of the family of hybrid tribunals.[7]

---

[1] ICTY, Appeals Chamber, *The Prosecutor v. Drazen Erdemovic*, Separate and dissenting opinion of Judge Cassese, 7 October 1997, I. A. 4; See also: Frédéric Mégret, 'International Criminal Law: A New Legal Hybrid?' (2003) <http://papers.ssrn.com/sol3/papers.cfm?abstract_id=1269382> accessed 3 July 2012; Roelof Haveman, Olga Kavran and Julian Nichols (trans), *Supranational Criminal Law: A System Sui Generis* (Intersentia 2003) 5.

[2] See for example Sarah Nouwen, "Hybrid Courts': The Hybrid Category of a New Type of International Crimes Courts' (2006), 2(2) *Utrecht Law Review* 190–214, <http://www.utrechtlawreview.org/publish/articles/000033/article.pdf> accessed 2 July 2012.

[3] See for example Cesare P.R. Romano, André Nollkaemper and Jann K. Kleffner (trans), *Internationalized Criminal Courts. Sierra Leone, East Timor, Kosovo, and Cambodia* (OUP 2004).

[4] Etelle R. Higonnet, 'Restructuring Hybrid Courts: Local Empowerment and National Criminal Justice Reform' (2005) 23 *Ariz. J. Int'l & Comp. L.* 352.

[5] William A. Schabas, *Unimaginable Atrocities* (OUP 2012) 27.

[6] Dafna Schraga, 'Mixed or Internationalized Courts' in Antonio Cassese (ed), *The Oxford Companion to International Criminal Justice* (OUP 2009) 424–426.

[7] Nadia Bernaz and Remi Prouvèze, 'International and Domestic Prosecutions' in C. Bassiouni (ed), *The Pursuit of International Criminal Justice: A World Study on Conflicts, Victimization, and Post-Conflict Justice. Volume 1* (Intersentia 2010) 312.

Hybrid tribunals are presented as integrating the best that both international and domestic justice have to offer. They are deemed to offer legitimacy by providing ownership without affecting independence and impartiality; to prosecute more perpetrators in less time and at lower costs while also building domestic capacity; to do domestic justice while upholding international law and complying with international fair trial standards, and thus also doing international justice.[8] Furthermore, hybrid tribunals can have the following impact on local institutions: building capacity; rebuilding judicial systems and promoting international human rights standards throughout the local community.[9]

It seems impossible to give a comprehensive definition of hybrid tribunals. Indeed, their most prominent feature is that they are all *sui generis*. The characteristics of hybrid tribunals are generally deduced from the elements which the tribunals have in common. In all cases, the tribunals are composed of international and domestic judges, prosecutor(s) and support staff. They also apply a compound of international and national substantive and procedural law.[10]

In this article, it will first be assessed if hybrid tribunals have so far managed to fulfill their initial expectations. Subsequently, the future necessity of hybrid tribunals will be considered, given the existence of the ICC as a permanent international criminal court. It will be argued that establishing hybrid courts in the future will remain indispensable, to fill the possible impunity gaps under the jurisdictional framework of the ICC, for reasons of limited capacity of both domestic courts and the ICC, and as a guarantee for fairness.

2. Did the Hybrid Tribunals Live upto their Expectations? A Concise Appraisal

Already two hybrid tribunals have closed their doors: the East Timor Panels and the Regulation 64 Panels, in 2006[11] and 2008[12] respectively. The SCSL

---

[8] Nouwen (n 2) 191.

[9] Parinaz Kermani Mendez, 'The New Wave of Hybrid Tribunals: A Sophisticated Approach to Enforcing International Humanitarian Law or an Idealistic Solution with Empty Promises?' (2009) 20 Crim. L.F. 75.

[10] Bernaz and Prouvèze (n 7) 294.

[11] Suzannah Linton, 'East Timor Special Panels' in Cassese (n 6) 307.

[12] The Kosovo Assembly substituted the Regulation 64 Panels with a law under which an EU presence, 'EULEX' operates, either separately or in mixed composition within the

will conclude after its Appeals Chamber has decided on the appeal of Charles Taylor for his conviction and 50-year sentence. While both the ECCC and the STL still have to fulfill an important portion of their respective mandates, the tribunals have been operating now for several years, which allow them to be assessed on a preliminary basis.

Since all the hybrid tribunals are, above all, *sui generis,* the results they produce will be too. For this reason, the following hybrid tribunals will briefly be assessed on an individual basis: the East Timor Panels; the Regulation 64 Panels; the SCSL; the ECCC and the STL. However, because of the communalities that these tribunals share, a general assessment will be given, in order to understand the hybrid model's strengths and weaknesses.[13]

2.1. *The Regulation 64 Panels*

The Regulation 64 Panels can be evaluated positively in terms of building the capacity of the Kosovar judicial system. Local judges and prosecutors have learned skills and knowledge in working within the hybrid system. Furthermore, the fact that the panels were integrated in the domestic system has allowed for cross-fertilization between the tribunal and the local system.

However, for most observers, the Regulation 64 Panels have failed to live up to their promises. Because of its hasty creation with little advance planning, there was no time for local consultation before and during the operation of the Panels and no premeditated plans for legacy were arranged.[14]

2.2. *The East Timor Panels*

Like Kosovo, the hybrid tribunal in East Timor is usually portrayed a story of missed opportunities. The close proximity to victims had the potential to promote justice and create benefits to the country's legal system. However, throughout the Panels' process, there was only minimal public consultation and inadequate capacity building efforts have reduced the positive impact which the tribunal could have had. The biggest problems the Panels were facing arose from the lack of cooperation from Indonesia. East Timorese

---

national system. See for more details Robert Cryer, Hakan Friman, Darryl Robinson, Elisabeth Wilmshurst (trans), *An Introduction to International Criminal Law and Procedure* Cambridge (2th edn CUP 2010) 190.

[13] Higonnet (n 4) 353.

[14] Mendez (n 9) 78.

officials were striving for good relations with Indonesia, and Indonesia bluntly refused to cooperate with the Panels. Following this experience, one may question the appropriateness of the hybrid model for international conflicts where foreign state cooperation is essential for the effective functioning of the tribunal. A more international, neutral tribunal with legally binding cooperation obligations would probably have been a better model.[15]

2.3. *The SCSL*

The SCSL is often taken as the example to demonstrate that hybrid tribunals can have positive results, as being the most effective and efficient hybrid tribunal to date. Although the SCSL has a very narrow mandate and has only prosecuted a few individuals, which is criticized by some as being merely a form of imperfect or symbolic justice,[16] the Court has had an impact in promoting the rule of law and in training professional and administrative staff. The SCSL outreach activities have helped to build civil society and foster some sense of participation of the local population in the judicial system. The focus on a few trials has made SCSL a relatively cheap enterprise in comparison with the *ad hoc* tribunals. This limited amount of trials was at least partly compensated by the coexisting Truth and Reconciliation Commission.[17]

2.4. *The ECCC*

Although the ECCC has only finished one trial, the concerns are growing that it will not be able to provide substantive justice. The main problem of the ECCC is ensuring impartiality. Because the high corrupt nature of the Cambodian court system and its submissiveness towards the Cambodian government, international judges have insufficient power to ensure impartiality. The lack of a majority of international judges has prevented the ECCC from opening new investigations and conducting fair trials, given the government's manipulation of Cambodian judges.[18] Because of this, many international judges have already resigned from their positions.[19]

---

15 ibid 85.

16 Chandra Lekha Sriram, *Globalizing Justice for Mass Atrocities: A Revolution in Accountability* (Routledge 2005) 102–103.

17 Mendez (n 9) 81.

18 ibid 85–86.

19 See Kevin Jon Heller, 'Disarray at ECCC' (*Opinio Iuris*, 1 April 2012) <http://opiniojuris.org/2012/04/01/disarray-at-the-eccc/> accessed 9 July 2012.

2.5. *The STL*

The STL, competent to prosecute and try those responsible for the murderous attack on Rafik Hariri and some connected attacks on other senior Lebanese political figures, has yet to start its first trial. Because of the inability of the Lebanese enforcement institutions to arrest four indicted members of Hezbollah, these trials will most probably be held *in absentia.* While trials *in absentia* are not impermissible *per se* under international law, an empty dock creates a sense of failure and toothlessness, both for the STL specifically, as for the project of International Criminal Justice in general.[20] The Tribunals legitimacy is also fragile because of the extremely limited (and thus selective) mandate of the STL. Many atrocities have been committed during the last three decades in Lebanon, including acts that can be qualified as war crimes and crimes against humanity. There has been impunity for all these crimes.[21] By definition, the justice rendered by the STL will be selective in nature vis-à-vis these crimes. This will probably further complicate the role of the STL in comparison with other international(ized) tribunals, which are significantly legitimized by their ability to represent and act in the interests of large numbers of victims.[22]

2.6. *A General Appraisal of the Hybrid Tribunals*

This concise overview of the operation of the hybrid tribunals to date demonstrates that these institutions have not entirely lived up to their promises. Local communities have probably a greater awareness and connection that they have proceedings conducted by purely international tribunals. In some cases, public outreach initiatives have been positive and the employment of local staff within the court system resulted in some hands-on learning. Lastly, according to locals, hybrid tribunals have helped to promote human rights and the rule of law.[23]

---

[20] Lynn Maalouf, 'Empty dock: a sense of failure? (*International Justice Tribune*, 5 February 2012) <http://www.rnw.nl/international-justice/article/empty-dock-a-sense-failure> accessed 8 July 2012.

[21] Marieke Wierda, Habib Nassar and Lynn Maalouf, 'Early Reflections on Local Perceptions, Legitimacy and Legacy of the Special Tribunal for Lebanon' (2007) 5(5) JICJ 1067.

[22] ibid 1072.

[23] Mendez (n 9) 87.

The hybrid model may have had some positive outcomes, but there is still a lot of room for improvement. We see three main concerns that should be remedied if the hybrid model wants to retain its legitimacy.

Firstly, when future hybrid tribunals are established, it is of utmost importance to find the correct balance between domestic and international elements.[24] As the case of the ECCC shows, the presence of a few international judges and prosecutors may be insufficient to ensure a tribunal is impartial and free from government manipulation. Creating a sense of local ownership can be attained through other means, for example by locating the tribunal on the territory where the crimes have been committed or by adding crimes under the national criminal laws of the country involved in the statute of the tribunal.

Another thorny issue concerns the appropriate mandate of hybrid tribunals. It is true that one of the justifications behind establishing hybrid tribunals was to create more cost-effective institutions than the *ad hoc* tribunals. One way by which this cost-effectiveness seems to have been realized is by narrowing down the jurisdiction *ratione personae*, *ratione materiae*, *ratione loci* and *ratione temporis* of the different hybrid tribunals. A jurisdictional framework that is too narrow however undermines the legitimacy of a specific institution and creates a sense of selectivity, exemplified by the case of the STL. This narrow jurisdiction can be compensated by the establishment of a coexisting Truth and Reconciliation Commission and/or by the capacity- building of the national judicial system, which could prosecute crimes that fall out of the jurisdictional ambit of the hybrid tribunal.

Finally, the issue of securing cooperation with local authorities or foreign states has also been of serious concern. Without cooperation, securing the presence of alleged perpetrators or witnesses, conducting investigations, and collecting evidence can be difficult if not impossible, as was shown by the non-cooperation of Indonesia with the East Timor Panels.[25] Creating a robust cooperation mechanism, akin to the framework that was set up by the Security Council for the *ad hoc* tribunals, is thus imperative for the future success of hybrid tribunals.

---

24 ibid.

25 Lindsey Raub, 'Positioning Hybrid Tribunals in International Criminal Justice' (2009) 41 N.Y.U. J. Int'l L. & Pol. 1045.

3. The Future Necessity of Hybrid Tribunals and Their Relationship With the ICC

The establishment of hybrid tribunals was deemed necessary to fill the impunity gap left by the *interregnum,* the period between the adoption of the Rome Statute establishing the ICC in 1998 and the coming into force of the Court in 2002. One might be tempted to think then that hybrid tribunals will become irrelevant in the future, given the fact the ICC is now fully operational. This view would be both short-sighted and simplistic, however. In the following sections, it will be argued that hybrid tribunals will need to be established in the future, both for crimes that fall out of the Court's realm, as for crimes committed within the ICC's jurisdictional reach.

3.1. The Future Necessity of Hybrid Tribunals When the ICC Has No Jurisdiction Ratione Temporis

The ICC has no retroactive jurisdiction and it is only allowed to prosecute crimes committed after July 1, 2002. The crimes for which the ECCC has jurisdiction could hence not have been brought under the jurisdiction of the ICC. The case of Syria can serve as an example. If, hypothetically, the situation in Syria is referred to the ICC one day, the Court will only be competent to prosecute and try the crimes committed by the Assad regime after July 1, 2002. If the Syrians themselves are unable to deliver post-conflict justice, a hybrid tribunal could then be established to fill this impunity gap. For example, the individuals responsible for the Hama massacre, which occurred in February 1982, when the Syrian army under the orders of Hafez al-Assad conducted a scorched earth operation in the town of Hama causing the death of several thousands, could be prosecuted before a hybrid tribunal.

3.2. The Future Necessity of Hybrid Tribunals When the ICC Has No Jurisdiction Ratione Loci

Potentially, the ICC has worldwide jurisdiction, since the Security Council can refer a situation to the Court under 13(b) of the Rome Statute.[26]

---

[26] As in the situation in Darfur, Sudan, referred to the Court by Security Council resolution 1593 (2005) and in the situation in Libya, referred to the Court by Security Council resolution 1970 (2010).

Likewise, article 12(3) allows a State, not party, to declare that it accepts the jurisdiction of the Court with respect to the crime in question.[27] However, because of geopolitical considerations of one of its five permanent members—and especially the United States, Russia and China—, the Security Council has already refrained to use its referral power.[28] The most recent example is the refusal by Russia to support any kind of resolution that would refer the situation in Syria where crimes against humanity are being committed to the ICC, despite the numerous calls by UN High Commissioner for Human Rights Navi Pillay.[29] Likewise, a State will only lodge an *ad hoc* declaration, under Article 12(3) of the Statute, if it is in its political interest to do so.

In order to fill this impunity gap, a hybrid tribunal could be established, for example by regional organizations such as the African Union or the Arab League. In this perspective, there have been calls to establish a tribunal under the auspices of the Arab League with competence over the crimes committed in Syria.[30]

3.3. *The Future Necessity of Hybrid Tribunals When the ICC Has No Jurisdiction Ratione Materiae*

The ICC currently only has jurisdiction over three core international crimes, namely genocide, crimes against humanity, war crimes. There have been unsuccessful proposals to include so-called 'transnational crimes', like drug trafficking[31] and terrorism[32] in the jurisdiction of the ICC. These

---

[27] Cryer, Friman, Robinson and Wilmshurst (n 12) 166.

[28] See for a fierce critique of the position of the Security Council towards the ICC: Richard Dicker, 'A Flawed Court in Need of Credibility' *New York Times* (New York, 1 May 2012).

[29] See for example 'Militarization of Syrian conflict must be stopped', says UN human rights chief Navi Pillay <http://www.ohchr.org/EN/NewsEvents/Pages/HCSecurityCouncil.aspx> accessed 4 July 2012.

[30] Aryeh Neier, 'An Arab War-Crimes Court for Syria' *New York Times* (New York, 4 April 2012).

[31] Trinidad and Tobago and Belize proposed to include the crime of international drug trafficking in the jurisdiction of the Statute, see 'Proposal for the inclusion of the Crime of International Drug Trafficking in the Rome Statute of the International Criminal Court',<http://www.icc-cpi.int/NR/rdonlyres/03DAF164-78C7-4129-A0BD-91534F80BF81/0/TrinidadTobagoCN737EN.pdf> accessed 4 July 2012.

[32] The Netherlands has submitted a proposal for the inclusion of terrorism in the subject matter jurisdiction of the ICC. See Assembly of States Parties to the Rome Statute of the International Criminal Court: Eighth Session, The Hague, November 18–26, 2009, U.N. Doc. ICC-ASP/8/20, Appendix III 65–66. However, it was decided not to consider this proposal at the Review Conference held in Kampala in 2010.

crimes can have a huge impact on people throughout the world and on global economic development.[33] Normally, transnational crimes can be adequately addressed by national judicial authorities, if necessary with the cooperation of other governments and other law enforcement agencies.[34] There may be instances however, despite the availability of international cooperation mechanisms, where the need still exists to establish a tribunal with international assistance and participation, like in cases where the State that would usually exercise jurisdiction is unable or unwilling to do so.

The establishment of the STL is the obvious example in this perspective. Because the Lebanese judiciary system present at the time of the murderous attack on Rafik Hariri and the other connected attacks was in a debatable state of inability to prosecute and unwillingness to seriously handle such crimes, an international solution was required.[35] Before the establishment of the Tribunal, a referral of the situation in Lebanon to the ICC was considered. The UN Secretary-General's report on establishing the STL considered and briefly presented a *prima facie* case that the assassination of Hariri and the other connected attacks arose to the level of a crime against humanity.[36] A debate in the Security Council resulted, however, in the exclusion of the label of crimes against humanity for the crimes committed in Lebanon.[37] This decision might be criticized,[38] but it closed the door to a possible referral of the situation to the ICC and thus necessitated the establishment of a hybrid tribunal.

3.4. The Future Necessity of Hybrid Tribunals When the ICC Has Jurisdiction. The Relationship With the Complementarity Regime of the ICC

As is widely known, the concept of complementarity is fundamental to the design of the ICC. If in a case or situation under the jurisdiction of the ICC

---

33 See Res. 56/120 the UN General Assembly expressed deep concern over 'the impact of transnational organized crime on the political, social and economic stability and development of societies'. UN Doc. A/RES/56/210 (2002).

34 Neil Boister, 'Transnational Criminal Law'? (2003) 14 *EJIL* 967–977.

35 Issam Kayssi and Weam Alawar, 'The Special Tribunal for Lebanon: International justice or international intervention?'<http://www.aub.edu.lb/sao/activities/outlook/archive/volume_44/issue_9/campus_news/Pages/4.aspx> accessed 7 July 2012.

36 Report of the Secretary-General on the Establishment of a Special Tribunal for Lebanon, UN Doc. S/2006/893 (2006) para. 24.

37 ibid para. 25.

38 See for a fierce critique: Matt Halling, 'Push the Envelope –Watch It Bend: Removing the Policy Requirement and Extending Crimes Against Humanity' (2010) 23 *LJIL* 843–844.

a *bona fide* examination of the alleged crime was undertaken and disposed of by the national judicial system of a state party to the Court, the matter will not be admissible before the ICC pursuant to Article 17 of the Statute.[39] What is the position of hybrid mechanisms within this dichotomous system? May a hybrid tribunal count as a national court? The ambiguous text of the Statute does not exclude such a scenario. Some national involvement should suffice, and a teleological interpretation in accordance with Article 31(1) of the Vienna Convention on the Law of Treaties supports the conclusion that hybrid tribunals may be included under the term national, since one of the primary aims behind the creation of the ICC was to end impunity.[40]

One important argument to be put forward for choosing in favor of hybrid tribunals over purely national tribunals is the argument of capacity, both from the perspective of the state parties to the ICC and the ICC itself. From the perspective of state parties, a country may be so devastated by war or a conflict with intense violence that its judicial capacity is too poor to deliver meaningful post-conflict justice. The creation of a hybrid tribunal may be indispensable then and, furthermore, it can be beneficial to a state's future judicial development and capacity-building.[41] For example, this 'capacity' argument is one of the most important rationales behind the plans to hybrid courts in the Democratic Republic of the Congo (DRC) to try international crimes committed between March 1993 and June 2003.[42] Because of budget constraints, the ICC itself will only be able to judge a very small fraction of human rights abusers in any given situation.

Furthermore, in its most recent prosecutorial strategy, the Office of the Prosecutor of the ICC consolidated its policy to investigate and prosecute those who bear the greatest responsibility for the most serious crimes.[43] In this respect, hybrid mechanisms should be seen as a useful complement to the ICC.[44]

---

39 Jonathan I. Charney, 'International Criminal Law and the Role of Domestic Courts' (2001) *AJIL* 95 120.

40 Markus Benzing and Morten Bergsmo, 'Some Tentative Remarks on the Relationship Between Internationalized Criminal Jurisdictions and the International Criminal Court' in Romano, Nollkaemper and Kleffner (eds) (n 3) 412.

41 ibid 416.

42 See Pascale Kambale, 'Plans for Hybrid Courts in Congo' <http://www.osisa.org/openspace/drc/plans-hybrid-court-congo-pascale-kambale> accessed 2 July 2012.

43 ICC, The Office of the Prosecutor, Prosecutorial Strategy 2009–2012 para 14.

44 Higonnet (n 4) 431; Padraig McAuliffe, 'Hybrid Tribunals at Ten: How International Criminal Justice's Golden Child Became an Orphan' (2011) 7 *JILIR* 63.

3.5. Fairness as an Argument in Favor of the Future Establishment of Hybrid Tribunals Both When the ICC Has or Has No Jurisdiction

Fairness is often put forward as one of the most important features and justifications for the project of International Criminal Justice[45] and of hybrid tribunals more specifically.[46] Admittedly, at a practical level, there seem to be great benefits to addressing mass atrocities at the domestic level. The proximity to the evidence and witnesses certainly facilitates expeditious trials. From the perspective of state cooperation, domestic prosecutions are easier because states are not asked to surrender jurisdiction to try their nationals, often seen as a critical aspect of state sovereignty. However, national tribunals face various drawbacks.

Given the fact that international crimes are often crimes committed with the support of the state, domestic mechanisms will often be unreliable and partial. Moreover, the danger of show trials and victor's justice exists where governments have been replaced after a conflict. This danger of partial trials and victor's justice is shown by the track record of two domestic tribunals specifically set up to try international crimes that fall out of the jurisdictional ambit of the ICC: the Iraqi High Tribunal (IHT) and the International Crimes Tribunal in Bangladesh (ICTB). Both tribunals are largely seen as illegitimate for its failure to deliver fair trials.

In the case of the IHT, the proceedings were marred by the assassination of defense counsel, the resignation of a presiding judge, the boycott of defense teams, disruptive conduct of defendants and by botched executions that were universally condemned.[47] As regards the ICTB, it has been labeled as a 'travesty of justice'[48] because of its failure to uphold the most fair trial rights and guarantees for impartiality. The list of reproaches is long, but the ICTB is criticized for, *inter alia*, conducting interrogations in secret; preventing foreign counsel from entering the country; the ill treatment of detainees and the subjection of defense lawyers and witnesses to threats of false arrest and intimidation.[49] In both instances, a hybrid

---

[45] See Stahn, 'Between 'Faith' and 'Facts': By What Standards Should We Asses International Criminal Justice?' (2012) 25 *LJIL* 266–270.

[46] Nouwen (n 2) 191.

[47] Michael P. Scharf, 'The Iraqi High Tribunal. A Viable Experiment in International Justice?' (2007) 5 JICJ 259.

[48] Tom Felix Joehnk, "A War Crimes Court and a Travesty of Justice" *New York Times* (New York, 29 November 2011).

[49] Toby Cadman, 'The International Crimes Tribunal Bangladesh: A Journey In Search Of Fairness' <http://www.internationallawbureau.com/blog/wp-content/uploads/2011/11/Toby-Cadman-Bangladesh-In-Search-Of-Fairness-copy.pdf> accessed 8 July 2012.

tribunal would have been a better option. The addition of a sufficient amount of international jurists, with experience in complex prosecutions and scrupulously respecting international fair trial standards, could ensure future similar tribunals are impartial and free from government manipulation.[50]

Concerning the crimes committed in situations that fall within the jurisdictional realm of the ICC, the establishment of hybrid tribunals for reasons of fairness could also be argued for. By allowing the internationalization of its domestic justice system, a state could create a genuine domestic proceeding to preclude admissibility of a case or situation before the ICC under Article 17 of the Statute.[51] An explicit requirement of fairness is contained in the chapeau of Article 17(2). The Court is mandated to determine admissibility with 'regard to the principles of due process recognized by international law'.[52]

4. Conclusion

Hybrid tribunals are the most obvious manifestations of a more global, pluralistic and holistic approach towards International Criminal Justice. Hybrid tribunals transcend the traditional dichotomy between the 'international' and the 'domestic', often presented as the only two legal orders where justice for the major international crimes could take place, by offering a more tailor-made, flexible and, at times, more desirable option. It is a necessary option sometimes too, to fill impunity gaps left by purely international tribunals, for reasons of limited capacity of both domestic courts and the ICC, and to uphold fairness that is lacking at the domestic level.

Although we still believe in the hybrid model's added value, one cannot stay blind to the flaws of hybrid tribunals. First and foremost, the inadequacies that the hybrid model has demonstrated up to date should be taken into consideration and remedied before the establishment of new hybrid tribunals is considered.

---

50 Sylvia de Bertodano, 'Where There More Acceptable Alternatives to the Iraqi High Tribunal?' (2007) 5 JICJ 297; Mendez (n 9) 87.

51 McAuliffe (n 44) 63.

52 See for more details: Stahn, 'Libya, the International Criminal Court and Complementarity: A Test for 'Shared Responsibility' (2012) 25 JICJ 345.

Normative Standards and Global Law-Making

Vanessa Mak
D.Phil, M.Jur (Oxon); Associate Professor of Private Law, Tilburg University
vanessa.mak@uvt.nl

Abstract
This contribution explores the meaning of 'global law' in private law. Private law relationships occur across borders more and more often, but does this also mean that the law governing these relations has become global? It is suggested that in law-making a connection can be made between different levels of regulation (international, national or regional) through the use of normative standards such as the 'average consumer' of EU law.

Keywords
private law theory; multi-level regulation

What does global law mean to a private lawyer? The words of Erasmus' famous adagium 'the World is my home' seem true for many of us today and consequently many private law matters have obtained an international flavour. We travel, we work, we marry, we buy, we do business – often within our own country but often also in other parts of the world. That *we* have become more globally active does not mean, however, that the *law* governing these private law issues has become global. The majority of transactions and private law relationships are still governed by national laws and only a small part by transnational or harmonised law.[1]

Global law in relation to private law, therefore, must mean something else; in this short contribution I will explore what meaning it can have for private law. I will focus in particular on law-making in private law. From this perspective, globalisation has had a significant impact on the way that law is perceived. National legislators are no longer central to law-making, in particular in multi-layered systems of regulation such as the EU. New actors and new sources of rules, whether they can be called 'law' or not, have

[1] For an overview and analysis of instruments of transnational law, see Roy Goode and others, *Transnational Commercial Law* (two volumes, Oxford University Press 2007).

appeared in the form of transnational or supranational law and perhaps are most visible in self-regulation.

This contribution consists of three parts. Part 1 sketches the development of 'global law-making' in private law and proposes a new theoretical model aimed at law-making across different levels of regulation. Part 2 tests the model through a short case study on European consumer law. Part three 3 draws together the lines that were set out in the previous parts.

1. Global Law-Making and Private Law

To start with, the idea of 'global law' is somewhat elusive. It is attractive to see it as a new paradigm or perspective on the nature of law in times of globalisation, but it could equally well be posited that it is an analytical tool that helps us understand processes of law-making and legal development in the world without those laws necessarily having a global (or international, or other non-local) nature.[2] The former view relates more to substance, the latter - to form.

The first view demands that we scrutinise the essence of law and ask 'what *is* law?', presuming that the answer to this question differs depending on whether rules stem from national legislation or from other, international, supranational or even private sources. The latter view, by contrast, does not so much ask as to what law is, but seeks to formulate an analytical framework, or organising concept, that helps us understand law in a world where the focus is shifting away from national legal orders. Either view has commendable points and I will, within the limited space of this contribution, not seek to choose between them.

There is, however, an interesting connection that can be made between substance and form in 'global law-making' within the sphere of private law. Global law-making – or: post-national law-making, both terms denoting the creation of legal rules in an international or multi-layered legal order – requires a perspective that is markedly different from law-making in national legal systems. Multiple actors can be involved (e.g. legislators but also private parties through self-regulation) who develop rules at different levels of regulation. The substance of these rules can diverge precisely because in this format of law-making several different actors are involved, with different roles and aims. One can think of legislators, courts, regulators, and private parties which self-regulate. The question is how their

[2] Cf William Twining, *General Jurisprudence* (Cambridge University Press 2009) 66.

law-making activities can be coordinated so that fragmentation of laws, which normally hinders the transparency of laws to private parties and threatens legal certainty, is kept to a minimum.

Existing strategies for better regulation, as seen, in particular, in European law, have not been very successful at decreasing such fragmentation. Harmonisation of laws in a top-down manner often does not work since the new rules do not fit with national laws and, moreover, are often not politically accepted.

The alternative, 'spontaneous harmonisation', would work in a bottom-up manner;[3] however, there is no evidence that it occurs. By suggesting a new approach that could qualify as a model for global law-making, this contribution submits that part of these problems may be countered by using normative standards as central reference points for law-making. Normative standards in this context are defined as open norms to which more concrete rules can be attached. If a standard is central to several forms and levels of regulation, it can provide a reference point for communication between those levels.

This theoretical model can be made more concrete by examining a case study. An illustrative example is that of the 'average consumer' in European consumer law. This open norm is used as a benchmark for consumer protection in several areas of EU consumer law and can provide a normative standard for law-making.[4]

2. The 'Average Consumer' of EU Law[5]

The 'average consumer' is a central standard in EU consumer law. What makes it interesting for law-making in a global law view is that its normative content is developed at (at least) two levels of regulation. First, the test

---

[3] See Norbert Reich, 'Competition between Legal Orders: A New Paradigm of EC Law?' (1992) 29 *Common Market Law Review* 861; Jan Smits, *The Making of European Private Law; Towards a Ius Commune Europaeum as a Mixed Legal System* (Intersentia, 2002).

[4] See in particular Directive 2005/29/EC concerning business-to-consumer unfair commercial practices [2005] OJ L149/22 (UCP Directive), Art. 5(1); Directive 2004/39/EC on Markets in Financial Instruments (MiFID) [2004] OJ L145/1; Directive 2006/73/EC implementing Directive 2004/39 [2006] OJ L241/26 (MiFID Implementing Directive), Art. 27(2). Cf. earlier Directive 97/55/EC on misleading and comparative advertising [1997] OJ L290/18.

[5] For a more elaborate discussion, see Vanessa Mak, 'The "Average Consumer" of EU Law in Domestic and European Litigation', in: Dorota Leczykiewicz and Stephen Weatherill, *The Involvement of EU Law in Private Law Relationships* (Hart 2012, forthcoming) chapter 14.

developed by the Court of Justice of the EU (CJEU) looks at the 'presumed expectations' of an average consumer rather than at factual evidence. Second, in national private laws the 'average consumer' is used as a normative reference point for the balancing of rights and duties between private parties.

It is important to realise, however, that the content of the standard does not only come from the balancing of private law rights and duties, but also from public law or in this case EU internal market policy. This can explain why the 'average consumer' of EU law is mostly regarded as a rational actor, rather than a weaker party in need of protection. A few words on this before coming back to the normative function.

2.1. The Internal Market Function

Who is the 'average consumer' of EU law? After earlier judgments – e.g., in *Mars*,[6] where the Court referred to 'reasonably circumspect consumers' as the standard by which to judge consumer confusion in intellectual property law – the 'average consumer' has reached its current definition in the *Gut Springenheide* judgment. The case concerned the marketing of eggs to consumers. Whereas the label on the packaging of the eggs stated '6-grain – 10 fresh eggs', the manufacturer of the eggs admitted that the chickens producing the eggs were fed the six varieties of cereals in question as only 60 per cent of their diet. But would consumers understand this, or would they assume that the chickens were only fed these six special cereals and that the eggs consequently were of a certain quality? The German court handling the main dispute was in doubt as to the standard that should be adopted in the interpretation of Regulation 1907/90 and referred the question to the Court of Justice.[7]

The Court's response that an average consumer is 'reasonably well-informed and reasonably observant and circumspect' opts for the empowered notion of a consumer.[8] EU law does not seek to protect the 'casual consumer' but rather regards consumers as responsible individuals. That view coincides with the neo-liberal policies that are reflected in EU

[6] Case C-470/93 *Verein gegen Unwesen in Handel and Gewerbe Köln eV v Mars GmbH* [1995] ECR I-1923, para 24.

[7] Art 10(2)(e) of Council Regulation (EEC) No 1907/90 of 26 June 1990 on certain marketing standards for eggs [1990] OJ L 173/5.

[8] Case C-210/96 *Gut Springenheide and Rudolf Tusky v Oberkreisdirektor des Kreises Steinfurt* [1998] ECR I-4657, para 31.

legislation, extending also into private law.[9] It also fits with the aims of the internal market.

By adopting a restrictive notion of the protection that an 'average consumer' deserves, the Member States' possibilities for maintaining stricter rules of consumer protection become limited. From this perspective, it can be explained why the Court of Justice often objects to national legislation on the ground that the 'average consumer' does not need extra protection (cf *Gut Springenheide*) and that it is therefore disproportionate. The Court thereby gives preference to internal market objectives, taking away barriers to trade that arise from differences in national consumer laws.[10]

By contrast, the Court of Justice tends to take a very pro-consumer stance in cases where it is asked to interpret EU consumer law Directives. In other words, whereas negative harmonisation is promoted by the Court's proactive objection to national legislation that may create barriers to trade, the positive harmonisation of national (private) laws through Directives is given a boost by interpreting them in a far-reaching and consumer-friendly manner. As noted by Unberath and Johnston, one wonders what the 'average consumer' of EU law would make of such cases.[11] These cases confirm that the Court regards the concept as a mediating tool between EU law and national laws, not only in its free movements case law but also in the interpretation of Directives.

2.2. *The 'Average Consumer' as a Normative Standard*

The content of the 'average consumer' notion may fluctuate and, as we see, be influenced by policy considerations. Nevertheless, it has a second function – namely its use as a standard for normative evaluation – that gives it potential for global law-making.

Its normative use can be seen in particular in national private laws, which are not directly influenced by the internal market problems discussed in the previous part. In the national context, the standard functions as a normative reference point for the balancing of rights and duties between

---

[9] Compare Martijn W Hesselink, 'The Politics of a European Civil Code' (2004) 10 *European Law Journal* 675, 687.

[10] Note that the Court, on the other hand, also objects to national legislation where it appears that national legislators (ab)use the 'average consumer' to justify consumer protection laws that hamper competition. Cf Case C-315/92 *Verband Sozialer Wettbewerb eV v Clinique Laboratoires SNC et Estée Lauder Cosmetics GmbH* [1994] ERC I-317.

[11] Hannes Unberath and Angus Johnston, 'The Double-Headed Approach of the ECJ Concerning Consumer Protection' (2007) 44 *Common Market Law Review* 1237, 1282.

private parties. Here, it mediates between the general premise of autonomy of the parties and the protective duties owed by businesses to consumers – e.g., duties of care – that seek to counter the imbalance of power that is paradigmatic for consumer contracts.

That does not mean that there is always a direct reference to the 'average consumer' standard in national legislation and case law, but its contours can often be made out in the balance that legislators and courts strike between the interests of businesses and consumers. Examples of this can be seen in domestic legislation in consumer credit and investment cases.[12]

The 'average consumer', therefore, functions as a benchmark or a normative standard against which the interests and responsibilities of businesses and consumers can be tested. That type of standard is common to national legal systems, in which a fictional 'officious bystander' or the 'man on the Clapham omnibus' can be used to determine whether or not there is ground for liability in contract or tort.[13] Examples also exist in other areas of law, such as in social security law. To determine the height of unemployment benefits, reference can be made to the salary that a fictional 'average employee' would earn in a similar employment position as the claimant.[14] In each case, a benchmark is sought on the basis of which concrete norms can be established.

The EU law concept of the 'average consumer' is also used for normative evaluation. That dimension can be gleaned from the judgment of the Court in *Gut Springenheide* from which, as seen above, the current definition of the average consumer stems. The test for misleading statements, read in full, is the following:

> [I]n order to determine whether the description, trade mark or promotional description or statement in question was liable to mislead the purchaser, the Court took into account the presumed expectations of an average consumer who is reasonably well-informed and reasonably observant and circumspect, without ordering an expert's report or commissioning a consumer research poll.[15]

---

[12] See references in (n 6).

[13] Both terms spring from English law. For the first, see Scrutton LJ in *Reigate v Union Manufacturing Co (Ramsbottom) Ltd* [1918] 1 KB 592, 605 and MacKinnon LJ in *Shirlaw v Southern Foundries (1926) Ltd* [1939] 2 KB 206, 227; for the second, Greer LJ in *Hall v Brooklands Auto-Racing Club* (1933) 1 KB 205.

[14] Compare the 'maatman' in Dutch social security law; Art 18(1) Wet op de arbeidsongeschiktheidsverzekering (WAO), Art 1 Wet Werk en Inkomen naar Arbeidsvermogen (WIA).

[15] Case C-210/96 *Gut Springenheide* [1998] ECR I-4657, para 31.

The definition adopted by the Court therefore is in principle a normative standard on the basis of which the 'presumed expectations' of consumers are assessed. The fact that it is not necessary to order an expert's report or to commission a research poll to establish if, and how many, consumers are misled by the statement emphasises the normative nature of the standard. It is possible, after all, that the facts of a case give sufficient information as to the context in which the statements were made to enable a court to *deem* it plausible that any reasonably well-informed and reasonably observant and circumspect consumer would have erred in interpreting a statement correctly. Thus, it is also not surprising that the Court feels competent to determine what standard of fairness was required and whether the contested statement was misleading or unfair.

The normative legal standard expressed in the 'average consumer' notion of EU law can still have a factual component in cases where additional information is needed to determine whether a statement is misleading or a practice unfair. In that respect, the Court adheres to its general case law on the interaction of the European and national courts. In many instances, the interpretation of EU legislation requires a court to refer to the national law context because the provisions of EU Directives and Regulations are interwoven with provisions of national law.[16] Situations in which a factual component comes into the test can be cases in which the expectations of the 'average consumer' relate to 'social, cultural and linguistic' aspects which are particular to a Member State.[17]

A second category is constituted by situations in which the national court wishes to use additional information on the actual behaviour of consumers. The Court of Justice does not rule out such further testing.[18] Moreover it adds that, in the absence of EU intervention on this point, it is up to the national court to decide which percentage of consumers must be misled to justify banning a measure.[19] Surprisingly, that can lead to different outcomes to what one would expect on the basis of a normative assessment of consumer expectations.

For example, it was possible for the German court in *Gut Springenheide* to hold the description of the '6-grain' eggs unfair on the basis that 10 to 15 per

---

16 Cf Case C-237/02 *Freiburger Kommunalbauten GmbH Baugesellschaft & Co. KG* v *Ulrike Hofstetter and Ludger Hofstetter* [2004] ECR I-3403.

17 Cf Case C-313/94 *Fratelli Graffione SNC v Ditta Fransa* [1996] ECR I-6039. See also Case C-220/98 *Estée Lauder Cosmetics GmbH v Lancaster Group GmbH* [2000] ECR I-0117. Compare UCP Directive, recital 18.

18 Case C-210/96 *Gut Springenheide* [1998] ECR I-4657, para 35.

19 ibid, para 36.

cent of consumers would be misled. Not only may one think that this number is relatively low, even more surprising is that the surveys on which these numbers are based did not use the reasonably well-informed consumer of EU law as their benchmark but instead referred to a 'casual consumer'.[20] Bearing this in mind, factual evidence may be helpful but the method by which it is acquired should be fine-tuned in order for the 'average consumer' truly to function as a normative standard.

3. Normative Standards and Global Law

Besides its function as a mediating tool between EU and Member State laws, the 'average consumer' therefore is ultimately a normative standard against which the expectations of consumers can be measured. This opens up possibilities for its use as a reference point in the development of law across different levels of regulation – or global law-making.

Still, the adoption of such a model in broader areas of global law-making is subject to a few conditions. It asks for a more open attitude towards sources of law and, importantly, towards the legitimacy of rules derived from non-legislative sources.[21] Furthermore, private lawyers need to be open to public law influences. The example of the 'average consumer' of EU law shows that its content is strongly influenced by EU internal market policy. Goals, often seen as part of regulation rather than private law, therefore also determine the way in which normative standards are given content. The fact that public law and private law often intertwine may not be surprising. Global law-making based on normative standards, however, should at least make transparent which content comes from regulatory goals and which is the result of a more principled private law approach.

Finally, for determining what substance rules should have – e.g. in terms of the level of consumer protection that is opted for – a normative reasoning in the context of a national legal system will no longer do. Comparison

---

20 See Stefan Dittmer, 'Misleading advertising: an end to the "cursory average consumer"?' (1998) 20 *European Intellectual Property Review* 313, 316; Cees van Dam, 'De gemiddelde Euroconsument – een pluriform fenomeen' (2009) 57 *Sociaal-economische wetgeving SEW* 7.

21 Legitimacy is a point of contention; for a recent contribution in the light of general principles of law, see Martijn W Hesselink, 'The General Principles of Civil Law: their Nature, Roles and Legitimacy', in: Leczykiewicz and Weatherill (n 5).

with other levels of regulation, but also empirical-legal research, can provide important guidance for legislators, policy makers and other actors engaged in law-making. Global law, therefore, is international and interdisciplinary and with those features, an excellent flagship for Tilburg Law School.

In Pursuit of the Global within: A Structure for the Global Law Project

Han Somsen
Professor of EU Law, Tilburg Law School;
Chair, Editorial Committee, Tilburg Global Law book series
han.somsen@uvt.nl

Abstract
This short essay takes as its point of departure the truism that 'the global' is omnipresent. 'Intimations of the global', to borrow from Neil Walker, are therefore as likely to be uncovered by studying domestic legal systems most familiar to us, as they are by pointing our lens at what is alien. If the global is understood in this way, i.e. as referring to the basic building blocks common to all legal systems, then two settings appear to offer prima facie fertile ground for unraveling the global. First, if laws employ open terminology or otherwise afford considerable discretion (e.g. as in the case of 'procedural autonomy'), it may be premised that when in such cases it is (empirically) established that in reality certain rules act to further constrain such freedom, those rules could be of a 'global' character. Obversely, when legal rules claim an absolute status, in the sense that they tolerate not exception (as in the case of the supremacy of EU law), factual departures from that absolute rule again may be regarded as intimations of the global.

Keywords
global law; EU law; procedural autonomy; supremacy of EU law

As the success of any journey of discovery worthy of the name obviously cannot be guaranteed in advance, it appears somewhat futile at this stage to speculate about the future contributions of the global law project to legal scholarship. This is particularly so because the vehicle that is to take us on our travels, 'global law', has yet to be put to the test, and moreover is set to remain imperfectly understood for quite some time to come. Any suggestion, therefore, that we can accurately predict how the unchartered territory of global law is set to enrich our understandings of the legal world we inhabit smacks of a lack of humility unworthy of the serious academic endeavour that the global law project represents.

Rather than to deny this charge, I hence plead guilty from the outset, and forfeit any claim that this short essay represents serious legal scholarship. Should what I have to say nonetheless turn out to be of use, then this is likely to be so due to the fact that these are the ponderings of an EU lawyer who, on a daily basis, must come to terms with complex interactions between different legal cultures represented at different levels of governance (global, regional, national and sub-national). I indeed presume that, whatever we may ultimately find global law precisely to add to our understanding of this contemporary legal universe, it will surely similarly concern the ways in which different legal realities coexist and relate. In our quest for answers to the challenges which those different realities increasingly generate, we should first unravel and then try to understand the DNA of our common legal heritage. This, I imagine, captures the justification for and general direction of the global law project. Let me try to explain.

Boundless curiosity apart - to my old-fashioned mind still the oxygen for a serious academic community - the practical use of the global law project insisted on by those representing the vocational element within law schools is found in the ramifications of globalization. Put simply: increasing globalization means that we are more frequently exposed to different legal realities, and that it does so in ways that we can no longer simply choose to ignore. It would be manifestly folly to infer from widespread nationalistic mutterings of parliaments across the globe that globalization is on its way out, if only because the essence of globalization is precisely the increasing irrelevance of those parliaments. As globalization is therefore most definitely here to stay, we need not worry about the shelf-time of the global law project.

As to the crucial question *how* global law can assist legal practitioners and scholars in engaging with globalization and its consequences, as a starter I posit that the lens of global law should help us understand both 'the self' and 'the other', and thereby ultimately should enlighten us as to how the self relates to the other and *vice versa*. Thus perceived, the global law project essentially is an existentialist endeavour.

At the beginning of the 17th century, in a similar attempt to make sense of the relation between his world and the surrounding universe, Galileo trained his telescope *outwards* towards the planets and the stars. The upshot of Galileo's pioneering observations and calculations is that we now realize that, in the bigger scheme of things, our earth is not central and quite possibly not even all that unique. Notwithstanding the passage of some four hundred years since Galileo's findings, humankind yet has to come fully to grips with this sobering truth, and we still stubbornly speak of 'sunset' and 'sunrise'. On the positive side, it has also allowed us to travel to other planets, to dream about forever expanding our horizons, and to start realizing that it is unlikely that we are on our own in this universe.

It was a contemporary of Galileo, Hugo Grotius, who almost simultaneously pulled off a comparable feat for the law, again by extending his focus outwards. Grotius' *De iure belli ac pacis* has laid the foundations for modern public international law and, on the occasion of this special issue devoted to the launch of Tilburg's global law project, it is warranted to lift one particularly fitting quote from this monumental work: 'Fully convinced (...) that there is a common law among nations, which is valid alike for war and in war, I have had many and weighty reasons for undertaking to write upon the subject'.[1]

Like Galileo's discoveries concerning the solar system, Grotius' conceptions of war and natural justice have forced us to give up claims of uniqueness, of belonging to some pre-conceived privileged inner-circle, or of being destined to be elevated above the other. But if humankind already has embraced the fact that 'there is a common law among nations', albeit perhaps imperfectly and inconsistently so, what remaining role can we foresee for global law?

I venture to suggest that the answer to this pertinent question is to be found in our understanding of 'the global'. Because the global law project is a response to *global*ization it is intuitive to presume that, like Galileo and Grotius, it will seek for its answers predominantly by peering into the distant expanse of the legal universe. This indeed has already been done by Grotius and by others who have followed in his footsteps. Legal disciplines such as public international law, comparative law and transnational law are fruits of their efforts.

Although the global law project obviously cannot exist in isolation from these disciplines, and indeed is to build on it, I am confident that it will make a discrete, fundamental and original contribution to legal scholarship and legal education. Earlier in this essay, despite a great deal of reluctance, I have used the worn and cliché metaphor of unraveling the DNA of our common heritage in an attempt to underline the attraction of adopting an internal perspective on the global.

There is a profound difference between an 'external' notion of the global, referring to some all encompassing legal system or principle spanning the globe, and an 'internal' understanding of the global denoting the basic building blocks of which all legal systems are made up. The former requires looking outward for something big enough to register on our radar, the latter can be pursued equally effectively by looking within ourselves for

---

1 Hugo Grotius, *The Law of War and Peace* (Francis Kelsey tran, Carnegie edition 1925) Prologue, pt 28.

something small but elementary. 'The self', in this context, can refer to any polity (arguably even to any source of regulation), because we are in search of the basic building blocks that hence are common to the laws of all those different polities. We have gazed through binoculars and telescopes at foreign legal landscapes for over four hundred years now, and we have done so with a degree of success. The global law project amounts to a new phase, however, in that we and our soul mates shall now peek though our microscopes in a systematic search for evidence of the global within ourselves.

Lest we think that such an exercise lacks in cosmopolitan glamour and promise, we do well to wonder why the most ground breaking discoveries were made by Nobel prize laureates such as Watson and Crick, Binning and Rohrer, or Kroto, Smalley and Curl, or why states are ready to invest some 4.5 billion Euros to build the Large Hadron Collider operated by CERN. The reason, I venture to suggest, is that the answers to the fundamental questions faced by humankind are found not by pointing our lens at what is alien and at a distance, but instead by directing it inwards, focusing on the familiar in pursuit of basic building blocks common to all and everything. The global law project, thus, seeks to unearth the global within.

So far so good, but how do we translate these possible lessons from the natural sciences into a concrete global law research agenda? If we are to take heed of our hunch that there is much to be gained from adopting an internal perspective on the global, at what do we actually point our lens? I do not sufficiently lack in modesty to claim to have the final answer here. Indeed, the most crucial and challenging part of the global law project is likely to consist of determining its focus.

Yet, using EU law as an example, as a first necessity we must identify spaces within the EU legal order that are presumed to represent legal voids, or no go areas; in the context of what I have said thus far the metaphor of black holes springs to mind, or of CERN's quest to find the Higgs-boson particle. Translated to the EU law context, we could say that global law scholars will have a hard and intense look at instances in which actors (individuals, Member States, and the institutions) claim unfettered discretion, simply because global law scholars are skeptical about the existence of such a state of lawlessness.

It flows from the internal perspective of the global, which I advocate here, that we premise that even black holes conceal rudimentary legal building blocks, which in turn act to discipline discretion. The flip side of the same coin, of course, is that global law scholars are equally dubious about claims pertaining to the absoluteness of rules, i.e. that certain rules tolerate no exceptions and exclude any discretion on the part of actors confronted with them.

To fend off predictable charges that my ideas are too general to be of use (which, mercifully, in universities is not synonymous for *practical* use), I should like to finish with two random examples of global law research topics that I considered for this essay, before I decided to discard them in favour of a more general and conceptual discourse.

The Myth of Procedural Autonomy in EU law

Conventional EU law wisdom holds that there is such a thing as 'procedural autonomy'. This simply means that, to the extent there are no applicable provisions of EU law, Member States are free to design their own systems of remedies that apply to the enforcement of rights derived from EU law, subject only to two open-ended and somewhat contradictory conditions:

1. The principle of equivalence;
2. The principle of effectiveness.

According to Oxford English Dictionary, 'autonomy' means 'the ability to act and make decisions without being controlled by anyone else'. Global lawyers are *prima facie* skeptical about the existence of such a black hole, and therefore critically query the existence of procedural autonomy.[2]

Principles of Judicial Review of Scientific Expertise in EU Risk Regulation

A second conventional wisdom inviting scrutiny by global law scholarship holds that EU institutions are free to base decisions aimed at regulating risks on the scientific expertise of their liking, subject only to review by the Court of manifest errors of judgment and misuse of power.[3] But does the freedom of EU regulators really extend this far, or is it possible to identify principles of global law that further curtail this freedom and, as a corollary, put greater demands on our courts?

---

2 And rightly so, according to scholars who have confirmed our suspicion. For EU environmental law see in particular Pal Wenneras, *Enforcement of EC Environmental Law* (Oxford University Press 2007). More generally see Michal Bobek, 'Why There is No Principle of Procedural Autonomy of the Member States' in Bruno de Witte and Hans Micklitz (eds), *The European Court of Justice and the Autonomy of the Member States* (Intersentia 2011).

3 See Case C-79/09, *Gowan Comércio Internacional e Serviços Lda v. Ministero della Salute* [Judgment of the Court (Second Chamber) of 22 December 2010]. The Court stipulated that Courts must assess 'whether the relevant procedural rules have been complied with, whether the facts admitted by the Commission have been accurately stated and whether there has been a manifest error of appraisal or a misuse of power.'

Countless other intriguing examples of possible future global law research of EU law spring to mind. Frequently, such examples involve seemingly absolute rules which, upon closer inspection, do not stand up to scrutiny. What to think of the EU principle of supremacy, for example, which surely should attract the attention of global law scholarship.

As this final example pointedly illustrates, the absoluteness of rules invariably denotes a very high position in hierarchies of norms. By querying the absoluteness of rules, the global law project is thereby set to shake legal orders at their foundations. Undisputedly, these are therefore immensely exciting and privileged times to be a scholar or student at Tilburg Law School.

The Global Challenge to Public International Law: Some First Thoughts

Randall Lesaffer[a] & Rianne Letschert[b]
a) Dean, Tilburg Law School; Professor of Legal History, Tilburg University and Katholieke Universiteit Leuven
r.c.h.lesaffer@tilburguniversity.edu
b) Professor, Victimology and International Law, Tilburg University; Deputy Director International Victimology Institute, Tilburg (INTERVICT)
r.m.letschert@tilburguniversity.edu

Abstract
Public international law has been 'global' in its application since at least the 1960s, when most Western colonial empires had disappeared. Still, it is far from being left untouched by the fundamental changes which law is undergoing worldwide and which scholars often catch under the term 'globalization'. The gradual decline of the monopoly of States in the field of international relations and the on-going globalization of the economy and the challenges mankind is facing threaten the autonomy of public international law and even stretch it to its vanishing point. The authors argue that while international lawyers should not react defensively, we should be even more careful not to sacrifice the central position of the State in international law too readily as it is the prime locus of democracy and the rule of law. They also plead for a shift in international legal academia from the traditional focus on the formal role of international law within the system of law and global governance to studying its societal impact and potential in facing global challenges.

Keywords
public international law; global law; globalization; legal history

Public international law as we know it is by and large the product of Western civilization. Its roots lay in the modern system of sovereign States which arose in Europe between the Late Middle Ages and saw its heyday in the 19th century. Through the processes of European colonization and decolonization, international law spread its wings over the globe. Since the 1960s at the latest, public international law has been 'global law' in the sense of universally applicable law. Notwithstanding this, public international law is not left untouched by the current debate on the globalization of law. Much to the contrary, the globalization debate has turned into a debate on the very nature of public international law. It has turned into a debate of whether there is a future for public international law as a law between States.

The challenge which the sovereign State faces is not novel; it goes back to the early 20th century. By and large, international lawyers and historians of international law have reflected upon the development of international law, during the 20th century, in terms of the gradual loss of the monopoly of States over international law. To this purpose, many writers have construed a dialectical opposition between the 'Westphalian' or 'Hobbesian' classical international law of the 19th century and the 'post-Westphalian' or 'Grotian' international law that arose during the 20th century.

Under the Hobbesian system, the sovereign State ruled supreme; it was, at the same time, the sole subject, author and enforcer of international law. Over the 20th century, the State's monopoly was gradually eroded through the rise of international organizations and more fundamentally, the return of the individual – mainly through the international protection of human rights and the emergence of international criminal prosecution – on the scenery of international relations and law.[1] By the midst of the 20th century, some leading voices in the debate claimed that the legal order of the world had reached a middle-point between the old historical Hobbesian reality and the Kantian cosmopolitan ideal: that of a 'Grotian' international law that was next to being the law of an international community of States, also that of a world community of people.[2]

Since the end of the Cold War (1989), changes that eroded the monopoly of the State over international law have increased in speed and depth.[3] Moreover, over the last few years, the debate on the relative decline of the State in international law has fallen within the orbit of the debate on globalization. While globalization is not a new phenomenon either – the integration of the world economy goes back to the Age of Discoveries and was much a fact by the 19th century[4] – it has gained a lot of traction over the last few decades. Through technological evolution, far more people than ever before are involved in activities that cross national borders.

---

1 Randall Lesaffer, 'The Grotian Tradition Revisited: Change and Continuity in the History of International Law' (2002) 73 British Yearbook of International Law 103, 103-110.

2 Hedley Bull, 'The Grotian Conception of International Society', in Herbert Butterfield and Adam Watson eds, *Diplomatic Investigations: Essays in the Theory of International Politics* (Allen and Unwin 1966) 51-73; Hersch Lauterpacht, 'The Grotian Tradition of International Law' (1946) 23 British Yearbook of International Law 1.

3 James Crawford and Sarah Nouwen eds, *International Law 1989-2010: A Performance Appraisal* (Select Proceedings of the European Society of International Law, Hart 2012) 3.

4 Kevin H O'Rourke and Jeffrey G Williamson, *Globalization and History: The Evolution of a Nineteenth-Century Atlantic Economy* (MIT Press 1999).

Globalization challenges the central position of the State in the world's political and legal order in two different ways. First, globalization enhances the role of non-State actors on the international scenery, from individual human beings to non-governmental organizations and global corporations, and stimulates the rise of a body of transnational law outside the confines of public international law. Second, the growing interdependency of the world and the global challenges mankind faces jeopardize the relevance of States, even the biggest ones, as vehicles for attaining the aspirations of people and peoples.

International legal theorists have not been slow to pick up on the decline of the State. In 1956, Philip Jessup proposed the term 'transnational law' to catch all laws that transcended national borders, thus indicating the growth of a global law distinct from public international law.[5] In the 1950s and 1960s, Wilfred Jenks laid out a roadmap for the construction of a cosmopolitan 'Common Law of Mankind'. In his view, existing international law could only be considered an early, underdeveloped version of the law the world needed.[6] In 1993, John Rawls pleaded for the reconstruction of world order as a society of peoples instead of States.[7] Over recent years, more and more voices have spoken out for the radical relocation of the nucleus of authority in world order away from the State and the construction of a cosmopolitan, Kantian order in which people and not States would be the ultimate focus and purpose. A good example thereof is the work of the Spanish legal historian Rafael Domingo.[8]

Jenks, Domingo and other scholars, all in a more or less radical way, propose the relocation of the locus of authority in 'international' or 'global' law from the State to the individual. This relocation plays out at two levels. First, there is the foundational question of who or what constitutes the purpose of international law. Is international law a law *for* States or a law *for* persons? It is meant to serve the interests of States or that of human beings

---

[5] Philip Jessup, *Transnational Law* (Yale University Press 1956).

[6] Wilfred C Jenks, *The Law of Mankind* (Steven & Sons 1958); Wilfred C Jenks, *Law in the World Community* (Longmans, Green 1967); Wilfred C Jenks, *A New World of Law? A Study of the Creative Imagination in International Law* (Longmans, Green 1969).

[7] John Rawls, 'The Law of Peoples' (1993), in Samuel Freedman ed, *Collected Papers* (Harvard University Press 1999); John Rawls, *The Law of Peoples, with the Idea of Public Reason Revisited* (Harvard University Press 1999).

[8] Rafael Domingo, *The New Global Law*, (Cambridge University Press 2010). An example of a more moderate approach to the relocation of the locus of authority in international law from State to person is offered by Ruti Teitel, *Humanity's Law* (Oxford University Press 2011).

themselves? The mere fact of the debate itself – which again, is not novel but goes back to at least the *Interbellum* – indicates the demise of the State's claim that its interests coincide with the interests of the nations and ultimately with those of its citizens; the core of the theory of popular sovereignty and the nation-State. Second, there are the practical questions about who are the subjects, authors and enforcers of international law? Is international law a law *of States* or is it a law *of* people?

On the latter level, Domingo and others construe a global law that directly recognizes individuals and private associations of individuals as bearers of rights and duties of global law, which they can enforce at any level of governance and jurisdiction. In this vision, 'global law' becomes next to being a universal law, which regulates relations between States and a myriad of other public and private actors, also a common law of minimal standards of human dignity, security and development.

In its more radical guise, as that of Domingo, the challenge of globalization stretches public international law to its vanishing point. Domingo, as did Jenks, conceives of existing (public) international law as an underdeveloped law of mankind, a stepping stone towards the 'new global law'. But once the point is reached where the State becomes one unprivileged player among many on the scenery of global law and where (inter-)State law becomes just one form of law, the existence of public international law as an autonomous body of law – which was hard 'won' in Europe between the 16th and 19th centuries – ceases. Domingo and others are, at the same time, not blind to the dangers these developments might entail. Indeed, some important *caveats* need to be brought into the debate on global law.

Firstly, whereas it is, according to the authors, undeniable that we are living through a paradigmatic shift that is profoundly changing international legal order, we must be careful not to avert ourselves from the lessons that can be learned from the past. *Primo*, as was indicated above, the developments we are living through are a radicalization of a development that already started in the early 20th century.

Secundo, the idea that 'international law' is *for* the people as much as *for* the State is not novel. It was an inherent part of the classical law of the European sovereign States system of the 17th and 18th centuries. Under that classical law of nations, the sovereign princes of Europe had as much a duty to serve the interests of the prosperity and wellbeing of their, and in some cases, other princes' subjects, as they had to their selves.

Later international lawyers have often been blind to this self-evident truism because these duties to mankind had been relayed to the world of natural law, while a prince's duties to his peers fell in the domain of the positive law of nations. That natural law only applied in conscience and was only upheld in the court of God made it no less relevant to an age where princes and politicians were deeply religious and sincerely concerned about their eternal souls. The correct understanding of this historic dualism of early-modern international legal order is highly relevant to the debate today. It indicates that an international legal order wherein States hold a central role can go very well together with the existence of international law as a law *for* people. What needs to be done, and what is indeed happening, is that what was relayed to natural law is merged into the domain of positive international law.[9]

Tertio, there exist historical precedents for a multilevel international legal order where the 'State' plays a central role, but without holding a monopoly over law making and law enforcement or even holding a monopoly over the core issues of 'international' relations. The main and most relevant historical example is no doubt late-medieval, pre-Westphalian Europe. That Europe, often referred to as the *respublica christiana*, was an amalgam of very diverse political players and entities who all held a certain modicum of 'sovereignty' while at the same time standing for some aspects of public government in a hierarchical relation to one another.

This Europe was also one of overlapping jurisdictions and legal systems that sometimes worked together but often vied with one another. It is out of this context that the sovereign State grew and successfully bid its claim to the monopoly over first matters of war and peace and ultimately all public authority and law. But before that point was reached in the 19th century, the European States system was one in which the State monopolized some law, but not all. It was a system in which State sovereignty was not absolute but relative. It only stretched to some domains of public governance. In other domains, it had to leave room to others or even recognize higher authority.

The latter historical remark, secondly, is a warning that, while we may rejoice in the ending of the State's claims to monopoly over law, we should not be too hasty to do away with the State altogether. As Domingo and others have warned, the State is historically and presently the primary locus of democracy and the rule of law. It has also played an instrumental role in the suppression of large-scale violence within societies. As we are striving to overcome, through international law and collective security, the terrible

9 Emmanuelle Jouannet, *The Liberal-Welfarist Law of Nations: A History of International Law* (Cambridge University Press 2012).

downside of the monopolization of force by the State, we should not ignore the lessons of the price of State failure from recent decades. This all implies that within the growing reality of 'global law' there is and will remain for the foreseeable future a separate spot for 'public international law'.

That public international law is this part of the wider 'global law' which deals with basic matters of the public order of the world, such as security, the enforcement against gross violations of human rights and the upholding of the world's basic values. While the inroads on the authority of States by third actors and increasingly vocal, if diffuse, world public opinions may be very beneficial to this public international law, the concern should as much go towards strengthening the legitimacy of State-based world order by making it more multi-polar and democratic.

Thirdly, and closely related to this, are the concerns we should feel about a too enthusiastic embrace of non-State law and alternative ways of dispute resolution. The rise of non-State 'soft' law as a function of civil society taking responsibility for itself is laudable, but we should be well aware that one of the great drives and merits behind the rise of public law in the 20th century is the protection of weaker players against the stronger in the field of private law relations. And while the stories abound of how the most redoubtable multinational corporations today must take heed of the power international pressure groups in the service of a good cause can harness, they cannot assure the neutrality formal State law can. In the same sense, the rise of alternative ways of dispute resolution is in itself not something to applaud or deplore. It is a fact which puts us in front of the double challenge of improving the accessibility and effectiveness of formal adjudication while at the same time strengthening the guarantees for fairness, effectiveness and accessibility that alternative dispute resolution can provide.

Fourth, all of this is not meant to mount a defense of the old in favor of the new or to deny that the world of international law is fundamentally changing. But at this point the debate seems to be too concerned with slashing the status quo and doing away with the old. This is understandable as it stems from unease with the paradigm of the sovereign State most legal scholars have been raised on and now find unsatisfactory to explain the complexities of current international order. Notwithstanding how strong the desire may be to do away with that paradigm and how influential some mental constructs scholars built may prove, these constructs cannot suffice, as they are, as of yet, not real.

Therefore, the debate on the 'globalization' of international law should move outside the confines of legal theory. This means that beyond looking from a new paradigm at what international law is, we also need to look at what international law does as an instrument of world policy. If we are dissatisfied with the paradigm from which we have learned to think about international law, we should also be dissatisfied with the way it is traditionally implemented at the level of its scholarly systematizations and doctrines. So the old system of international law, as it was laid down in the great textbooks of the 20th century, does not satisfy any more to comprehend the purpose, meaning and life of international law. Therefore, a new doctrine of international law, with a new structure and maybe even a new vocabulary will have to be developed. This will be a long and tedious process and one that will be the work of more than one generation. But it is a task we should not wait to start with until a new paradigm of international legal theory has crystallized. A more pragmatic approach to the new realities is, as if not, more expedient. What we need are new doctrines which depart from the global challenges that international law is faced with today.

Comparative Law in a Globalizing World: Three Challenges

Maurice Adams
Professor of Law, Tilburg Law School (the Netherlands)
Part-time Professor of Comparative Law, University of Antwerp (Belgium)
m.adams@tilburguniversity.edu

Abstract
Contemporary comparative law and comparative legal scholarship have generally been marked by constructivist purposes, as a means for state building and local law reform. In this sense they have lent support to the idea of law being an exclusively national phenomenon. However, as a result of globalization, the question is whether the discipline, as it stands now, is fit for dealing with an ever more interdependent world. The answer might well be in the negative, with a result that comparative lawyers have to adapt their analytical and educational toolkits to ones other than constructivist purposes, and also to the realities of a largely fragmented and fluid regulatory landscape. At least three challenges stand out with regard to changing comparative law from a marginal and static discipline into a central and dynamic one: the objects of comparative law; the role of comparative law in the law curriculum and the type of research a dynamic approach to comparative law requires.

Keywords
comparative law; comparative legal research; globalization; legal dynamics

1. Comparative Law as a Marginal and Static Discipline

Patrick Glenn has aptly and repeatedly observed that for a long time comparative law and comparative legal scholarship[1] have generally been marked by constructivist purposes: as a means for state building and local law reform.[2] In this sense comparative law lent support to the idea of law

[1] In the remainder of this text the term 'comparative law' is taken to include 'comparative legal scholarship'.

[2] PJ Glenn, 'The Nationalist Heritage' in P Legrand and R Munday (eds), *Comparative Legal Studies: Traditions and Transitions* (Cambridge University Press 2003) 76-99 and PJ Glenn, 'A Transnational Concept of Law' in P Cane and M Tushnet (eds), *The Oxford*

being an exclusively national phenomenon and an instrument in the nationalization of the law. Looking at the region where I come from, i.e. continental Europe: up until the nineteenth century, when the nation state was in formation for some time already,[3] there were quite some non-binding - secondary or supplementary - legal sources available, which interacted or competed with each other: e.g., canonical law, local statutes, custom, case law, Roman law (the overarching and unifying source), and, yes, the Bible (the latter the most 'binding' of all!). It was more specifically the ideal of codification - prominently entering the legal scene in the wake of the French revolution[4] - which wanted to put an end to this situation: law was identified exclusively with *written* and *national* law.[5] National codified law was on the one hand to be the exclusive source of law, identifiable through a local *Grundnorm* or *rule of recognition*,[6] and should on the other hand contain the solution for about every situation conceivable (law's adequacy).[7]

So although, paradoxically, the content of national law was the result of the mining of comparative sources,[8] extra-national inspiration was not

Handbook of Legal Studies (Oxford University Press 2003) 839-862. In what has arguably for a long time been the most influential handbook of the discipline of comparative law, this constructivist approach is very much promoted: K Zweigert and H Kötz, *Introduction to Comparative Law* (Oxford University Press 1998) 11: 'In its *applied* version, comparative law suggests how a specific problem can most appropriately be solved under the given social and economic circumstances.' (similar statements can be found throughout the introductory and methodological chapters of the book by Zweigert and Kötz).

3 The rise of the nation state is of course a complex, and dialectic development. Usually one is referred to the Peace of Westphalia (1648) as the starting point of the nation state, although the concept of the state as such has developed from the thirteenth century onwards. For nuance and details I refer to M van Creveld, *The Rise and Decline of the State* (Cambridge University Press 1999). The use of the term 'state' came into use in the first part of the seventeenth century.

4 Just as the concept of the nation state, the concept of codification didn't emerge during a fixed and clearly identifiable period in time. It was however after the French revolution that it gained momentum. For nuance and details I refer to P van den Berg, *The Politics of European Codification. A History of the Unification of Law in France, Prussia, the Austrian Monarchy and the Netherlands* (Europa Law Publishing 2006).

5 It even suffered, as Gény said, from a 'fétichisme de la loi écrite codifiée.' F Gény *Méthode d'interprétation et sources en droit privé positif: essai critique* (Librairie Génerale de Droit et de Jurisprudence 1919) 70.

6 These terms of course come from H Kelsen and HLA Hart respectively. On the neglect of Hart of comparative legal scholarship see the recent (posthumously published) monograph by AWB Simpson, *Reflections on 'The Concept of Law'* (Oxford University Press 2011) 157-160. The universalistic aspirations of his concept of law didn't seem to really invite Hart for comparative observations. It could and should have, though.

7 PC Kop, *Legisme en Privaatrechtswetenschap* (Kluwer 1982) 2-3.

8 See Glenn (n 2) 84.

really felt to be a necessity anymore. National law was thought to be self-supporting, and the legal system was predominantly understood as an entity in which '*demos*', law creation and a specific and delineated area were intimately bound. Since the nineteenth century it was: *La Nation, la loi, le roi* - in that order.[9] As a result comparative law 'blossomed' as a static discipline in the margin, both in terms of the law school's curriculum and in terms of research;[10] an intellectual pastime if there ever was one.

In recent years comparative law has witnessed a revival, especially due to European unification processes.[11] However, as a result of globalization – which with Twining can loosely be described as the developments and interactions which are making the world more interdependent with respect to ecology, economy, communications, language, politics, etc[12] - the question is if the discipline as it stands now is fit for purpose, i.e., dealing with this ever more interdependent world. In my opinion the answer is in the negative, and comparative lawyers have to adapt their analytical and educational toolkits to other than constructivist purposes, and also to the realities of a largely fragmented and fluid regulatory landscape.[13] At least three challenges stand out.

2. Comparative Law as a Central and Dynamic Discipline: Three Challenges

As a result of the foregoing ('constructivism') most comparative law is still typically concerned with traditional legal questions: what is the law in at least two jurisdictions and how do they compare? The applicable legal

[9] Rousseau's thinking has been of great influence here. See J Miller, *Rousseau. Dreamer of Democracy* (Yale University Press 1984). A similar development as just described with regard to the process of codification in continental Europe could be witnessed in the common law through the evolution of the doctrine of *stare decisis*, which was only firmly rooted in the English legal system by the end of the nineteenth century. On this J Evans, 'Change in the Doctrine of Precedent during the Nineteenth Century', in L Goldstein (ed), *Precedent in Law* (Oxford University Press 1987) 35-72.

[10] A comparative approach in any case seems sometimes to be more a matter of being *en vogue*, instead of really bringing useful insights to the issue being researched. M-C Ponthoreau, 'Le droit comparé en question(s). Entre pragmatisme et outil épistémologique' 57 *Revue internationale de droit comparé* 2005, 9.

[11] A process which is very much building on the traditional constructivist ambitions of comparative law too.

[12] W Twining, *Globalisation and Legal Theory* (Cambridge University Press 2000) 4.

[13] P Zumbansen, 'Transnational Comparisons: Theory and Practice of Comparative Law as a Critique of Global Governance' in M Adams and J Bomhoff (eds), *Practice and Theory in Comparative Law* (Cambridge University Press 2012) 189-190.

norms in the different jurisdictions have to be identified and described with an eye to their subsequent systematization and the identification of similarities and differences. In a globalizing world however, comparative law should also self-consciously and explicitly encompass a dynamic approach to supplement its customary and more static perspective, to be able to answer questions such as: how do the societal changes that occur as a result of globalization impact on the configuration of legal traditions or cultures; how do these adapt or maintain their distinctiveness; how is law used in relation with other legal cultures and traditions; how do new legal configurations become assimilated, rejected or refashioned in a host legal system, etc?[14] In doing so we have to expand comparative law's traditional focus on municipal law of western nations.[15]

Another clear implication of globalization is that the nature of legal education will have to change. 'Neither a nationally confined doctrinal instruction in the rules and methods of a particular field in a given country nor the, more often than not, relatively randomly chosen jurisdiction of comparison, can provide for an adequate training of the soon to be graduate legal scholar – or practitioner', Zumbansen recently wrote.[16] Legal education has to shift from a purely local approach, to what we might call an integrated approach that can make more sense of legal dynamics and diversity. This is comparative law broadly defined. We are nevertheless still struggling to build in such an approach into the law school curriculum; an approach that also deals with the questions identified in the previous paragraph.[17] Many options present themselves (all having advantages and disadvantages): starting law school with teaching broadly accepted legal principles as they are currently unfolding, thereafter integrating how different jurisdictions have integrated these principles, and finally situating this in an ever more interdependent (legal) world; or teaching comparative law as a separate graduate curriculum (after having gone through a thorough traditional national education); or integrating a global and dynamic perspective

---

[14] H Muir Watt, 'Globalization and Comparative Law' in M Reimann and R Zimmermann (eds), *The Oxford Handbook of Comparative Law* (Oxford University Press 2006) 589 (with further references).

[15] This is the so-called 'Country and Western' tradition, contrasting especially between the 'parent' civil and common law systems, and mostly dealing with private law. Twining (n 12) 185-187.

[16] Zumbansen (n 13) 188.

[17] Interesting proposals and ideas can be found in J Husa, 'Turning the Curriculum Upside Down' (2009) 10 *German Law Journal* 913 and S Chesterman, 'The Evolution of Legal Education: Internationalization, Transnationalization, Globalization' (2009) 10 *German Law Journal* 877 (with many references).

throughout the curriculum (i.e., an approach that also puts perspective - even subversive perspective[18] - to national law); etc.

In line with all this, globalization also requires a renewed research agenda. This however calls for a resort to other disciplines than the law; interdisciplinarity is the key here. But how much or what type of interdisciplinarity is needed for answering the type of questions that are raised by globalization? In particular, the humanities and social sciences are important. We should nevertheless avoid as much as possible the legal researcher from becoming a 'jack of all trades (and a master of none)'. From a practical point of view, this issue is relevant because depending on the mode or intensity of interdisciplinarity, comparative lawyers may experience fewer or more difficulties while doing research. I would be pragmatic here: all this does not mean that scholars engaging in comparative law need to be fully versatile in other disciplines besides their own, at least not in terms of being able to do the type of research that is typical of these other disciplines. But they must in any case be able to build on these other disciplines.[19]

3. Final Observations

The issue for comparative law is not whether or not the nation state will sooner or later fade way. I don't think it will, at least not in the foreseeable future. Let it also be clear that depending on the topic to be dealt with, it is to a greater or lesser extent still possible and sensible to engage in traditional multi-jurisdictional – i.e. state-centered – comparative law. So, too, will the long established purposes and aims of comparative law continue to be relevant for many years to come (including its constructivist purposes).[20] Globalization is nevertheless challenging the state-centered approach to comparative law as being the exclusive one. Globalization is a very complex and hybrid phenomenon, and law is no longer parochial nor fully

---

[18] G Fletcher, 'Comparative Law as a Subversive Discipline' (1998) 46 *The American Journal of Comparative Law* 683.

[19] This is by the way not a plea for excluding *strong* interdisciplinary perspectives altogether, but realistically that might well require group work. For a helpful overview of dimensions of interdisciplinary legal research, see BMJ van Klink and HS Taekema, 'On the Border: Limits and Possibilities of Interdisciplinary Research' in BMJ van Klink and HS Taekema (eds), *Law and Method. Interdisciplinary Research into Law* (Mohr Siebeck 2011) 7-32.

[20] See on these aims: G Dannemann, 'Comparative Law: Study of Similarities or Differences?' in Reimann and Zimmermann (n 14) 401-406.

cosmopolitan: 'it includes empires, spheres of influence, alliances, coalitions, religious diasporas, networks, trade routes, migration flows, and social movements. It also includes sub-worlds such as the common law world, the Arab world, the Islamic world and Christendom, as well as special groupings of power such as the G7, the G8, NATO, OPEC, the European Union, the Commonwealth, multi-national corporations, crime syndicates, cartels, social movements, and non-governmental organisations and networks. All of these cut across any simple vertical hierarchy and overlap and interact with each other in complex ways. These complexities are reflected in the diversity of forms of normative and legal ordering.'[21]

If comparative law does not want to become a marginal discipline again, or even fade away into oblivion, we have to rethink its role as a scholarly discipline and as an integrated and dynamic part of the law school curriculum. It should in any case be clear that in an increasingly interdependent era that makes ever greater demands on our ability to understand the world with which we are confronted, comparative law can be of tangible benefit and a center-piece of legal education and research. All this of course makes the task of comparative law even more complex than it already was: integrating globalization into the legal discipline raises questions of feasibility and practicality, of what still should/can be national to legal education, of how much non-law should be part of the curriculum, of making lawyers sensitive of the non-orderly world of borders and non-borders, etc. The challenges are formidable indeed, but they cannot be ignored.

---

[21] W Twining, 'Globalisation and Comparative Law' in E Örücü and D Nelken, *Comparative Law: A Handbook* (Hart Publishing 2007) 70.

What I Talk about when I Talk about Global Law*

Morag Goodwin
Associate Professor, International Law, Tilburg Law School, The Netherlands
m.e.a.goodwin@uvt.nl

Abstract
In this contribution I attempt to sketch what I mean when I talk about 'global law', finishing up with a brief consideration of what I think our responsibilities are, as legal scholars, when we engage in such talk.

Keywords
global law; law in context; ethics for global legal voyaging?

How are we to understand the phrase 'global law'? In his recent Montesquieu Lecture, Neil Walker, following Twining, noted the dangers of the phrase 'global law' as a term that simultaneously implies some sort of exaggerated and false coherence or unity between what are many and disparate practices and yet fails to capture the plurality of interactions that we see occurring around us that are not limited to the state but that are not necessarily global either, where global tends to mean spatially all-encompassing.[1]

Given these dangers, and the seemingly irresistible pull of the holistic with 'global law', why do we not simply heed Twining's warning and refuse to acknowledge the phrase altogether? One reason for not doing so is, as Walker suggests, the increasing prevalence of the term; that what should interest us as legal scholars is the first order significance of 'global law'. Yet

---

* This short paper is based on a talk given in the context of a Tilburg Law School Faculty Seminar dedicated to the idea of global law in April 2012; thanks to all those present for their comments.

1 Neil Walker, Intimations of Global Law, Montesquieu Lecture delivered in Tilburg on 21 June 2012 (forthcoming with Wolf Legal Publishing); William Twining, *General Jurisprudence* (Cambridge University Press 2009).

there is another reason why 'global law' should not only interest us but demands our engagement – as Walker also highlighted, there is a double element to the 'global law' 'project':[2] at the same time that the idea of 'global law' is used, however it is being used,[3] as an analytical tool to understand or map the shifting legal landscape around us, it is also sculpting that landscape. We have therefore (albeit expressed in rather a heavy-handed way) a responsibility to engage.

In this short paper I will attempt to sketch what I mean when I talk about 'global law' and end by considering what I think our responsibilities are, as legal scholars, when we engage in such talk.

1. What Global Law is Not

One way to begin our reflection of what we mean by 'global law' is to consider what we are not talking about; otherwise put, how does 'global law' compare to other labels that are used to either map and/or consciously shape the legal landscape in a global setting? What is global law not? I will reflect on three attempts or descriptive categories to elucidate the most important elements of what 'global law', for me, is not.

Let us begin with international law. International law, put simply, governs relations between sovereign states. Despite a modest opening up of international law to other actors, such as international organisations or natural persons, it remains the case that only states have what we might call primary legal personality within international law. All other international legal personality is derived from the will of states. The continuing dominance of states at the heart of international law is the reason that many assume international law fails to address the changing nature of legal interactions beyond the state; in particular, that international law does not, perhaps cannot, address the shifting nature of power away from states to other actors.

In one of the first monographs to be published on global law, Rafael Domingo suggests that international law is in crisis because the state as a

---

2 To describe 'global law' as a project suggests that those who use 'global law' have a certain destination in mind, albeit that the direction and route is unknown. I wish to reject this use of 'global law'.

3 Walker has suggested seven helpful categories for the way in which 'global law' is being used or can be viewed; Walker, ibid.

means of organising political and legal affairs is dying a slow death.[4] From this premise, he goes on to suggest that global law – as a people-centred law with human rights at its normative core – is replacing international law, just as international law once replaced the Roman conception of *ius gentium*.

In this characterisation, 'global law' forms part of a narrative of progression, as a system of law in which 'global law' occupies the apex of the legal pyramid. However, one does not need to agree with Domingo's premise that international law is in crisis or with his understanding of global law as progressing beyond and supplanting international law – and I agree with neither – to concur that global law, whatever it is, is not international law.

The term that has most often been used to describe the changes to the legal landscape has been transnational law.[5] Jessup used the term to refer to all law that is used to regulate actions or events that transcend national frontiers; we might think of *lex mercatoria* or *lex sportiva* as examples of systems of law that by their nature are not limited by the territorial boundaries of individual states. Transnational law, unlike international law, recognises the increasing importance of private or non-state and sub-state type actors in cross-border relationships; at the same time, it is not limited to private transactions, but includes the interaction between public and private actors in networks of regulation.

But while transnational law as a descriptive category is capable of capturing much of what we see occurring all around us, and while it may, as Zumbansen suggests, work to expose a world that Philip Allott has described as international 'unsociety', it does nothing to address the lack of humanity in the international system that Allott's work so beautifully highlights.[6] Rather there is something soulless about transnational law, denoted by its primary focus on economic interactions. 'Global law' must be something more than this.

---

4 Rafael Domingo, 'The Crisis of International Law' in Rafael Domingo, *The New Global Law* (Cambridge University Press 2010).

5 See Phillip Jessup, *Transnational Law* (Yale University Press 1956); Michael Likosky (ed), *Transnational Legal Processes: Globalisation and Power Disparities* (Butterworths 2002); Peer Zumbansen, 'Transnational Law', in Jan Smits, *Encyclopedia of Comparative Law* (Edward Elgar Publishing 2006) 738-754.

6 Philip Allott, *Eunomia. New Order for a New World* (Oxford University Press 1990) 244; Zumbansen, ibid 739-740.

One attempt to carve out a heart amongst the transnational interactions we see going on around us is Ruti Teitel's 'humanity's law'.[7] Teitel uses this phrase to denote what she sees as a discursive paradigm shift to a new rule of law based upon a merger of humanitarian and human rights law that seeks to manage conflict and violence through law. This shift consists in an extended spatial and temporal reach,[8] an extended jurisdictional scope towards obligations *omna erges*, the re-conceptualisation of international personality away from states to persons and peoples, and the institutionalisation of 'humanity's law' in new structures, such as the International Criminal Court.

This globalisation of the law of war, according to Teitel, in the form of international criminal justice has become the basis for an emerging global rule of law. Moreover, it is the operation of this 'humanity's law' through its tribunals, proceedings, and public discussions that forms the source of authority and legitimacy in this legal realm beyond the state. This attempt to bring the legitimacy question front and centre is of course welcome, and Teitel's approach shares much with the many efforts to elucidate forms of global constitutionalism (as well as with Domingo's account); however, such efforts to create a people-centred rule of law with human rights at its heart lacks the normative and moral pluralism that is central to what I talk about when I talk about 'global law'.

So what is 'global law' not? It is not limited by actor. It is not a descriptive term for a more or less neatly arranged hierarchical system with 'global law' at its apex. It is not limited to interactions of a cross-border nature. It must be more than simply what actors do; yet its normative heart is not predetermined and cannot be understood by reference to a single organ. 'Global law' cannot be reduced to 'law' in the singular or to a single 'map'.

2. What does 'Global Law' Mean to Me?

By asking what 'global law' might be, it is important to remind ourselves that what we are of course asking is what it should be, what purpose, or

---

[7] See Ruti Teitel, 'Humanity's Law: Rule of Law for the New Global Politics' (2002) 35 Cornell International Law Journal 355-387; Ruti Teitel, *Humanity's Law* (Oxford University Press 2011).

[8] Extended spatial reach in the sense of cross border; extended temporal reach in the sense of 'justice talk' no longer being solely applied to conflicts and violations after they have occurred but assuming a much bigger role prior to conflict occurring. Teitel, ibid 360.

multiple purposes, the rhetorical shift to this phrase serves. Making a positive statement about what 'global law' means is of course a lot harder than saying what it is not and it necessitates a woolly answer at this stage. So what do I mean by 'global law'? I think I understand 'global law' as referring to the relations and interactions between systems of law, all systems of law, whether formal or informal.

For example, an individual asserting a right in a local context, whether before a juridical instance or not, is an example of global law, again whether or not in so doing this individual refers to a document or decision from another legal system, such as an international or regional human rights treaty or constitutional jurisprudence from another system. By simply asserting a right, this individual, consciously or not, is speaking to the history and sociology of rights-talk, and it is this that makes it an instance of 'global law'. Her actions in asserting a right have an effect far beyond the given circumstance in which the claim is made. The recent decision by the Landgericht Köln, where the rights of the child to bodily integrity trump the rights of the parents to religious freedom in relation to whether circumcision can be permitted, is perhaps an example of a local decision that is at the same time 'global law'.[9] In this sense, 'global law' is everywhere.[10]

While locating 'global law' everywhere is clearly rather unhelpful, I think it is nonetheless a necessary starting point in order to embed into the idea of 'global law', at this early stage, a radically pluralistic approach: to actors, to the idea of what law is and to the purpose(s) of law. Refining the concept can and will come later. So 'global law' is a way of thinking about, an analytical tool for framing, the inter-connectedness of actors, of relationships and of concepts and/or legal tools. Yet there is something else that 'global law' must be: in approaching the inter-connectedness and relationships between actors and legal systems it must concern itself explicitly with power relations, with domination, with questions of justice. Moreover, 'global law' necessarily, for me at least, must speak to the 'public-ness(es)' of law, and bring the virtues of public space to the global (as defined above).

Talking about what 'global law' might *be* only takes us so far, of course, at the outset of the journey. The real question at this stage concerns what the look and feel of global legal scholarship should be.

---

9 'Beschneidung von Jungen aus religiösen Gründen ist strafbar', *Süddeutschen Zeitung*, 26 June 2012; available at: <süddeutsche.de> accessed 29 July 2012.

10 The sense of 'global law' suggested here is very close to Twining's idea of general jurisprudence; Twining (n 1).

3. The Look and Feel of Global Legal Scholarship

If global legal scholarship must primarily be concerned at present with mapping the flux of interconnections and relationships in the 'global' space in the context of ideas about justice and public virtue, global legal scholarship needs to consist of a law in context approach. This may require the involvement of multiple disciplines, but it may not, and we should not prize inter-disciplinarity for its own sake. Further, such scholarship needs to take as a starting point that law is a social practice – it is *not* a market mechanism – and begin from the premise that there is something of the sacred about the social functions of law that are non-reducible to criteria like efficiency.

In place of a primary focus on questions of what works, therefore, global legal scholarship should instead concern itself with questions of what regulation works for *whom*, *when* and in *what way*, using the idea that there are always winners and losers in any legal 'moment' as points by which to navigate through the legal terrain. We need to be suspicious of the language and thinking of economics and cautious about the use of indicators as a technology of governance. At the same time, while good legal research is necessarily knowledge-driven, what constitutes 'knowledge' must be radically open. 'Knowledge' cannot mean something that we can measure solely by quantitative analysis, and must include alternative epistemologies and forms of legal reasoning.[11]

What might this mean for legal scholars interested in exploring 'global law'? More specifically, what might our responsibilities be as legal scholars exploring, mapping and sculpting this new legal landscape?

As a young human rights researcher, I was sent to South Africa to accompany and provide advice to a large Romani delegation to the 2001 UN World Conference Against Racism. Once there, the delegation voted to include a demand for non-territorial nationhood in the NGO declaration presented to the main conference. I worked hard to persuade the group that this was a bad idea, given that such status does not exist under international law, and counselled that they would be ridiculed for including it. I was right about the ridicule. I was wrong to attempt to prevent the presentation of an

[11] See for example, Boaventura de Sousa Santos (ed), *Another Knowledge is Possible: Beyond Northern Epistemologies* (Verso 2007); Karin Mickelson, 'Rage and Rhetoric: Third World Voices in International Legal Discourse' (1998) 16 Wisconsin International Law Journal 353-419.

alternative way of seeing the world because it was strange and because it did not fit within the realm of existing legal possibility.

An ethical code for voyaging through the global legal terrain requires that we consciously reflect on and take responsibility for the choices that we make in framing our research and, in so doing, carving the global legal landscape from the world around us. For me, the ethical starting point of the voyage must be two principles: that we must listen to all the voices that we encounter on our legal travels, whether we like the message or not, whether we understand it, and even where it makes us deeply uncomfortable; and that we must be careful not to use the tools of our trade – our legal 'knowledge' – to close down or exclude strange and alternative perspectives or visions. In this way, the 'global law' voyage has the potential to be a genuine voyage of discovery.

Global Law: The Spontaneous, Gradual Emergence of a New Legal Order

Joshua Karton
Assistant Professor, Queen's University Faculty of Law, Kingston, Ontario, Canada
joshua.karton@queensu.ca

Abstract
This article argues that the debate over whether international law can apply to non-state actors misses the point. The useful distinction is not between rules that regulate the obligations of states and those that regulate the obligations of non-state actors, but rather between rules that regulate the reciprocal obligations of states to each other (international laws) and rules that set global standards that must be obeyed by all entities, state and non-state alike, regardless of national laws and boundaries. This latter category is the emerging phenomenon of global law. Global laws take varying forms, but they all seek to bind the entire globe to a singular global standard—they do not so much cross national boundaries as ignore them. Global law remains inchoate, but is increasing in both scope and coherence. Those seeking to predict the course that global law will take can look to the current example of international commercial arbitration, which is global law *par excellence*.

Keywords
global law; legal harmonization/unification; transnational legal practice; international arbitration

In recent years, the international law commentariat has been preoccupied with the question of non-state actors as subjects of international law. As classically defined, international law deals only with the rights and obligations of sovereign states; it is the law between – 'inter' – nations. And yet, vast fields of law exist that regulate the transnational conduct (i.e., conduct that crosses national borders) of individuals, companies, and NGOs, laws that are clearly not domestic and yet do not concern relations between states. Such laws are not national, but debate persists as to whether they constitute part of the corpus of 'international law'.

This debate misses the point. The useful distinction is not between rules that regulate the rights and obligations of states and rules that regulate the rights and obligations of non-state actors. Rather, it is between rules that regulate the reciprocal obligations of states *to each other* and rules that set global standards that must be obeyed by all entities across the globe, state and non-state alike, regardless of national laws and boundaries. For me, it is this latter category that is described by the label 'global law'.

Global laws take one of two forms: either treaties or model laws adopted simultaneously by several states that uniformly regulate the conduct of their citizens; or the customary practices of transnational groups of non-state actors (including the decisions of non-national tribunals), which are final and binding and employ state laws and legal processes only as enforcement mechanisms. Both forms of rulemaking share one characteristic: they aspire (whether successfully or not) to bind the entire globe to singular global standards. Whereas international law exists to resolve the problems that arise from the conflicting interests of countries vis-à-vis each other, global law exists to resolve problems that arise from conduct (whether public or private) that crosses national boundaries and is not amenable to regulation by individual states. In terms of form and method, global law overlaps with both domestic and international law. It is distinguishable on its object and purpose; global law is global teleologically.

The distinction between international and global law is not an entirely clean one. Laws may be global but not international (such as the *lex mercatoria*), international but not global (such as regional trade agreements or the European Union governance regime), or both global and international. They can even coexist within a single instrument, as in the United Nations Convention on the Law of the Sea (UNCLOS).[1] Part II of UNCLOS deals, *inter alia*, with a paradigmatically international law issue: the delimitation of boundaries between states whose territorial seas are adjacent.[2] However, Part VII of UNCLOS contains some distinctly global law provisions. It establishes a global obligation for ships' masters to render assistance on the high seas to persons in distress[3] and creates a global standard for what constitutes piracy.[4] To be sure, UNCLOS does not impose obligations (to render assistance, to not commit piracy) directly upon non-state actors like ships' masters. Instead, it enlists state legislative processes in furtherance of its global standards by use of such language as 'every state shall take effective measures to ...' or 'every state shall require the master of a ship flying its flag to ...' But the intention and the effect of Part VII of UNCLOS is to create

---

1 The United Nations (UN) Convention on the Law of the Sea A/CONF.62/122; 21 ILM 1261 (1982).

2 ibid at Articles 3-16.

3 ibid at Article 98.

4 ibid at Article 101.

unified global obligations to which (for example) all masters of ships sailing on the high seas must adhere, regardless of nationality or location.

I do not pretend that there already exists a full-fledged system of global law. We still live in an essentially Westphalian world order, so global law continues to depend on the operation of national legal processes: treaties must be ratified by states and model laws implemented by their legislatures; standards must be adopted by national regulatory agencies; the decisions of international tribunals must be enforced in state courts. However, the endpoint would be for global laws to apply globally the same way national laws apply domestically: they would bind all state and non-state entities regardless of their consent.

In the meantime, elements of what may come to be a comprehensive global law do exist. The socio-legal scholar Lawrence Friedman has described 'a kind of internationalized law, or globalized law, which exists side by side of, or on top of, the national or local sector. It may well represent a minority, even a small minority, of lawyers' work, but its importance is clearly on the rise.'[5] These various bits of global law have evolved piecemeal, as specific responses to the needs of different globalized communities. Global law arises spontaneously as an epiphenomenon of globalization; it is the legal response to the increasing interconnectedness of people and organizations across national borders. Just as nature abhors a physical vacuum,[6] society abhors a legal vacuum.

Accordingly, we should expect to see global laws emerge in areas of law that are amenable to global rulemaking and that do not require a unified global administrative apparatus. These areas are not amenable to the traditional division of laws into public and private. What they have in common is that they involve global interactions. For example, not all commerce is amenable to global rulemaking, but transnational commerce is;[7] not all aspects of family relationships are amenable to global rulemaking, but their transnational aspects are; there is no burning need for a global law of theft or murder, but global rules regarding transnational criminal enterprises are beginning to emerge.[8]

---

[5] Lawrence M Friedman, 'Erewhon: The Coming Global Legal Order' (2001) 37 Stanford Journal of International Law 347, 355.

[6] As first proposed by Aristotle in the Book Four of the *Physics*.

[7] For example, members of the international commercial arbitration community often describe national legal systems as being unable to meet the 'specific needs' of international commerce. See, eg, Markus A Petsche, *The Growing Autonomy of International Commercial Arbitration* (QUADIS 2005) at 10; ICC Case No. 9427 of 1998 (2002) XXVII Yearbook Commercial Arbitration 153 [7].

[8] For example, The UN Convention Against Transnational Organized Crime ('Palermo Convention') 2000.

* * *

It is not surprising that the development of global law is most advanced in the commercial arena. Commerce was the earliest and remains the greatest beneficiary of globalization. National boundaries have been described as 'international merchants' worst enemy'.[9] Global commercial law makes cross-border contracting easier and more profitable by making choice of law irrelevant and removing the problem of dealing with foreign law. It reduces uncertainty, lessens risk, promotes accurate pricing of contractual obligations and, in turn, increases the total volume of trade. Globalization of commerce has led to 'an urgent need for a corresponding legislative policy' that is consistent globally and independent of national legal systems.[10]

Global law is not limited to commerce, just as globalization is not limited to cross border flows in goods, services, and capital. A good example is global family law, exemplified by the four Hague Children's Conventions: the 1980 Convention on the Civil Aspects of International Child Abduction,[11] the 1993 Convention on Intercountry Adoption,[12] the 1996 Convention on Jurisdiction, Applicable Law, Recognition, Enforcement and Co-operation in Respect of Parental Responsibility and Measures for the Protection of Children,[13] and the 2007 Convention on the International Recovery of Child Support and Other Forms of Family Maintenance.[14] These treaties were enacted because national-level efforts were seen to be inadequate to confront the challenges posed by increasing numbers of cross-border marriages and increasing numbers of migrants with children.[15] Familial globalization could only be addressed by legal globalization.

---

[9] Errol P Mendes, 'The U.N. Sales Convention & U.S.-Canada Transactions: Enticing the World's Largest Trading Bloc to Do Business under a Global Sales Law' *Journal of Law and Commerce* 109 at 112 (1988).

[10] Franco Ferrari, 'The International Sphere of Application of the 1988 Ottawa Convention on International Factoring' (1999) 8 International Business Law Journal 895, 895.

[11] Hague Convention on the Civil Aspects of International Child Abduction, 1343 UNTS 89, 19 ILM 1501-05 (1980).

[12] Hague Convention on Protection of Children and Cooperation in Respect of Intercountry Adoption, 32 ILM 1134-46 (1993).

[13] Hague Convention on Jurisdiction, Applicable Law, Recognition, Enforcement and Co-operation in Respect of Parental Responsibility and Measures for the Protection of Children, 35 ILM 1391 (1996).

[14] Hague Convention on the International Recovery of Child Support and Other Forms of Family Maintenance, 47 ILM 257 (2008).

[15] Stephen I Winter, 'Note: Home is Where the Heart Is: Determining "Habitual Residence" under the Hague Convention on the Civil Aspects of Child Abduction' (2010) 33 Washington University Journal of Law & Policy 351, 351.

Since global law emerges largely as a reaction to socio-economic conditions, its emergence is largely driven by individuals and organizations that are independent of governments. Given the reality of state sovereignty, most existing global law is embodied in forms to which states have given their consent: treaties and model laws. For this reason, the aspects of global law that already exist tend to fall into two categories where states have less incentive to restrict the development of global standards. They either deal with areas of law where states' national rules differ only slightly (e.g., the abduction of children) or where fundamental national interests are not implicated (e.g., private contracts for trade in goods).

In the last two decades, we have begun to see areas of global law emerge that butt directly against the interests of sovereign states. The best example is the international law of investment protection. Through the decisions of investment arbitration tribunals and the practice of states and investors (including the provisions included within bilateral and multilateral investment treaties) a coherent global law of investment protection is currently emerging. It is still inchoate; for example, there is general agreement that states may not expropriate the property of foreign investors with impunity, but there is no global agreement on what constitutes expropriation. However, the emerging global investment law is remarkable in that it subordinates the regulatory decision-making processes of sovereign states to global standards of treatment – standards to which states never expressly agreed. The existence, extent, and autonomy of investment law are stark evidence of the expanding reach of global law.

From the above, it may seem that global law, as I have defined it, is simply international uniform law by another name. In fact, the two are related but they are not the same thing, and the difference is instructive about the nature and prospects of global law.

Going back at least to the foundation of the Hague Conference of Private International Law in 1893, the uniform law movement has sought to unify or harmonize disparate national laws. Its primary tools are codifications – 'hard law' instruments like treaties and model laws that are adopted by states into their domestic legal systems—and 'soft law' instruments like the Lando Commission's Principles of European Contract Law that act as exemplars to states and may apply directly in arbitrations or other ADR processes.

In other words, uniform law is fundamentally a centrally managed process, in which experts from around the world meet and agree on a uniform text, then try to persuade states to adopt the text. In contrast, global law develops organically through a gradual accretion of legislation and adjudicative decisions and a gradual solidification of standard practices. Codifications do play an important role in the development of global law, but it is primarily a supportive one. The most successful codifications have been those that consolidate and rationalize already-prevalent principles and practices (such as the International Bar Association's Guidelines on Conflicts of Interest in International Arbitration, which are now the *de facto* global standard) or principles elaborated in the international case law (such as the UNIDROIT Principles of International Commercial Contracts, whose drafting was informed by international arbitral experience). Berger has evocatively labeled this process 'creeping codification'.[16]

On their own, codified international uniform law instruments often fail to achieve true global standardization due to low ratification rates and, more fundamentally, inconsistent application by courts. National courts, in particular, have often displayed a 'homeward trend', infusing domestic notions into their interpretations of uniform law instruments.[17] Globalization is as much a cultural phenomenon as anything else, and legal globalization is no exception.[18]

Accordingly, for global legal standardization to become a reality, the adjudicative bodies must not only interpret common text, but must approach the act of interpretation with a common mindset; they must share a

---

[16] Klaus Peter Berger, *The Creeping Codification of the Lex Mercatoria* (Kluwer 1999).

[17] The literature on the homeward trend is particularly well developed in international sales law scholarship. See, e.g., Ingeborg Schwenzer and Christopher Kee, 'International Sales Law – The Actual Practice' (2011) 29 Pennsylvania State International Law Review 425; Franco Ferrari, 'Homeward Trend and Lex Forism in International Sales Law' [2009] International Business Law Journal 333; Camilla Baasch Andersen, *Uniform Application of the International Sales Law. Understanding Uniformity, the Global Jurisconsultorium and Examination and Notification Provisions of the CISG* (The Hague: Kluwer 2007); John O Honnold, 'The Sales Convention in Action – Uniform International Words: Uniform Application?' (1988) 8 Journal of Law and Commerce 207.

[18] Scholars now regularly speak of declining legal nationalism and greater acceptance of supranational and transnational decision-making bodies. The literature on so-called 'judicial transnationalism' is vast. See, e.g. Elaine Mak, 'Why do Dutch and UK judges cite foreign law?' (2011) 70(2) Cambridge Law Journal 420; Brian Flanagan and Sinead Ahern, 'Judicial Decision-Making and Transnational Law: A Survey of Common Law Supreme Court Judges' (2011) 60(1) International & Comparative Law Quarterly 1; Sam Muller and Sidney Richards (eds), *Highest Courts and Globalization* (The Hague: TMC Asser, 2010); Harold Hongju Koh, 'The Ninth Annual John W Hager Lecture, The 2004 Term: The Supreme Court Meets International Law' (2004) 12 Tulsa Journal of Comparative & International Law 1; Robert B Ahdieh, 'Between Dialogue and Decree: International Review of National Courts' (2004) 79 New York University Law Review 2029; Charles H Koch Jr, 'Envisioning a Global Legal Culture' (2003) 25 Michigan Journal of International Law 1; Anne-Marie Slaughter, 'Judicial Globalization' (2000) 40 Virginia Journal of International Law 1103.

common adjudicative culture. This is why I believe that global law will not be advanced primarily by the kinds of codified instruments that the uniform law movement has prioritized since the 19th century, but rather by the organic evolution of legal principles in response to the needs of transnational communities.

Moreover, a distinct variety of global legal practice is emerging alongside global law itself. Modern law practice is increasingly specialized, so that practitioners in transnational fields often have more in common with each other than with other lawyers from the jurisdictions in which they were trained. Whenever actors are placed outside existing systems of governance and interact repeatedly with each other, it is not surprising that new cultural norms, specific to the new field of interaction, might develop. Teubner has called this process 'auto-constitutionalisation' – the tendency of private governance regimes operating outside the state to develop their own sets of norms.[19] Where economic globalization has given rise to the establishment of a corpus of specialist transnational legal practitioners who work primarily with each other and outside the governance of any one state, professional cultures specific to global legal practice will coalesce – a globalization of the legal profession. The development of a distinct global legal community of practitioners can only strengthen the emergence of a distinct global law.

* * *

If rules change fundamentally without an accompanying change in culture, parties and adjudicators will resist the new rules and will subvert them in a variety of ways. Therefore, if global law is to evolve toward a comprehensive, internally consistent system, it will have to develop organically, and not through negotiations at international conferences or scholarly drafting committees. These processes are already underway. Discrete fields of global law have already spontaneously emerged and are gradually evolving. The patchwork character of existing global law 'matches the one experienced in the first stages of judicial development described by legal historians and anthropologists ... law percolates up from the bottom'.[20]

---

19 Gunther Teubner, 'Global Private Regimes: Neo-Spontaneous Law and Dual Constitution of Autonomous Sectors?' in Karl-Heinz Ladeur (ed), *Public Governance in the Age of Globalization* (Ashgate 2004).

20 Florian Grizel, 'Control of Awards and Re-Centralisation of International Commercial Arbitration' (2006) 25 Civil Justice Quarterly 166, 168.

It is difficult to predict what global law will look like once it has evolved into a mature legal system,[21] or even whether it will in fact become a comprehensive system. However, there is at least one solid source of information about the likely future development of global commercial law: the decisions and practices of international commercial arbitral tribunals. International commercial arbitration is global law *par excellence*. It is a global system of dispute resolution that exists outside the legal system of any state. It aspires to eliminate the legal significance of state boundaries ('delocalization') and to establish global rules, both procedural and substantive, for the resolution of cross-border commercial disputes.

Of course, arbitration requires the cooperation of states – the international arbitration system is undergirded by treaties such as the New York Convention,[22] which obliges contracting states to enforce valid arbitral agreements and arbitral awards, and by national laws that regulate arbitrations (which must of necessity take place within *some* state). However, the role of states in international arbitration – or at least the role that the arbitration community sees for states – is simply to enforce the decisions of arbitral tribunals. To a large extent, states have agreed that 'arbitration-friendly' policies are advisable and have pledged not to interfere unless state mandatory laws are contravened.[23] Thus, when international arbitrators apply national laws, they may not do so in the same way as national courts, but their decisions generally cannot be overturned for errors of law.[24]

The effect of these developments is that all of the dynamism in international arbitral rulemaking comes from outside the state context. Rules of international arbitration are not generally made by states, or on their behalf, or even by reference to them. In addition to interpreting national laws in

---

21 I attempt this with respect to contract law in a forthcoming book, *The Culture of International Arbitration and the Evolution of Contract Law* (OUP 2013).

22 Convention on the Recognition and Enforcement of Foreign Arbitral Awards (1958) 330 UNTS 4739.

23 The phrased often used is that international arbitration has become progressively 'delocalized'- detached from the laws and courts of the countries in which arbitrations are conducted. Of course, arbitration cannot be entirely delocalized so long as national courts are needed to enforce arbitral awards.

24 For concrete examples of divergences between arbitral and judicial applications of the same national laws, see Joshua Karton, 'Interpretation of Contracts in International Commercial Arbitration' (2012) 28(4) International Business Law Journal / Revue de Droit des Affaires Internationales 383; Joshua Karton, 'Contract Law in International Commercial Arbitration: the Case of Suspension of Performance' (2009) 58(4) International & Comparative Law Quarterly 863.

ways that may be inconsistent with national jurisprudence, arbitrators may apply non-national rules of law, including free-floating 'general principles'. Arbitration is also radically decentralized – no arbitral tribunal is bound by the legal determinations of another (although tribunals do regularly cite each other, especially in investor-state disputes). Finally, arbitration is more flexible than national court proceedings and more sensitive to changes in commercial practice.

Whenever an arbitral tribunal applies an international instrument or recognizes a general principle of international private law, it helps to develop global law. International arbitration is currently the most dynamic source of new global commercial law. Present trends in arbitration may well presage the future evolution not just of international arbitral practice, but of global commercial law more generally. As Pierre Karrer put it, 'Arbitration may not be a window to the future. But it is a good seismograph. It registers what is moving down the road. It gives us a glimpse of what the law tends to become.'[25]

---

25 Pierre A Karrer, 'The Alexander Lecture 1998: Is Arbitration a Window to the Future?' (1999) 65(3) Arbitration 170, 176.

A Global Law Perspective of the WTO

Panagiotis Delimatsis
Associate Professor of Law and Co-Director, Tilburg Law and Economics Center (TILEC)
Tilburg University, The Netherlands
p.delimatsis@uvt.nl

Abstract
This note attempts to map the relevance of global law advocacy for the WTO. In this regard, it understands global law as an attempt to describe a growing decrease of the regulatory State and an ensuing increase of private rule-making. Global law intends to generate new thinking about global governance and its patterns of influence and power. Few instances of creeping global law are identified, whereas the note concludes with some thoughts on much-needed future research on a range of topics ranging from the role of NGOs to the struggle against intrinsic inequalities of the multilateral trading system.

Keywords
global law; WTO; transnational law; producer welfare; consumer welfare; NGOs

1. Introducing the WTO

Created only in 1995, the potentially broad scope of the World Trade Organization (WTO) attracted the attention and critique of many, including international law scholars and political scientists, export-oriented companies and import-competing groups, domestic authorities and the public, including domestic consumer groups and global non-governmental organizations (NGOs). This was only a matter of time: the creation of the WTO and its evolution in the last fifteen years arguably constitutes a paradigm shift in the way trade matters are regulated, through a combination of *centripetal* forces, bringing more integration in terms of, for instance, regulating intellectual property protection, the use of technical regulations or sanitary and phytosanitary measures, and *centrifugal* forces, which result from the nature of contemporary globalized trade occurring at the very peripheries of the four corners of the world by individual economic operators or companies.

The WTO is the institutionalized umbrella of the multilateral trading system (MTS) succeeding the previous diplomacy-based General Agreement on Tariffs and Trade (GATT).[1] The WTO is a semi-autonomous regime that promulgated its own administrative, legislative and judicial procedures and therefore exemplifies a certain degree of self-sufficiency. At the same time, when viewing the everyday activities, institutional structures, ways of decision-making and settlement of disputes among Members, the WTO is quite similar to other international organizations (IOs).[2] In addition, general international law applies to the WTO unless there is a WTO rule going explicitly to the contrary. Thus, to all intents and purposes, the WTO is an international treaty (the international equivalent of a contract) concluded among States, which is to be interpreted in accordance with general international law.[3] At equipoise, WTO is yet another contextualized regime of international law.[4]

The WTO is an immediate derivative of the development of global trade, but also the development of an increasingly globalized society. It has resulted from ever-increasing global economic interdependence and has admittedly been instrumental in *accentuating* this phenomenon. Through its manifest paradigm shift towards higher levels of rule-orientation, particularly when performing its executive and judicial functions,[5] the WTO has arguably instigated institutional reform in IOs such as the Codex Alimentarius Commission whose activities may constitute inputs for the WTO activities or which may otherwise be somehow connected to the WTO.

This short note does not aim to delve in the abstract into the current theoretical debates about the exact contours of the concept of global law and its cognates, such as post-national law.[6] It understands global law as an attempt to describe a growing *decrease* of the role of the State in regulatory matters, coupled with a frenetic *increase* of the regulatory activity of private parties at the transnational level, stemming from the globalization

---

1 Also J Jackson, 'The Evolution of the World Trading System – The Legal and Institutional Context' in: D Bethlehem, D McRae, R Neufeld, I van Damme (eds), *The Oxford Handbook of International Trade Law* (Oxford University Press, 2009) 30-53.

2 P Delimatsis, 'The Fragmentation of International Trade Law' (2011) 45(1) *Journal of World Trade* 87.

3 Cf J Pauwelyn, 'The Role of Public International Law in the WTO: How Far Can We Go?' (2001) 95 *American Journal of International Law* 535, 538.

4 Cf Appellate Body Report, *US – Gasoline* 17.

5 Cf J Weiler, 'The Rule of Lawyers and the Ethos of Diplomats: Reflections on the Internal and External Legitimacy of WTO Dispute Settlement' Harvard Jean Monnet Working Paper 9/00, 2000.

6 For this, see N Walker, 'Intimations of Global Law', in this special issue.

of economic activity. It also considers the concept of global law, much as appealing as it is, to be yet another effort to think anew as to the normative question of future global governance and the morphology of global patterns of power and influence.[7] Indeed, just like debates relating to constitutionalism or constitutionalization of international law; global administrative law; constitutional pluralism and so on, discussions about global law constitute an alternative intimation of the law of the future.

The WTO can be viewed through the lens of most of these endeavors.[8] Having said this, one should note at the outset that one of the trends that results in so much discussion about law's normativity at the global level is the fact that an ever-globalized and interdependent economy also contributes to the creation of more law in general. Everything is legalized from economic transactions to politics at the international level. Thus, it is the evolution of law that allows for so much debate over the institutions, rules and principles. However, the sources of law multiply and thus reconceptualizing what we consider to be law will alter the way we understand legal science.[9]

This note constitutes a very tentative and humble attempt to map the relevance of global law advocacy for the WTO. Few instances of creeping global law are identified, whereas the note concludes with some thoughts on much-needed future research on a range of topics ranging from the role of NGOs to the struggle against intrinsic inequalities of the multilateral trading system.

2. WTO Law as an Instance of Incremental Global Law?

Increased globalization of economic activity leads to a shift of regulatory power from public to private and from national to global.[10] Indeed, the WTO as a forum (albeit State-centered) for the regulation of international

---

[7] Cf D Kennedy, 'The Mystery of Global Governance' in J Dunoff and J Trachtman (eds), *Ruling the World? Constitutionalism, International Law, and Global Governance* (Cambridge University Press 2009) 38.

[8] Cf T Cottier, P Delimatsis and K Gehne, 'Fragmentation and Coherence in International Trade Regulation: Analysis and Conceptual Foundations' in T Cottier and P Delimatsis (eds), *The Prospects of International Trade Regulation – From Fragmentation to Coherence* (Cambridge University Press 2011) 1; see also J Dunoff, 'The Politics of International Constitutions: The Curious Case of the World Trade Organization' in Dunoff and Trachtman (eds), (n 7) 178.

[9] Cf Kennedy, (n 7) 55.

[10] F Cafaggi, 'New Foundations of Transnational Private Regulation' (2011) 38(1) *Journal of Law and Society* 20.

economic activity is interesting for a global law theorist because boundaries are blurred between various layers of law and governance: public and private, national, supranational/regional and international are inextricably intertwined. As an institution, the WTO is overtly overwhelmed by such abundance of self-interested pullers, suggesting different (sometimes even conflicting) directions and exerting varying influence.

From a global law perspective, the transformation of international trade regulation reflects one of the most intriguing challenges that the WTO faces nowadays: how to square an institutional legal tradition and culture based on the sovereign equality of the States, a State-centered mentality and the infamous secrecy and confidentiality of trade negotiations (keyword: Member-driven organization) with the incremental, yet perceivable – and, in fact, pervasive nowadays – Stateless reality of commercial transactions as well as the rising of NGOs arguing for increased participatory rights? This competition for participation and voice can easily transform into a competition for authority in an ever-increasing number of instances, raising a whole new bundle of questions relating to hierarchy or, as some would argue, the adequate (that is, manageable) level of heterarchy.

If one considers global law as a field where lack of a commonly agreed ordering among legal orders reins, then the WTO could very well fit the confines of such a construct; then, whereas the WTO remains a Member-driven IO, much of its output can no longer be deemed as the outcome of work and activity exclusively originating in States and their organs. Rather, much of this output reflects views and input by domestic special interest groups; transnational corporations; non-governmental organizations representing what is commonly termed 'the global civil society' and other private constituencies. This transformation of the global trade regulator *par excellence* is irreversible and thus much of 'blue-sky' thinking takes place in the relevant scholarship as to the future governance and indeed structure of the multilateral trading system, overestimating[11] or underestimating[12] the role that the WTO can play, as well as identifying the potential side-players and stakeholders beyond the States.

In the meantime, the evolution of transnational private regulation continues apace. The term 'transnational private regulation' describes the

---

[11] See, for instance, A Guzman, 'Global Governance and the WTO' (2004) 45 *Harvard International Law Journal* 303.

[12] See, for instance, R Howse, 'From politics to technocracy – and back again: The fate of the multilateral trade regime', (2002) 96 *American Journal of International Law* 94.

emerging body of rules created by private actors in a manner that leapfrogs national borders. Driven by the forces of globalization of business, these actors offer handy solutions to globally active economic operators through rule-making activities that take place 'in the shadow of the law' and the traditional forms of State regulatory making.[13] The constant increase of the role of private parties in regulatory activities and the desire of such parties to assume a regulator-like role, very similar to the one that was traditionally taken up by the State, constitutes a phenomenon that is driving legal change and continuous reflexion as to the normativity of the future law of world trade and the group of constituencies which will promulgate it. At present, with respect to the idea of global law theory upgrading individuals to the driving force of change,[14] nothing revolutionary is to be reported on the front of the WTO when one looks at the current state of affairs: indeed, human beings are at the center of the WTO actions only in part, that is, in their capacity as traders or producers.[15]

In its early case-law, the *US – Section 301* Panel recognized that the multilateral trading system is composed not only of States but mostly of individual economic operators and thus one of the primary objectives of the system is to generate and maintain certain market conditions which would allow this individual activity to flourish. It went on to confirm the importance that the WTO and its predecessor, the GATT, had attributed to the indirect impact of legislations on individuals. Thus, the Panel found that, contrary to traditional public international law, in a treaty like the WTO 'the benefits of which depend in part on the activity of individual operators the legislation itself may be construed as a breach, since the mere existence of legislation could have an appreciable "chilling effect" on the economic activities of individuals'.[16]

In addition, producer welfare and its protection is an essential *raison d'être* for the contingent protection agreements of the WTO, that is, the agreements relating to safeguards, anti-dumping and subsidization. Consumer welfare, on the other hand, is a concern only indirectly and no

---

[13] For an economic perspective on alternative modes of governance, see the treatise by A Dixit, *Lawlessness and Economics – Alternative Modes of Governance* (Princeton University Press 2004).

[14] For the sake of argument, let's assume that such a theory exists. In this respect, we follow here the scholarship developed by R Domingo.

[15] See, inter alia, Panel Reports, *Argentina – Hides and Leather*, paras 11.76-11.77, *EC – Selected Customs Matters*, paras 7.107-8.

[16] Panel Report, *US – Section 301*, paras 7.73-7.91.

requirement exists as to it being taken into account when formulating domestic trade policies or, indeed, global trade rules.[17]

Therefore, instances of global law, at least as understood by Rafael Domingo,[18] whereby the individuals take center stage in a post-modern legal landscape, cannot yet be found in the WTO. Having said this, the WTO does constitute an important complementary layer of governance exerting unprecedented influence in the regulation of economic activity domestically. If the erosion of national sovereignty is happening in any global institution, then this is the WTO. Discussions about the infamous 'S word' and the legitimacy of the WTO,[19] notably its judicial branch,[20] have quickly become mainstream in the wake of controversial rulings by the WTO adjudicating bodies and notably the Appellate Body, the WTO's last instance standing court, over politically charged and highly mediatized disputes, particularly in the developed world. Such rulings, for instance, condemned the EU ban on genetically modified products (GMOs); the EU preferences for the importation of bananas from the EU former colonies (the so-called ACP countries); or the US import prohibition of shrimps based on environmental grounds.[21]

The debate over sovereignty has quickly been contextualized to include borderless issues such as global subsidiarity;[22] efficient power allocation and institutional choice in a multi-layered environment;[23] inequality and global responsibility or ethics;[24] cooperation for the production and protection of global public goods;[25] cooperation to address global

---

17 Cf P Mavroidis, 'Come Together? Producer Welfare, Consumer Welfare, and WTO Rules' in E-U Petersmann, *Reforming the World Trading System – Legitimacy, Efficiency, and Democratic Governance* (Oxford University Press 2005) 277.

18 See R Domingo, *The New Global Law* (Cambridge University Press 2010) 121ff.

19 Cf A Buchanan and R Keohane, 'The Legitimacy of Global Governance Institutions' (2006) 20 *Ethics and International Affairs* 405.

20 Cf R Howse, 'The Most Dangerous Branch? The WTO Appellate Body Jurisprudence on the Nature and Limits of the Judicial Power, in T Cottier and P Mavroidis (eds), *The Role of the Judge in International Trade Regulation* (University of Michigan Press 2001).

21 Ironically, it was the most powerful countries that insisted in the inclusion of an effective dispute settlement system during the Uruguay Round negotiations: J Trachtman, 'The Constitutions of the WTO' (2006) 17 *European Journal of International Law* 623, 634.

22 See R Howse and K Nicolaidis, 'Enhancing WTO Legitimacy: Constitutionalization or Global Subsidiarity?' (2003) 16(1) *Governance* 73.

23 See, in particular, J Jackson, *Sovereignty, the WTO, and Changing Fundamentals of International Law* (Cambridge University Press 2006).

24 Cf Kennedy (n 7) 66.

25 See, for example, G Shaffer, 'Recognizing Public Goods in WTO Dispute Settlement: Who Participates? Who Decides? The Case of TRIPS and Pharmaceutical Patent Protection' (2004) 7(2) *Journal of International Economic Law* 459.

concerns[26] and so on. This reflects a broader fading of the once alluring concept of sovereignty. As noted by the International Criminal Tribunal for the Former Yugoslavia (ICTY) in *Tadic*, '[d]ating back to a period when sovereignty stood as a sacrosanct and unassailable attribute of statehood, this concept recently has suffered progressive erosion at the hands of the more liberal forces at work in the democratic societies'.[27] Beyond doubt, sovereignty is a concept in crisis and there does not seem to be much to do to avoid the transition beyond the traditional notion of the Westphalian Nation-State.

In addition, one should not lose sight of the fact that the regulation of global commerce is binary and thus it would be a naïve understatement to suggest that no trace of global law, understood as an individual-centered law, is identifiable in the regulation of global commerce. Indeed, much of global commerce nowadays is largely conditional on the regulatory activities of private bodies, the so-called *lex mercatoria*. This regulatory usurpation that is taking place in the area of commerce is not something extraordinary. States were acquainted with it very early in the human history and the situation has not changed much ever since, despite few intervals of 'State bullying' from time to time. In addition, it may even be misleading to consider as antagonists the State and the private quasi-regulators in this respect: cross-fertilization and complementarity may be the keywords rather than fervent rivalry.[28]

The role of the WTO is fairly modest in this regard: its regulatory activity evolves around facilitating trade, for instance, through the requirement that WTO Members abide by procedural obligations relating to transparency, due process, proper notification and publication of amendments to law and so on, with a view to ensuring predictability and security in the marketplace. In an era where disorderliness of rules and institutions is the very trait of economic globalization and the importance of the source of rulemaking seems to have vanished, the WTO needs to stick to the basics: ensuring non-discrimination and equality of competitive opportunities in the marketplace. This may be more difficult than one would think at first blush: to start with, economists would predict that, in case of an ongoing,

---

26 T Cottier and Sofya Matteotti-Berkutova, 'International Environmental Law and the Evolving Concept of "Common Concern of Mankind" in T Cottier, O Nartova and S Bigdeli (eds), *International Trade Regulation and the Mitigation of Climate Change* (Cambridge University Press 2009) 21.

27 *Prosecutor v Tadic* (Jurisdiction) (1996) 3 Intl Human Rights Rep 578, para 55.

28 Cf R Michaels, 'The True Lex Mercatoria: Law Beyond the State' (2007) 14(2) *Indiana Journal of Global Legal Studies* 447.

important flow of private rules that companies prefer to use over public rules, States may have no incentive to switch towards more efficient rules due to the uncertainty as regards 'buyers' of their product, i.e. regulatees that use such regulations.[29]

Legally speaking, various legal concepts within the WTO legal system are anachronistic at best: take the case of the definition of what constitutes a 'measure' for the purposes of dispute settlement in the WTO.[30] Some form of involvement by the State is a *conditio sine qua non* for the application of any obligation under the agreements on trade in goods.[31] Such interpretations, a legacy of the GATT State-centered tradition, are becoming less and less defensible.

3. A Future Research Agenda for the WTO from a Global Law Perspective

A global law-related research agenda for the WTO would evolve around three axes: first, the identification of a set of principles akin to the global law advocacy; second, the empowerment of non-State constituencies and a more intensive bridge-building with the transnational private regulators; and, third, improving the still unconvincing actions to create a more inclusive world trading system that is brimful with development opportunities for all.

With respect to principles, traces of a cosmopolitan or global law view are already discernible in dispute settlement. In *US – Underwear*, the Appellate Body, in an attempt to give flesh to the fundamental principle of transparency, found that promoting full disclosure of governmental acts affecting Members and private persons and enterprises, *whether of domestic or foreign nationality*, is an overarching objective of the multilateral trading system. For the Appellate Body, there is on the ground a community of traders that is worth protecting irrespective of nationality. Due process

---

[29] See E Carbonara and F Parisi, 'Choice of Law and Legal Evolution: Rethinking the Market for Legal Rules' (2009) 139 *Public Choice* 461.

[30] Cf T Voon and A Yanovich, 'What is the Measure at Issue?' in A Mitchell (ed), *Challenges and Prospects for the WTO* (Cameron May 2005).

[31] Having said this, the definition of measure under the General Agreement on Trade in Services (GATS) is more promising, as it covers private regulation and adopts an all-encompassing definition of a measure affecting trade in services. See also the rather unique case of export subsidies made and funded by private parties in Appellate Body Report, *Canada – Dairy (Art 21.5 – New Zealand and US II)* para 95.

shall be universally applicable implying that persons (that is, not only States) affected, or likely to be affected, 'by governmental measures imposing restraints, requirements and other burdens, should have a reasonable opportunity to acquire authentic information about such measures and accordingly to protect and adjust their activities or alternatively to seek modification of such measures.'[32]

Few years later, the controversial issue of amicus curiae briefs and the ensuing right to communication and information arose. In *US – Shrimp*, the Appellate Body, against all odds, accepted the filing of *amicus curiae* briefs by NGOs, only to find that they were not helpful in resolving the dispute. In *EC – Sardines*, the Appellate Body would go a step further to also accept and consider an *amicus curiae* brief submitted by a private individual. However, the Appellate Body also stated earlier that *no legal right* exists for individuals or NGOs to make submissions or to be heard by the WTO adjudicating organs; this remains a matter of their discretion.[33]

When it comes to the empowerment of non-state actors and increased participation, a caveat has to be mentioned at the outset: it appears that access to the WTO decision-making is unbalanced to the benefit of global companies and less of transnational private regulators such as professional bodies or standard-setting organizations. This is because of obvious public choice reasons that go beyond the scope of this note.[34] On the other hand, any calls for more democracy within the WTO shall also be treated with caution. Recall that the WTO is a reflection of its Members' national systems with all the imperfections that such democracies have in terms of participation, deliberation, inclusiveness and the like. The fact remains that more transparency brings with it more interest in the activities of the WTO and thus more interest in influencing those activities.

The attribution of observer status to NGOs has been a first step. Clearly, the red line is attributing to the NGOs something more than an observer status.[35] NGOs have been very active and quickly managed to become considerably savvy in the relevant technical issues under discussion at the WTO. This applies with particular force in the so-called 'trade and (...)' issues. Thus, by involving the NGOs more in its work along functional lines, the WTO and its Members receive a valuable support, which can enhance

32 Appellate Body Report, *US – Underwear* 21.

33 Appellate Body Report, *US – Lead and Bismuth II*, para 41.

34 The reference work in this respect is G Grossman and E Helpman, 'Protection for Sale' (1994) 84(4) *American Economic Review* 833.

35 Cf S Charnovitz, 'The WTO and Cosmopolitics' in E-U Petersmann (ed), (n 17) 438, 444.

the WTO legitimacy, authority and effectiveness.[36] Sticking with States is increasingly becoming old-fashioned and imprudent.[37] In addition, empirical evidence suggests that NGOs may be less critical once they become 'part of the system', thereby contributing to enhancing public support for trade liberalization.[38]

In this respect, a more important concern may relate to the representative function of the NGOs currently active at the WTO yard. There is an increased feeling that there are unorganized, ordinary people who mistrust the WTO, as exemplified by the demonstrations during MCs or other high-level meetings at the WTO. These people do not feel to be represented by any State official nor NGO. There seems to be an overall perception that State representatives join WTO negotiations or meetings with a significant bias to the detriment of the people on the ground. If this is indeed the case, openness, that is, open-door bargaining, decision-making, and dispute settlement, may be the only possible and sustainable modus operandi for the WTO if the organization wants to gain public support.

Public hearings of disputes are now reality and additional initiatives towards this direction such as the WTO Public Forum or the WTO Open Doors Initiative can only be praised. The same goes for live webcasting or press releases where non-technical language is used. Indeed, what is sought after is not transparency in the form of increased communication of technical documents, which few outside the WTO are able to assess and act upon.[39] This type of transparency may actually be perilous and have the opposite effect if it produces piles of documents that few understand and thus read.

As to transnational private regulators, the WTO can only benefit from more intensive cooperation with such constituencies. To be sure, there is a misalignment of incentives in this case, as private bodies have few incentives to cooperate due to their desire to maintain existing rents. As the interest of multilateral trade negotiations is moving towards the identification and elimination of non-tariff barriers almost exclusively, the cooperation of private regulators is critical. Thus, a more inclusive governance

---

36 See D Esty, 'Linkages and Governance: NGOs at the World Trade Organization' (1998) 19(3) *University of Pennsylvania Journal of International Economic Law* 709, 716.

37 Cf A Kuper, *Democracy Beyond Borders – Justice and Representation in Global Institutions* (Oxford University Press 2004) 164-165.

38 D Esty, 'The World Trade Organization's Legitimacy Crisis' (2002) 1 *World Trade Review* 7.

39 Cf Kuper (n 37) 180.

of the WTO, open to private parties, seems to be a self-fulfilling prophecy in the field of global commerce.

Finally, with respect to the creation of a more inclusive system allowing for the development of all WTO Members, two things are worth mentioning: first, whereas we have witnessed an increasing integration of the developing world in the global trading system in recent decades, such integration has been highly unequal, with some countries benefitting more than others. The adoption of redistribution mechanisms and the participation of domestic constituents in the deliberation process of the WTO can be highly informative and, for this simple reason, beneficial. Such initiatives do not necessarily entail direct money transfers from the WTO to specific groups or countries. Global distribution of benefits is perhaps addressed for the first time through the Cotton initiative, involving four cotton-producing countries, Benin, Burkina-Faso, Chad and Mali, but the final deal is yet to be concluded. More determined action is needed, along with innovative legal drafting.

Arguably, support for development cannot be confined to the introduction of transitional periods during which developing countries and LDCs are exempted from application of certain rules. This has led to the alienation of several Members vis-à-vis the key WTO objective of achieving liberalization and restructuring the domestic market to allow for this. Indeed, transformation of the global regime regulating trade will most likely lead to more responsible governance domestically as well. Global challenges such as climate change, environmental degradation, protection of human dignity and public health cannot wait for long to be addressed. As interdependent regimes will increasingly realize the cul-de-sac that a solitary stance leads to, they will be looking for reconciling strategies which have to be carefully designed, along with the relevant actors, to enhance consumer welfare. For the WTO and other economic organizations, setting the improvement of consumer welfare as a priority for a modern trade agenda becomes pressing. The same goes for the largely neglected issue of the role of the WTO in *enabling* trade.

A new generation of researchers will have to pick up those issues and give satisfactory answers and effective solutions. Global law constitutes a new window to look at the evolution of the real world and its vicissitudes. Great expectations surround legal science. Legal engineering will either make or break economic globalization, but will also change law as we know it. Interesting times are ahead, indeed.

Global Justice and Global Criminal Laws: The Importance of *Nyaya* in the Quest for Justice after International Crimes

Antony Pemberton[a] **& Rianne Letschert**[b]
a) Associate Professor and Research Coordinator, International Victimology Institute Tilburg
a.pemberton@tilburguniversity.edu
b) Professor, Victimology and International Law, and Deputy Director International Victimology Institute Tilburg
r.m.letschert@tilburguniversity.edu

Abstract
This brief contribution to the debate concerning global law draws on the authors' analysis of international criminal justice. It argues that the extent to which international criminal law is in fact contributing to global justice in the aftermath of international crimes remains to be seen. In particular, the smooth relationship between international criminal law and the perception of justice can be called into question, as it relies too heavily on the idea that going through the motions of westernized forms of international criminal law will automatically inculcate a sense of justice in victimized populations, while *en passant* contributing to the resurrection of the rule of law. The connection to broader issues in global justice and global law will draw heavily on Amartya Sen's recent critique of John Rawls' Theory of Justice, in which the former employs the ancient Sanskrit notions of *niti* and *nyaya*.

Keywords
victimology; international criminal law; global justice; international crimes

1. Introduction

One of the primary difficulties in discussing the development or emergence of global law is that the construct is used loosely and can mean different things in the eyes of different scholars.[1] In this short contribution we will sidestep this problem by positing that a clearer understanding of global law

---

[1] T Nardin, 'Justice in the Global Order' (2011) 37 Review of International Studies 259.

can be found in the application of this broad idea to relevant areas of law, in which progression – at least rhetorically – towards a global legal order is underway and where the notion of contributing to global justice is explicit.

This applies in particular to our own area of expertise; that of criminal law. The developments in the past decades in the field of international criminal law have been, in many ways, spectacular. There is the definition of a special class of international crimes; genocide, war crimes and crimes against humanity; the installment of *ad hoc* tribunals - first for Rwanda and the former Yugoslavia (the ICTR and ICTY), followed by judicial bodies for Sierra Leone, East Timor, Lebanon and Cambodia, ultimately culminating in the establishment of the permanent International Criminal Court.[2] The connection of international criminal law to global justice is evident in the stated key aim of holding the *'hostis sui generis',* the enemies of all mankind, to account for their atrocities. It is also made explicit in the view of the current prosecutor of the ICC, Luis Moreno Ocampo, that the ICC seeks global justice.[3] The latter sentiment is echoed in the work of scholars of globalization who view the materialization of international criminal law as key elements of the development towards global justice.[4]

However, the extent to which international criminal law is, in fact, contributing to global justice in the aftermath of international crimes remains to be seen. In our recent work we questioned the smooth connection between international criminal law and the perception of justice, which relies too heavily on the idea that going through the motions of westernized forms of international criminal law will automatically inculcate a sense of justice in victimized populations, while *en passant* contributing to the resurrection of the rule of law.[5]

---

[2] B Broomhall, *International Justice and the International Criminal Court. Between Sovereignity and the Rule of Law* (Oxford University Press 2003).

[3] L Moreno-Ocampo, 'The International Criminal Court: Seeking Global Justice' (2007) 40 Western Reserve Journal of International Law 215.

Of course it is possible to take issue with the notion that the ICC indeed has global reach, as neither the United States, nor the majority of Islamic and Asian countries have ratified the Rome Statute.

[4] D Held, 'Cosmopolitanism: globalisation tamed?' (2003) 29 Review of International Studies 465.

[5] RM Letschert, RH Haveman, A de Brouwer and A Pemberton (eds), *Victimological Approaches to International Crimes: Africa* (Intersentia 2011); A Pemberton, RM Letschert, A-M De Brouwer and RH Haveman, Het internationale strafrecht: een victimologisch perspectief' [2011] Tijdschrift voor Criminologie 385; A Pemberton, RM Letschert, A-M De Brouwer and RH Haveman, *Coherence in International Criminal Justice: A Victimological Perspective* (forthcoming). See also: MA Drumbl, *Atrocity, Punishment and International Law* (Cambridge University Press 2007); LE Fletcher and HM Weinstein, 'Violence and Social Repair: Rethinking the Contribution of Justice to Reconciliation', (2002) 24 Human Rights Quarterly 573.

In this brief contribution to the debate concerning global law we will sketch these problems in greater detail, before connecting this to more abstract notions of justice. The latter will draw heavily on Amartya Sen's recent critique of John Rawls' Theory of Justice, in which he employs the ancient Sanskrit notions of *niti* and *nyaya*.[6] Finally, in conclusion, the analysis of international criminal law will be used as a base to provide more general notions about global justice and global law.

2. The (Mis)match between International Criminal Law and Global Justice?

As a means of ensuring justice, criminal law is by no means perfect. Its faults are legion, from a poor coverage rate, through bias in its administration to a large discrepancy between its stated aims of retribution and prevention and its actual outcomes.[7] It is no small wonder that politicians who tout the adjudication and enforcement of criminal law as a resolution to social problems are viewed by the academic community with suspicion: well captured in the concept of penal populism.[8]

In the move to the international level the shortcomings of criminal law have been given short shrift, replaced instead by a triumphant and aspirational rhetoric of 'ending impunity' and 'delivering safety and justice on a global scale'.[9] This is remarkable, considering the fact that the characteristics of international crimes render the delivery of justice through criminal law, *more* rather than *less* difficult. Just to mention a number of additional difficulties: establishing individual guilt for crimes committed as a collective and/ or in the name of a collective,[10] in other words the abundance of evidence of collective evil, coupled with a lack of proof of individual

[6] A Sen, *The Idea of Justice* (Allen Lane 2009); J Rawls, *A Theory of Justice* (Harvard University Press 1972).

[7] JJM van Dijk, *World of Crime*, (Sage 2007); L Wacquant, *Punishing the Poor: The Neoliberal Government of Social Insecurity* (Duke University Press 2009); M Tonry, *Retributivism has a Past: Has it a Future?* (Oxford University Press 2012).

[8] JV Roberts, L Stalans, D Indermaur and M Hough, *Penal Populism and Public Opinion: Lessons from Five Countries* (Oxford University Press 2003).

[9] MA Drumbl, 'Collective Violence and Individual Punishment: The Criminality of Mass Atrocity' (2005) 99 Northwestern University Law Review 539 & MA Drumbl, *Atrocity, Punishment and International Law* (Cambridge University Press 2007).

[10] See Drumbl, 'Collective Violence' ibid; DJ Levinson, 'Collective Sanctions' (2003) 56 Stanford Law Review 345 & M Osiel, 'The Banality of Good: Aligning Incentives Against Mass Atrocity' (2005) 105 Columbia Law Review 1751.

wrongdoing; the uncertain line between culpable and inculpable parties,[11] including the role of so-called innocent bystanders,[12] the difficulty of finding a remedy suitable to the enormity of the crimes committed[13] and, coupled with the previous points, the diminished likelihood of reaching goals of criminal justice such as retribution and general or special prevention.[14]

In practice moreover, these shortcomings have been exacerbated by problems of selectivity, insufficient proportionality and lengthy procedures. The punishment meted out for international crimes is *lower* rather than *higher* compared to ordinary crimes, while the treatment of the often top-level suspects and convicts in international criminal justice is vastly superior to the facilities available in most domestic criminal justice systems.[15] The latter also applies to the emphatic and time consuming emphasis on meeting all criminal-procedural nicities. In stark contrast to the trials of Nuremberg, which were over and done with within the space of 11 months and trials in the domestic sphere – the Rwandans managed to try over 5000 cases with one tenth of the funding of the ICTR, before the latter handed down one verdict – international criminal law proceeds at an almost glacial pace.[16]

The reason given for this, as noted by ICTY-appeals court judge Patricia Wald, is that 'we have to assure that justice is seen to be done'.[17] This is also

---

11 Osiel, ibid.

12 Drumbl, *Atrocity, Punishment and International Law* (n 5); LE Fletcher, 'From indifference to engagement. Bystanders and International Criminal Justice' (2005) 26 Michigan Journal of International Law 1013 & E Staub, *The Roots of Evil: The Origins of Genocide and Other Group Violence* (Cambridge University Press 1989).

13 Osiel (n 10) & RM Letschert, T Van Boven, 'Providing Reparation in Situations of Mass Victimization: Key Challenges Involved' in Letschert (n 5).

14 MA Drumbl, 'Collective Violence and Individual Punishment: The Criminality of Mass Atrocity' (2005) 99 Northwestern University Law Review 539; DJ Levinson, 'Collective sanctions' (2003) 56 Stanford Law Review 345; M Osiel, 'The Banality of Good: Aligning Incentives Against Mass Atrocity' (2005) 105 Columbia Law Review 1751; MA Drumbl, *Atrocity, Punishment and International Law* (Cambridge University Press 2007); LE Fletcher, 'From Indifference to Engagement. Bystanders and International Criminal Justice' (2005) 26 Michigan Journal of International Law 1013; E Staub, *The Roots of Evil: The Origins of Genocide and Other Group Violence* (Cambridge University Press 1989); MJ Aukerman, 'Extraordinary Evil, Ordinary Crime: A Framework for Understanding Transitional Justice' (2002) 15 Harvard Human Rights Journal 39.

15 MA Drumbl, *Atrocity, Punishment and International Law* (Cambridge University Press 2007).

16 GJ Bass, *Stay the Hand of Vengeance: The Politics of War Crime Tribunals* (Princeton University Press 2001); J Rabkin, 'Global Criminal Justice: An Idea Whose Time has Passed' (2005) 38 Cornell International Law Journal 753.

17 Rabkin (2005) uses this quote to make a similar point.

the explanation for international criminal law's recurring emphasis on the *independence* of international criminal law, which attempts to protect it from so-called victor's justice, but, simultaneously, erects a Chinese wall separating it from domestic attempts to provide justice, from other, concurrent attempts to rebuild state structures and from the history, tradition and political realities of affected societies.[18]

International criminal law is *remote* justice, meted out by an 'international community' which may have positive connotations for many commentators, but whose actions in the experience of inhabitants of war-torn societies are most often characterized succinctly as 'too little, too late'.[19] The legitimacy of the process and actors involved in the process of international criminal law in the eyes of these populations is suspect, which further strains the smooth and easy connection of international criminal law to the provision of a sense of (global) justice.[20]

3. Niti and Nyaya: Applying Ancient Sanskrit Notions to International Criminal Law

In our view much of the difficulties in the development of international criminal law can be traced to the over-emphasis on procedure and more precisely the faith that striving for global justice encompasses the development of a perfect procedure, which is capable of ensuring just outcomes, irrespective of the context in which it is placed.[21] This procedural view of justice has a decidedly Rawlsian quality. The requirement of the so-called *veil of ignorance* in Rawls' original position as a starting point for deliberations about justice necessitates a view of justice which is independent

---

[18] LE Fletcher and HM Weinstein, 'Violence and Social Repair: Rethinking the Contribution of Justice to Reconciliation' (2002) 24 Human Rights Quarterly 573; HM Weinstein, 'Editorial: The Myth of Closure: The Illusion of Reconciliation. Final Thoughts on Five Years as Co-Editor in Chief' (2011) 5 International Journal of Transitional Justice 1.

[19] Eg MJ Aukerman, 'Extraordinary Evil, Ordinary Crime: A Framework for Understanding Transitional Justice' (2002) 15 Harvard Human Rights Journal 39.

[20] See for instance T Longman, P Pham and HM Weinstein, 'Connecting Justice to Human Experience: Attitudes Toward Accountability and Reconciliation in Rwanda' in E Stover and HM Weinstein (eds), *My Neighbor, My Enemy: Justice and Community in the Aftermath of Mass Atrocity* (Cambridge University Press 2004). See also the subsequent population surveys of the Berkeley Human Rights Center.

[21] In greater detail: A Pemberton, RM Letschert, A-M De Brouwer and RH Haveman, Het internationale strafrecht: een victimologisch perspectief' [2011] Tijdschrift voor Criminologie 385; A Pemberton, RM Letschert, A-M De Brouwer and RH Haveman, *Coherence in International Criminal Justice: A Victimological Perspective* (forthcoming).

of specific situations: the participants in the deliberation do not know what their position is in society or indeed to which society they belong. The justice of a procedure is then judged by its fairness as a procedure, rather than the outcomes it delivers in specific situations.

Recently, Amartya Sen developed a critique of Rawls' theory which is probably most succinctly summarized in his description of the Sanskrit justice concepts *niti* and *nyaya*.[22] The former concept proposes that justice should be conceptualized in terms of organizational arrangements, regulations and procedures; it is in other words an arrangement-focused view of justice, which fits well with Rawls' theory. The latter instead concerns the world that actually emerges; it is a realization-focused understanding. Niti measures justice by the extent to which it meets some standard of perfection, while nyaya does so on the basis of a comparison with other realistic alternatives, a comparison that includes the independent value of organizational arrangements, but does not allow this to override all other concerns.

Seeing the poor fit between the reality of international crimes and principles of criminal justice, we have argued previously that *nyaya*, rather than *niti* is a base to assess international criminal law.[23] Using *niti* as a benchmark entails striving for a standard of perfection within the justice procedure, blinded to the reality that in situations of mass victimisation it is a wholly unattainable ideal. A focus on *niti* restricts justice in the aftermath of mass victimization in three ways: it reduces it to what the criminal justice procedure can provide, isolates criminal justice from other relief efforts and – importantly - ringfences resources that may stand a better chance of providing a measure of justice if allocated elsewhere.

The extent to which justice is done should be measured by the actual, although probably at best modest, contribution to rebuilding society rather than its adherence to the blueprint of (Western) criminal justice procedure. Maybe more so than in the domestic sphere justice after international crimes is done, when it is *seen to be done*.[24] Historical and cultural aspects may give rise to different solutions, while the interplay between the crimes committed and the views of victimized populations may differentiate the

22 A Sen, *The Idea offjustice* (Allen Lane 2009).

23 A Pemberton, RM Letschert, A-M De Brouwer and RH Haveman, Het internationale strafrecht: een victimologisch perspectief' [2011] Tijdschrift voor Criminologie 385.

24 MA Drumbl, *Atrocity, Punishment and International Law* (Cambridge University Press 2007); J Feinberg, 'The Expressive Function of Punishment' in J Feinberg (ed), *Doing and Deserving: Essays in the Theory of Responsibility* (Princeton University Press 1970).

reactions from one instance of victimization to another, even *within* the same societies: as Fletcher and Weinstein note, an *ecological* view of justice may be most appropriate.[25]

A key element of the use of nyaya rather than niti as lense for viewing international criminal law is therefore the insight that delivering global justice after international crimes is unlikely to proceed through a one-size-fits-all solution. We should never lose sight of the fact that lawmaking never entails a simple translation of morals: we have to reckon with the spin that the social and political reality will place upon this connection.[26] The question to what extent international criminal law delivers justice needs an empirical answer: this can not be resolved on the basis of theory and assumptions alone.

The yardstick involved in this measurement should include procedural concerns, but not allow them to overrule other, often more substantive measures of justice. Of course this is a highly complicated matter – the space of this article does not allow us even to attempt to broach the myriad complexities of developing such a measurement tool, in the face of the different and often competing notions of justice involved – but work of this kind is possible and in fact conducted even in the most difficult of circumstances (again we point to the work of Berkeley Human Rights Center as a promising practice example).[27]

4. Conclusion: Nyaya and Global Justice

Our analysis of the experience, particularly in the last 20 years, with international criminal law, has led us to the insight that *nyaya* rather than *niti* provides an appropriate base for assessing justice in the aftermath of international crimes. If generalization from this field of law to others is valid, the following general observations can be made.

First, legal scholars and policy makers should resist the temptation to view the *terra incognita* of global law as a licence to abstract its development and construction from the messy and uncomfortable realities connected to its application in practice. The vacuum of global law is not a blank slate: it is *pre*-shaped by the constraints of culture, politics and economics

[25] LE Fletcher and HM Weinstein, 'Violence and Social Repair: Rethinking the Contribution of Justice to Reconciliation', (2002) 24 Human Rights Quarterly 573.

[26] D Runciman, *Political Hypocrisy: The Mask of Power from Hobbes to Orwell and Beyond* (Princeton University Press 2008).

[27] M Sandel, *Justice: What's the Right Thing to do* (Farrar, Straus & Giroux 2009).

and *post*-shaped by the interactions between law and legal actors, in the patterns visible in the growing body of work in the field of empirical legal studies. Indeed, as a rule the contribution of a system of global law to global justice is to a matter of empiricism, rather than of assumption.

And finally, global justice will likely entail global laws rather than global law: the political, social and cultural specificities of a given situation necessitate different solutions, also in the legal sphere. Rather than one-size-fits-all, the extent to which the global legal order will contribute to global justice, depends on the extent to which it meets these demands of ecological appriopriateness.

Globalisation and Regulation: (Where) do they Meet?

Rob van Gestel
Professor of Theory and Methods of Regulation at Tilburg University, The Netherlands
r.a.j.vangestel@tilburguniversity.edu

Abstract
Globalisation is the new buzz word in legal education, but nobody really seems to know what 'global law' entails and to what extent legal practice is waiting for global lawyers. What is needed is a better understanding of how globalisation affects the market for legal practitioners. Does the current law school curriculum meet the demands of legal practice in the 21st century? The argument in this contribution is that this is not the case. The law school curriculum is still dominated by the role model of the judge and the advocate, whereas the rise of the regulatory state has hardly led to serious curriculum changes. One of the changes that is necessary is the introduction of courses in legislation and regulation, at the bachelor level, to teach students what it means to translate policy goals into legal rules. This would not only serve the demands of legal practice, but also open up the law school programme to new theories and methodologies of legal research.

Keywords
legislation; regulation; legal practice; regulatory state

1. Introduction

Writing this story in the hills of Fiesole, overlooking the Duomo of Firenze built between 1296 and 1472, anticipating the possible effects of globalisation on law and legislation seems virtually impossible. After all, who could have imagined during those days that in 2012 we would discuss the emergence of a 'global law'? Even the thought that in 1976 the doors of the Badia Fiesolana would be opened for the first generation of students of the newly established European University Institute in the field of 'European law' would have sounded awkward at the time.[1]

[1] The term University Institute instead of just European University was chosen because the member states did not want to put the EUI on the same level as the national universities,

As such the idea of having a harmonised system of laws across the borders of the nation state was, however, something quite familiar to the medieval Italian lawyer. From the 11th century onwards, the renaissance of Roman law had spread its wings from Bologna to other Italian universities and from there on to universities in most European countries. Around the year 1500 getting a law degree meant that one needed to study Roman law, next to perhaps local law and/or canonical law. It did not matter whether one studied in Italy, Germany, France or the Netherlands. Everywhere, Roman law dominated the study of law. There was even a lingua franca in law, which was not English though, but Latin.[2] Transnational law, therefore, is not a new phenomenon, although the globalisation of markets and services was still far away back then.

A bright Florentine lawyer, such as Niccolò Machiavelli, would probably have had more questions about the sort of practice future students of the EUI or the global law bachelor in Tilburg are aiming for. As we know from his famous 'Il Principe', which is often considered to be the first work in modern political philosophy, in which the effective truth is taken to be more important than any abstract ideal, Machiavelli was a legal realist *avant la lettre*. He would probably have asked: who will want to hire these lawyers? I think that would have been, and still is, a good question.

For EUI students, we know the answer. Many of them get a position in academia somewhere in Europe, others will receive a job at one of the EU institutions (EC, ECJ, agencies et cetera) and a lot of them also end up as EU law specialists in the public administration of the member states. The reason they usually succeed in finding a job, not only has to do with the fact that a degree from the EUI is a post-graduate degree, which implies that one already has a law degree from one of the member states, but EUI students have something extra. By the time they graduate, the intertwinement of EU-law and national law has become second nature to them. Apart from that they will have developed their language skills (English and Italian are inadmissible) and acquired an international network. This gives them an advantage on the job market.

---

which was also why the EUI did not receive regular students but only post-graduates. What the member states did not realise, however, was that exactly these features would turn the EUI into a prestigious fore post in the area of European law research.

[2] As Bruno de Witte has shown this is a huge contrast with the situation today where even in the field of European law there is no unified, cross national community of scholars, not in the last place because of language differences. See Bruno de Witte, 'European Law: A Unified 'Academic Discipline?' (2008) EUI Working Papers RSCAS no 34.

For the graduates of a global law bachelor it is much harder to predict where they will end up. Inspired by Machiavelli I am a bit worried that global law will remain an abstract ideal, which legal practice can do without. Does that mean that I do not believe in the forces of globalisation? Of course not. Everyone can see, almost on a daily basis, how international financial markets have gained power over national governments, how institutions of the European Union (EU) have acquired powers to strike down or rewrite national legislation, while international tribunals have acquired power over transnational trade and commerce (WTO/Nafta), and a whole range of other areas varying from maritime law to peace and security, whereas both national and international higher courts increasingly engage in judicial dialogues across jurisdictions.

The latter does not, however, imply that we need global law. As Paul Berman has argued, globalisation can, and probably will, go in different directions.[3] Some states may try to seal themselves off from outside influence (e.g. China's censuring of the Internet use of its citizens), either by retreating from the rest of the world and becoming more insular or by falling back on territorially based jurisdiction or choice-of-law rules. Others may call for far-reaching harmonisation, more supranational governing bodies or the creation of 'world law'.

Somewhere in the middle there will be people and organisations arguing in favour of procedural mechanisms to deal with global legal pluralism. Which way we will go in the Netherlands is still hard to tell. One thing I am pretty sure about, however, is that national law is not going to disappear for a long while. History shows that successful legal regimes have always been built on diversity, on metis and phronesis, and on a bottom up capacity to adapt to changing circumstances.[4] Moreover, we should not underestimate the power of language differences, cultural identity and history. Hence, it would be foolish to do away with national or European law in any global law school curriculum.

In my view, globalisation implies that teaching the next generation of students to 'think like a lawyer' presupposes more and other qualities than in the past.[5] What it essentially requires is the incorporation of a meta-perspective. What futures students will need, more than past generations,

---

[3] Paul Schiff Berman, *Global Legal Pluralism: A Jurisprudence of Law Beyond Borders* (Cambridge University Press 2012).

[4] James C Scott, *Seeing it Like a State: How Certain Schemes to Improve the Human Condition have Failed* (Yale University Press 1998).

[5] See for example Harry Arthurs, 'Law and Learning in an Era of Globalization' (2009) 10 German Law Journal 629.

is to be able to understand the 'laws of law-making': the various theories and methods underlying regulation, adjudication and governance. This in combination with a familiarity of an increasing plurality of legal sources (national/international; hard law/soft law; private/public) and a healthy amount of content-based legal knowledge about different legal systems.

2. Legislation and Regulation: The Stepchildren of Legal Education

Tilburg law school could make a difference if it succeeds in combining and translating two of its strengths in the field of research to legal education, namely the expertise and past performance in legislation & regulation and the experience with a variety of legal research methods ranging from comparative research to law and economics and socio-legal and empirical legal research.

But why legislation and regulation, one might ask. Is the fact that Tilburg's law faculty happens to have past performance in these fields a good reason to bet on these features in the battle to overcome the challenges of globalisation? The answer is yes and no. No because globalisation also requires substantive training in other areas, such as an introduction to the most important legal systems of the world, knowledge about international trade and finance, European and international law et cetera. Yes because legislation and regulation are underdeveloped topics in the law school curricula in most law schools in the world of today.

In the overwhelming majority of both European and U.S. law schools the role model of the judiciary is still dominant. Learning to think like a lawyer currently means learning to think like a judge. Since the heydays of Roman law we have been teaching students to apply the law to cases. The model for doing this in a very systematic way is in the U.S. even called the 'case method', which was introduced around 1870 by Christopher Columbus Langdell, the famous former Dean of Harvard Law School, who literally changed the way law was (and still is) being taught in American law schools.[6] What is interesting though is that another Harvard Law School Dean, Elena Kagan, who has now become a Supreme Court judge, also introduced an important and much debated curriculum reform at Harvard in 2006.[7] She motivated the move away from the Langdellian model,

---

[6] See Edward Rubin, 'What's Wrong with Langdell's Method and What to do About it?' (2007) 60(2) Vanderbilt Law Review 609.

[7] Elena Kagan, The Harvard Law School Revisited, Green Bag, (2008) 475-481 <http://www.greenbag.org/v11n4/v11n4_kagan.pdf> accessed 28 July 2012.

which has been so successful at Harvard for so long by arguing: 'From the beginning of law school, students should learn to locate what they are learning about public and private law in the United States within the context of a larger universe - global networks of economic regulation and private ordering, public systems created through multilateral relations among states, and different and widely varying legal cultures and systems.'[8]

Introducing a course on legislation and regulation (better known as 'LegReg') was one of the major changes, next to the introduction of comparative law methods and complex problem solving. The LegReg course: 'considers the justifications for modern regulation, the structure of the modern administrative state, the incentives that influence the behaviour of the various actors, and the legal rules that help to structure the relationships among Congress, the agencies, and the courts.'[9]

Now, what has puzzled me ever since 2006 when the curriculum change at Harvard was first introduced, followed by other law schools,[10] is: how is it possible that a top law school in the U.S., which has never been accused of being too progressive, in a common law country with a strong and long tradition of judicial law-making, is capable of understanding that globalisation and the rise of 'the regulatory' state are so strongly intertwined, whereas most European law faculties apparently still fail to see this? Or if they don't fail to see it, why have especially civil law countries, with a tradition of legislative law-making, not introduced obligatory courses on legislation and regulation in their bachelor curricula? I think there are a number of possible reasons: 1) legislation and regulation are considered to be matters of politics and policy-making that lawyers better not engage in 2) we think that most law students end up in law firms or working in or for the judiciary 3) we believe that what lawyers should do is apply the law, which does not necessarily presuppose knowledge about how laws and regulations are being made and 4) learning how to create statutes and regulations requires a firm knowledge about non-doctrinal legal methods.

Without going into too much detail I think the first three assumptions are wrong and only the fourth one is correct, but not fatal.

Of course legislation and regulation have a strong political dimension, but so has judicial law-making, especially in the case of decisions by the

---

[8] See: CNS News (2012) <http://cnsnews.com/news/article/harvard-law-dean-kagan-did-not-require-study-us-constitutional-law-did-require-study> accessed 28 July 2012.

[9] Harvard Law School, News (2012) http://www.law.harvard.edu/current/careers/ocs/employers/about-our-students/the-new-1l-curriculum.html accessed 20 July 2012.

[10] Ethan J Leib, 'Adding Legislation Courses to the First-Year Curriculum, Journal of Legal Education' (2008) 58(2) Journal of Legal Education 166.

highest/constitutional courts. Apart from that, regulation also has features that are closely linked to fact finding, effectiveness and efficiency where decisions need to be even more evidence-based than judicial decisions in individual cases. Furthermore, I don't have all the job market figures at hand but for the situation in the Netherlands I know for sure that the majority of law students do not end up in a law firm or in the judiciary. The biggest employer by far for lawyers is the government.[11] I would not be surprised if the same applies elsewhere, since the tremendous growth of law-making by the administration is certainly not unique for the Netherlands. Most of the rule-making both in Europe and the U.S. has been outsourced by parliaments to executive bodies, private regulators (e.g. standardisation bodies) and specialised agencies.

From that perspective it is absurd that we do have a successful Academy of Legislation in The Hague with hundreds of applicants each year, but one that is staffed by the government instead of being part of our universities where legislation and regulation are still absent apart from a handful of courses on the master level. Apparently, there is a market for legislative drafters and regulators, but universities avoid the competition. Why? Even at the European level we see organisations, such as EIPA (European Institute of Public Administration) taking a large part of the market for the professional training of EU lawyers. Law schools with aspirations to meet the needs of globalisation should not let that happen.

The fourth reason mentioned above of why law schools both in Europe and in the US have overlooked legislation and regulation in their education programmes has to do with the fact that designing rules and regulations requires more and other research methods than judicial law-making. In particular the translation from policy plans to legal rules involves knowledge of public administration (policy design), evaluation methods (*ex ante and ex post*), law and economics (cost and benefits of regulations/risk analysis), comparative law methodology (how do other regimes deal with similar problems?), sociology of law (consideration of alternative modes of regulation, such as self-regulation/co-regulation and for instance compliance issues), law and psychology (behaviour modification) and so on. Presented like this, the development of LegReg seems a mission impossible but it so happens that our faculty has expertise in most of these domains in the field of research. Therefore, the main challenge would be to bring this

---

[11] See for the facts and figures, Menno Bouwes, De vorming van de wetgevingsjurist, in: Hedi Schouten (red), *De opleiding van wetgevingsjuristen en wetgevingsonderzoekers in vergelijkend perspectief* (Wolf Legal Publishers 2011).

knowledge together and translate it to legal education. Not an easy task but certainly not impossible for those who believe in the solidarity of our faculty staff.

3. A Proposal for a LegReg Course in Tilburg

Would this LegReg course not be very nation-state oriented instead of answering the needs of a globalised legal practice, one might ask? I think this does not have to be the case, especially if LegReg will concentrate on theories and methods of law-making instead of on topics like statutory interpretation, institutions and competences. Therefore, I believe the emphasis should lie on the preparatory phase of the rule-making process because that is where most of the action is. There, one will need to think about the problem definition, about what causes the problem, about regulatory alternatives, about respecting higher law and legal principles, about compliance and enforcement issues et cetera.

For a large part these issues arise in every legal regime and as long as the topics/problems that are chosen to illustrate the choices that need to be made in the regulatory process appeal to a broad and international audience such a course could be a success. Having given such courses abroad in different places for different audiences (practitioners and students) I believe it is certainly doable. In my view a LegReg course should, however, go beyond *ex cathedra* teaching and needs to include clinical work (drafting practice, internships, policy research) that will only make the course more interesting to students, since they will have to get more involved, in the meanwhile, developing both their research skills and their ability to cooperate with others in complex problem solving.

These are exactly the things that are still missing in the regular curriculum, which we are currently trying to solve by upgrading the academic level of the regular bachelor curriculum. For a LegReg course as such we do not need a separate 'global law bachelor'. What we could do instead is offering the same course both in English and in Dutch. Technically, this is manageable, but of course doing it on the Harvard level of sophistication would require that we put our heads and talents together and invest serious time and energy in developing course materials, assignments and new ways of examination. These could even be tested first if we are afraid, like they initially were at Harvard, that the students will not appreciate the course.

What might give us hope is that at Harvard the LegReg course has proven to be the most popular new course in the first year. Although I realise that

Tilburg University is not Harvard, I have no doubt this can be done. My colleague Edward Rubin, the former Dean of Vanderbilt and strong adherent of curriculum reform in U.S. law schools, who was in Tilburg last September to speak about the role of legislation in legal education, has convinced me of the fact that we should be able to do it even better than most law schools in the U.S. This is due to our longer tradition with legislative law-making and also due to the fact that our legislative and regulatory policy is better developed and has already been heavily tested by the forces of globalisation through the exposure to European law. Moving from Europeanisation to globalisation is a much smaller step than what was needed to be taken in the U.S., where looking to developments in the rest of the legal world was, until recently, not well-developed. So perhaps, Tilburg could actually become the Harvard of the Low Countries in the field of legislation and regulation. Who would not want that?

A Regulatory Approach to Global Constitutional Analysis*

Anne Meuwese
Associate Professor of Public Law, Tilburg Law School, The Netherlands
anne.meuwese@tilburguniversity.edu

Abstract
This contribution draws attention to one of the challenges for contemporary public law thought: the emergence of 'problem-solving thinking' among public actors, alongside or in competition with, the more traditional 'competence-oriented' thinking. It is then proposed to supplement constitutional analysis with regulatory analysis so as to include 'alternative mechanisms' with the capacity to aid the *Rechtsstaat*. These mechanisms could be based on 'community' or 'competition' as alternative control modes.

Keywords
constitutionalism; regulation; competence

1. Introduction

Constitutional analysis is having a hard time fulfilling its traditional 'core business': answering questions of 'who may decide what, under what conditions?' Globalization means that actors responsible for public decision-making often transgress territorial and legal boundaries, causing the state not quite to disappear, but to disaggregate 'into its separate, functionally distinct parts'.[1] This is not only true for specialized public authorities, but also for those public actors with tasks defined in more general terms, such as Ombudsmen, audit institutions and even courts and parliaments. The culture within these institutions and the professional identity of the people working there is influenced by norms which transcend a national context.

---

* Comments on an earlier draft by Tilburg Law School PhD students in the context of their reading group on regulation are gratefully acknowledged.

[1] Anne-Marie Slaughter, 'The Real New World Order' (1997) 76 Foreign Affairs 183, 184.

Although public law traditionally prefers to abstract from the fact that 'public action' is 'human action', acknowledgement of social and institutional practices as part of constitutional realities is now wide-spread. However, we still lack research strategies for *how* to capture these practices in a way that is still relevant to legal debates. As part of the scholarly quest to grasp the interaction between the changing social reality and the development of that part of the law aimed at delineating the exercise of public power, we use various headings and lenses, often zooming in on specific challenges. For instance, there is the waning of the principle of territoriality in public law as one such a challenge, as well as the increasing informality of relationships between public actors.

This contribution takes a related challenge for contemporary public law thought as one possible lens for gauging the effects of globalization on public law: the emergence of 'problem-solving thinking' among public actors, alongside or in competition with, the more traditional 'competence-oriented' thinking. The main problem here is a diminishing relevance of constitutional analysis: how can we meaningfully say something about the role of law in constraining the exercise of power if the latter – our research object – is a moving target we have no means of keeping up with? This contribution proposes a 'regulatory approach' as one way of incorporating 'problem-driven' actions that have objectives similar to the objectives of constitutional law in the analysis.

Theoretical efforts, aimed at addressing various challenges in our collective understanding of constitutional dynamics in a globalizing world, have come from constitutional pluralism and constitutional dialogue theory. The central idea of constitutional pluralism is to 'stretch' the idea of constitutional discourse to multiple polity settings and even non-polity settings. Thus, normative sites that could at most be qualified as 'constitutional' in an aspirational or relational sense, may be seen as 'worthy of consideration in constitutional terms'.[2] This choice is made because the 'continuous reflection on the legitimacy of authoritative decision-making'[3] is seen as an essential element of constitutionalism.

Constitutional dialogue theory shares this view of constitutionalism, but emphasizes the loss of a monopoly of constitutional interpretation on the part of the three classic branches and analyses a wide range of actors as

---

[2] Neil Walker, 'The Idea of Constitutional Pluralism' (2002) 65 Modern Law Review 317, 341-342.

[3] ibid 358.

constitutional actors.[4] Although both theories are controversial, we can see their influence in terms of the emergence of more discourse-centered and actor-centered approaches in global constitutional analysis. This contribution builds on these approaches and suggests a complementary approach that is effect-centered and relies on the idea that constitutional law, too, can be usefully viewed as 'regulation'.

2. Two Types of Thinking among Public Law Actors

This section juxtaposes 'competence-oriented thinking' and 'problem-solving thinking' and illustrates the impact of these parallel ways of thinking on public law's capacity to exercise control over exercises of public power.

2.1. *Competence-oriented thinking*

If there would be one term to distinguish the legal approach from any other disciplinary approach, it would be 'competence'. As expressed in this fairly typical quote: '[c]ontrary to other disciplines (...) law is less interested in how decisions are made in practice, but rather poses the question of whether the relevant actors were competent, taking into account the legal (...) basis of the decision'.[5] In many public law courses in law school curricula, competence is presented as the main trigger and limit for intervention by actors exercising and supervising public power. However, a focus on 'competence' in answering questions regarding task allocation among public actors or the bindingness of decisions and measures, can amount to the exclusion of *de facto* exercise of public power. This is for instance the case when commercially sold private standards are consistently being excluded from public law controls by the courts, even if they are elevated to a privileged position through references in public law rules.[6]

---

[4] Bradley M Bakker, 'Blogs as Constitutional Dialogue: Rekindling the Dialogic Promise?' (2008) 63 NYU Annual Survey of American Law 215; Christine Bateup, 'The Dialogic Promise: Assessing the Normative Potential of Theories of Constitutional Dialogue' (2006) 71 Brooklyn Law Review 1109.

[5] Ramses A Wessel, 'A Legal Approach to EU Studies' in Knud Erik Jørgensen, Mark A Pollack and Ben Rosamond (eds), *Handbook of European Union Politics* (Sage Publications 2006) 109.

[6] HR 22 June 2012, LJN: BW0393.

The limits of this type of thinking are also apparent when clear instances of public exercise of power are the object of analysis. Public law research often focuses on 'official' norms (e.g. 'public actors shall not impede free speech' or 'the minister bears responsibility for actions taken in the policy area assigned to him') and the legal enforcement thereof. However, when these norms fail to achieve their intended effect – as certainly happens in the case of the examples provided – we often lack the scholarly tools to creatively look for a diagnosis and a solution.

2.2. *Problem-solving thinking*

One possible consequence of the globalization of relations between public law actors is the contestation or marginalization of 'competence' as a trigger for actions under public law.[7] Increased transnational interaction among peers and ensuing socialization are likely to foster a more instrumental attitude among various public law actors. Public tasks and norms become driven by problems and the will to solve them, rather than by competences as such. This is not the place to delve into empirical accuracy or normative implications of this claim. These matters are part of a larger research agenda. In any case, 'competence-oriented thinking' and 'problem-solving thinking' are not necessarily mutually exclusive as drivers for actions under public law. For instance, whereas it is clear that parliaments still operate mainly within the former framework, they are also characterized as 'watchdogs',[8] which should work with 'assessments', 'benchmarks' etc.

'Problem-solving thinking' can easily be linked to changes in the nature of regulatory governance, not only in the narrow sense of the rise of agencies and the broad delegation of powers to them, but also in the broader sense of 'a new culture of control over regulators'.[9] One concrete example concerns the rise of audit as 'meta-regulation'.[10] Traditionally, courts of auditors mainly possess competences to appraise the regularities of public

---

[7] Andrea Hamann and Hélène Ruiz Fabri, 'Transnational Networks and Constitutionalism' [2008] International Journal of Constitutional Law 481; Christian Joerges, Inger-Johanne Sand and Gunther Teubner (eds), *Transnational Governance and Constitutionalism* (Hart Publishing 2004).

[8] Ian Cooper, 'The Watchdogs of Subsidiarity: National Parliaments and the Logic of Arguing in the EU' (2006) 44 Journal of Common Market Studies 281.

[9] Terence Daintith and Alan C Page, *The Executive in the Constitution, Structure, Autonomy and Internal Control* (Oxford University Press 1999).

[10] Sasha Courville, Christine Parker and Helen Watchirs, 'Introduction: Auditing in Regulatory Perspective' (2003) 25 Law & Policy 179.

finance. Increasingly, they carry out 'performance audits' on concrete projects, using strictly defined methodologies. However, arguably, as the result of increased networking among national and supranational audit institutions, the idea that '[q]uality and results of regulatory management shall be subject for public audit'[11] has become popular.

The telling aspect of this example is the reasoning – presented as self-evident – that *because* legislative and regulatory activity generally are important, they *should* be subject to the kind of control audit that institutions are good at delivering. The European Court of Auditors did in fact carry out such a concrete audit,[12] stretching the 'audit' format to the maximum when arriving at what were essentially normative statements about the proper institutional relations within the European Commission and between the EU co-legislators. Especially among non-judicial review institutions, constitutional 'competence creep' appears often not too experienced as such by the institution in question – possibly because the institution is in 'problem-solving thinking' mode.

3. Developing a Regulatory Approach to Constitutional Analysis

This section explores a different way of reacting to the phenomenon that actors (public and private ones) involved in shaping the control over the exercise of public power define their role in instrumental terms. Different, that is, from the typical public law scholar's reflex to try to bring constitutional problem-solving behaviour in line with competence-oriented thinking, or, - if that is not possible - declare it unconstitutional. The main reason for this is not so much that this reflex is 'wrong' *per se*, but rather that a lot of 'controlling of public actors' escapes constitutional analysis – and therefore possibly the test of constitutional values – altogether.

A regulatory approach to constitutional analysis may be one useful strategy to cast the net wider so as to include *de facto* exercises of public power. The 'regulatory perspective on law' has been reasonably successful in the past.[13] In general it emphasizes the objective of shaping socially valued

11 Speaking notes by Dr Tuomas Pöysti, Auditor General European Court of Auditors' Seminar on 'The Future of Public Auditing and Accountability in the European Union', Luxembourg, 18 October 2007.

12 European Court of Auditors, 'Impact Assessments in the EU institutions: Do they support decision-making?' Special Report No 3/2010 (Publications Office of the European Union 2010).

13 Christine Parker and others (eds), *Regulating Law* (Oxford University Press 2004).

behaviour through standard setting and monitoring and the analytical separation of 'problem definitions', 'objectives' and 'instruments'.[14] Following Scott, locating stable, but not necessarily codified limitations on the exercise of legislative and executive power implies identifying examples where institutionalized solutions have been developed.[15]

Challenging the assumption that all constitutional norms and institutions emanate from an authoritative constitutional text frees up conceptual space for alternative norms and institutions which are contributing to the control of public power.[16] Applying this approach to the constitutional realm implies a revival of the 'regulation inside government' literature,[17] which initiated the application of insights from regulation theory to non-sectoral governance.

An important additional step is to extend to the possibility that private actors perform regulatory functions and engage in generic control of exercises of public power.[18] In the regulatory approach a 'constitutional framework' is defined as the social structures and institutions that allocate and restrain power at the macro-political level. Scott has put forward a definition of constitutionalism reflecting this approach, which is inspired by the discipline of 'regulation': 'the commitment to effectively limit the exercise of legislative and executive power'.[19] Institutionalization of regulatory mechanisms can occur through law, through social mechanisms or through both simultaneously. For instance, not only classical constitutional instruments such as review powers can help political principals keep tabs on agents, 'disclosure' can also have an equivalent effect.[20]

Regulation studies may also go a long way not just in analyzing but also in accounting for the rise of 'problem-solving' actions that are functionally equivalent to public law controls, when it postulates that regulation is a

14 Bronwen Morgan and Karen Yeung, *An Introduction to Law and Regulation: Text and Materials* (Cambridge University Press 2007).

15 Colin Scott, 'Regulatory Governance and the Challenge of Constitutionalism', in Dawn Oliver, Tony Prosser and Richard Rawlings (eds), *The Regulatory State: Constitutional Implications* (Oxford University Press 2010).

16 Colin Scott, 'Regulating Constitutions', in Parker (n 13).

17 Christopher Hood and others (eds), *Regulation inside Government. Waste-Watchers, Quality Police and Sleaze-Busters* (Oxford University Press 1999).

18 Jody Freeman, 'The Private Role in Public Governance' (2000) 75 New York University Law Review 543.

19 Scott (n 15).

20 Mathew McCubbins, Roger G Noll and Barry R Weingast, 'Structure and Process, Politics and Policy: Administrative Arrangements and the Political Control of Agencies' (1989) 75 Virginia Law Review 431.

substitute for social trust. In the words of Levi-Faur and Jordana, '[i]t might well be that the Regulatory State and the demand for more transparency and accountability are both outcomes of the shift in the balance of trust between different professions and social groups'.[21] Indeed, governments start regulating when they do not trust citizens. Why should it not work the other way around in times when trust among citizens in their governments is in decline? One example is the emergence of NGOs such as OMB Watch in the US, which review the actions of a certain part of government across the board and 'name and shame' it when falling short of its own standards.

A clarification is in order. First, developing a 'regulatory approach to constitutional analysis' undeniably has an instrumental ring to it. However, the instrumentality proposed here is different from the one employed in 'new constitutionalism' experimented with in the nineties. This deemed that constitutionalism should not only be concerned with the control of the exercise of public power, but also with institutional design so as to achieve economic efficiency.[22] The regulatory approach does put the 'traditional preoccupations' upfront, but uses 'smart mechanisms' to achieve them. Thus, the approach taken is not a purely instrumental one: these instruments are connected to normative discourses through which constitutions are 'justified, defended, criticized, denounced or otherwise engaged with'[23] and may have capacity for empowerment.

Considering law as regulation is already commonplace in many sector-specific legal fields, but is underdeveloped in constitutional law even though this field of law is explicitly aimed at regulating the behavior of public actors. Developing a regulatory approach to constitutional analysis includes attention for the fit between the mechanisms used in constitutional and administrative law on the one hand and insights from behavioral sciences on the other. For instance, if we observe a lack of interest in parliaments to scrutinize legislative bills for compatibility with the constitution, we may lament this and point to political constraints, but rarely do we ask how we can provide incentives to change this behavior.

Elaborating somewhat the idea of 'smart mechanisms' can illustrate what a regulatory approach to constitutional analysis might look like. One central premise of the approach is the existence of a plurality of control modes. An oft-used and classic typology of control mechanisms distinguishes

---

21 Jacint Jordana and David Levi-Faur (eds), *The Politics of Regulation in the Age of Governance* (Edward Elgar 2004).

22 Stephen L Elkin and Karol E Soltan (eds), *A New Constitutionalism. Designing Political Institutions for a Good Society* (The University of Chicago Press 1993).

23 Walker (n 2).

four types of underlying modalities of control: 'law', 'social norms', 'markets' and 'architecture'.[24] These have been relabeled 'hierarchy', 'community', 'competition' and 'design' in the regulation literature,[25] which has produced rich insights on the functioning of 'alternative instruments' that depend on control modalities other than law/hierarchy.[26]

Regulatory scholarship has produced rich insights on how 'alternative instruments' may use 'competition' and 'community' as control mechanisms. In the world of transnational governance these insights are being put to practice in functional solutions for disciplining national public actors. Examples are best practice exchange in horizontal transnational networks of public actors (e.g. courts of auditors), peer review (e.g. OECD peer reviews) and naming and shaming (e.g. World Bank rankings).

4. Concluding Remarks

Public law – or constitutional law as the law *for* government rather than the law *of* government – does not have a monopoly when it comes to regulating the exercise of public power. This is the case both within the nation and in processes of a global nature. This paper argues that instead of trying to reclaim that monopoly, for instance by emphasizing constitutionalization processes and the importance of 'competence', we are better off embracing the regulatory function of public law mechanisms as part of our research approach.

Much of the role-shifting that is going on among public actors – not to mention the public task poaching by private actors – will never enter the radar of public law *scholars* as long as they keep the same competence-oriented focus the public law *system* has. Infusing constitutional analysis with elements of regulation studies may help develop an effect-centered approach that can be complementary to discourse-centered and actor-centered approaches.

The regulatory approach replaces the famous paradox that constitutional law is deemed inadequate yet vital[27] with a new one. Although constitutionalism is primarily a commitment to restrain the exercise of public

---

[24] Lawrence Lessig, *Code and Other Laws of Cyberspace* (Basic Books 1999).

[25] Andrew Murray and Colin Scott, 'Controlling the New Media: Hybrid Responses to New Forms of Power' (2002) 65 Modern Law Review 491.

[26] Robert Baldwin and Martin Cave, *Understanding Regulation: Theory, Strategy and Practice* (Oxford University Press 1999).

[27] Walker (n 2) 327.

power, we must be prepared to abandon the archetypical form of restraint, namely hierarchical mechanisms, in favor of heterarchical mechanisms. In terms of a research agenda, this implies a systematic analysis of the conditions under which community-based and competition-based instruments are effective in solving constitutional problems. The extent to which mechanisms such as these, which escape the very concept of competence, are functionally similar to controls from administrative or constitutional law is a matter of empirical investigation.[28] This is not to say that all constitutional law scholars should take a regulatory approach and become empiricists; complementarity of research approaches and cooperation between researchers with different specializations and skills are an inescapable feature of the future of global constitutional analysis.

28 See also Maurice Adams' contribution in this issue.

Some Preliminaries to Global Law and Human Rights

Daniel Augenstein*
Assistant Professor at Tilburg University, Department of Philosophy, The Netherlands
d.h.augenstein@tilburguniversity.edu

Abstract
The article considers the relationship between economic globalisation and the universalisation of legal human rights obligations.

Keywords
human rights; globalisation; economic; obligation; multi-national; corporation

1. Delineating Global Law and Approximating Global Legal Studies

Rather than attempting a positive definition of 'global law', it may be more fruitful – and less controversial – to set out by noting what it is not. Such a 'negative' approach that delineates the boundaries of the concept appears particularly appropriate if the 'intimations' of global law[1] are considered piece and parcel of a legal paradigm shift that draws its transformative power from a present diagnosis of crisis but that will only be fully comprehended after its completion, that is, with historical hindsight.[2] Accordingly, after some reflection on the negativity of global law and the thrust of global legal studies, I shall sketch out three symptoms of crises of the Westphalian state-based paradigm of human rights protection brought about by

* For helpful comments and suggestions, I am grateful to my colleagues Morag Goodwin and Hans Lindahl.

1 N Walker, 'Intimations of Global Law' (June 2012) Tilburg Law Lectures Series, Montesquieu Seminars.

2 On the notion of 'paradigm shift' see T Kuhn, *The Structure of Scientific Revolutions* (3rd edn, University of Chicago Press 1996).

patterns of (economic) globalisation. In line with the not-yet-realised nature of the paradigm shift, the final section places human rights in the context of transformations of statehood in globalising economies.

Global law is not, and will not be for the time being, a law of planetary extensions that aspires to regulate all human beings in all places at all times. More specifically, global law is neither constituted as a national legal order of global scale, nor is it congruent with an international legal order that populates the entirety of the globe with sovereign state entities. As regards the former, it is tempting to invert William Twining's call to revive 'general jurisprudence' in and for an age of globalisation in order to shed light on the negativity of global law:[3] global law lacks comprehensive legal authority, that is, it does not 'claim authority to regulate all forms of behaviour' within a unified and all-encompassing global legal order.[4] As regards the latter, at least in its 'thin' positivist, contractual and functionalist variations, the global ambitions of international law are limited to ensuring the peaceful co-existence of territorially localised state entities.

The important point of this crude description of the Westphalian state-of-affairs is that what may be called 'public' approaches to global law[5] have to come to terms with the segmentation of legal and political authority in the global realm. The national/international divide dissects authority into, on the one hand, a constitutional relationship between rulers and ruled within the sovereign state and, on the other hand, an international relationship between sovereign states.[6] Hence, while the attraction of appeals to global public law stems from the shortcomings of the international

---

[3] William Twining discards global jurisprudence (that is, 'looking at law solely or mainly from a global perspective') in favour of a general jurisprudence that inquires whether and to what extent 'it is meaningful, feasible and desirable to generalise – conceptually, normatively, empirically, legally – across legal traditions and cultures', see W Twining, *General Jurisprudence* (Cambridge University Press 2009).

[4] See J Raz, *The Authority of Law* (Oxford University Press 2009) 117.

[5] Which includes global constitutional and global administrative law, as well as cosmopolitan readings of international law, see, e.g., A Rosas, 'State Sovereignty and Human Rights: towards a Global Constitutional Project (1995) 18 Political Studies 61; A Peters, 'Compensatory Constitutionalism: The Function and Potential of Fundamental International Norms and Structures' (2006) 19 Leiden Journal of International Law 579; A Peters, 'The Merits of Global Constitutionalism' (2009) 16 Indiana Journal of Global Legal Studies 397; J Habermas, *The Postnational Constellation* (Polity Press 2001); and B Kingsbury N Krisch & R Stewart, 'The Emergence of Global Administrative Law' (2005) 68(15) Law and Contemporary Problems 15.

[6] See, e.g., R Jackson, 'Sovereignty in World Politics: A Glance at the Conceptual and Historical Landscape' (1993) XLVII Political Studies 431, 433.

compartmentalisation of the globe into territorial state entities, it cannot lay claim to a global political community akin to that of the nation that would render its authority legitimate in the light of a global public good.

If 'public' approaches to global law strive to transform the international legal order into a global *ordre public*, a prominent variation of 'private' global law postulates the development of a new 'conflicts of laws' approach to mediate the tensions between the partial rationalities of functionally differentiated global regimes.[7] Arguably, the segmentation of 'public' authority in the global realm correlates with a sectoral differentiation of 'private' transnational regimes that claim global validity.[8] The mismatch between a highly globalised economy and weakly globalised politics leads to a privatisation of political power and presses 'for the emergence of a global law that has no legislation, no political constitution and no politically ordered hierarchy of norms'.[9] However, far from positing a unitary legal order of planetary extensions, Gunther Teubner's 'global law without a state' is intrinsically heterarchical and pluralistic. While global regimes claim worldwide validity unconstrained by the territorial national/international divide, they are delimited by virtue of their functional logic in a socially fragmented world:

> In the place of an illusory integration of a differentiated global society, law can only, at the very best, offer a kind of damage limitation. Legal instruments cannot overcome contradictions between different social rationalities. The

[7] See G Teubner's seminal contribution '"Global Bukovina": Legal Pluralism in the World Society', in G Teubner (ed), *Global Law Without a State* (Dartmouth 1997); A Fischer-Lescano & G Teubner, 'Regime Collisions: The Vein Search for Legal Unity in the Fragmentation of Global Law' (2004) 25 Michigan Journal of International Law 999; C Joerges work in the EU and WTO contexts represents a different 'global' approach to conflicts of law, see e.g. his edited collection *After Globalisation. New Patterns of Conflict and their Sociological and Legal Re-construction* (RECON Report No 15 2011).

[8] Whether one considers these global developments as co-evolutionary or incommensurable may ultimately depend on one's view of the relationship between political integration and social fragmentation in the state legal order. As Hans Lindahl perceptively notes, 'if the emergence of the nation-state both inaugurates and arrests social differentiation, the constitutionalisation of [global] social subsystems heralds the completion of *das unvollendete Projekt der Moderne*. Not the realisation of individual and collective autonomy through the foundation of a global polity, as Habermas would have it, but rather the autonomisation of systems, that is, the "worldwide realization of functional differentiation" marks the historical completion of modernity', see H Lindahl, 'Societal Constitutionalism as Political Constitutionalism: Reconsidering the Relation between Politics and Global Legal Orders' (2011) 20(2) Social & Legal Studies 230, FN 2.

[9] G Teubner, 'Foreword: Legal Regimes of Global Non-state Actors', in G Teubner (ed), *Global Law Without a State* (Dartmouth 1997).

> best law can offer – to use a variation upon [Martti Koskenniemi's] apt description of international law – is to act as a 'gentle civilizer of social systems'.[10]

Hence, and contrary to what the label may suggest, global law does not encompass the globe in any holistic sense but remains embedded in its (trans-) national, (trans-) territorial, and (trans-) sectoral contexts. At the same time, it may be this very moment of *trans*ition on a continuum from the national and international to the global and the local that best captures the essence of global approaches to law. In this vein, global legal studies could be said to concern itself with ways in which law positions itself in relation to globalisation. Yet different from variations of intra-, inter-, trans-, and post-national law whose primary concern remains with conceptualising law's extension and escape from the state (whether spatial, structural, or normative), global legal studies also inquires law's re-contraction and re-capture in the local context of the global.

On the national/international continuum, global legal studies comprises approaches that broaden the analytical tool-box of traditional state-centred jurisprudence,[11] as well as normative approaches that strive to compensate for negative externalities on the territorial state and its citizens created by global interdependencies.[12] On a global/local continuum, it comprises approaches that reconstruct law along the complementary lines of 'globalised localisms' and 'localised globalisms'[13], for example, by tracing out trajectories from intra-state to global legal pluralism,[14] or by vesting

---

10 Fischer-Lescano & Teubner, (n 7) 1045, with reference to M Koskenniemi, *The Gentle Civilizer of Nations: The Rise and Fall of International Law 1870-1960* (Cambridge University Press 2001).

11 See for example, W Twining's *General Jurisprudence* (n 3) and his earlier *Globalisation and Legal Theory* (Cambridge University Press 2000); B Tamanaha, *A General Jurisprudence of Law and Society* (Oxford University Press 2001).

12 For example, Jürgen Habermas' call for the development of a *Weltinnenpolitik* or Anne Peters compensatory global constitutionalism, n (5).

13 The distinction between 'globalised localisms' and 'localised globalisms' is taken from B de Sousa Santos' *Toward a New Legal Common Sense* (2nd edn, Butterworths: 2002). While 'globalised localisms' refer to local phenomena that are successfully globalised, 'localised globalisms' occur when local conditions change in response to global influences.

14 See, e.g., the works of R Cotterrell and P Zumbansen on 'legal transnationalism' and 'transnational legal pluralism': R Cotterrell, 'Transnational Communities and the Concept of Law' (2008) 21(1) Ratio Juris 1; R Cotterrell, 'Spectres of Transnationalism: Changing Terrains of Sociology of Law' (2009) 36(4) Journal of Law and Society 481; P Zumbansen, 'Transnational Legal Pluralism' (2010) 1(2) Transnational Legal Theory 141.

legal authority in the regulatory spaces of (global) governance without (territorial) government.[15]

2. Moments of Crises: Human Rights and Economic Globalisation

For my present and rather limited purposes, global law may thus be understood as comprising *legal* responses to the crises of the Westphalian state-based paradigm of human rights protection brought about by patterns of (economic) *globalisation*. In a nutshell, the Westphalian distinction between national-constitutional and international law compartmentalises human rights within and between sovereign states. On the one hand, the universal 'rights of man' of the Declarations – the human being endowed with inalienable rights by virtue of being human – translate into a political relationship between the state and its people and are legally institutionalised in the national-constitutional order.[16] On the other hand, human rights increasingly feature as international standards of political legitimacy to which states strive to (pretend to) live up to in their dealings with each other.[17]

In both dimensions, the principal concern remains with obligations of public authorities to protect human rights in relation to their own citizens and on their own territory. This leads to what Gibney, Tomaševski and Vedsted-Hansen, in an early seminal contribution to the debate, have labelled a 'paradox' of human rights law: 'human rights are declared to be universal, yet state responsibility for their violations is limited by territoriality as well as citizenship'.[18] Moreover, it explains how a state's legal human rights obligations within its constitutional polity are transformed into mere human rights policies in its international relations with other states.

The descriptive accuracy and normative appeal of the ensuing divide between a state's 'internal' human rights obligations and its 'external'

---

[15] L Cata Backer, 'Governance without Government: An Overview', Draft Paper presented at the Tilburg Centre for Transboundary Legal Development (May 2012), on file with the author; instructive on the OECD Guidelines for Multinational Corporations; L Cata Backer, 'Small steps towards an autonomous transnational legal system for the regulation of multinational corporations' (2009) 10(1) Melbourne Journal of International Law 258.

[16] See, e.g. J Habermas, 'On the Internal Relation between the Rule of Law and Democracy' in C Cronin & P De Greiff (eds), *The Inclusion of the Other* (MIT Press 2000).

[17] See, e.g., J Donnelly, *Universal Human Rights in Theory and Practice* (2nd edn, Cornell University Press 2003).

[18] M Gibney, K Tomaševski & J Vedsted-Hansen, 'Transnational State Responsibility for Violations of Human Rights' (1999) 12 Harvard Human Rights Journal 267.

human rights policies is increasingly put under strain by patterns of economic globalisation,[19] particularly in the context of operations of multinational corporations. Put crudely, the progressive emancipation of globalising economies from the state blurs the boundaries between domestic politics and foreign policies constitutive of the Westphalian conception of state sovereignty.[20] Yet this has not been accompanied by a parallel process of universalising the state's human rights obligations that remain vested in its territorial legal order. An often noted consequence of these developments is that human rights law fails where it is most needed: for the benefit of individuals in 'weak' host states of corporate investment that lack the capacity (and at times also the willingness) to protect human rights against business operations conducted with the (active) support or (passive) connivance of 'strong' home state governments.[21]

Let me briefly sketch out three related moments of this crisis. First, and from within the state-based paradigm, patterns of economic globalisation challenge the adequacy of the Westphalian reading of the distinctions between public and private, and between territorial and extraterritorial, in allocating human rights obligations within and between sovereign states. Economic globalisation has created increasing gaps between the operational capacities of global business entities and the regulatory capacities of territorial states. At the same time, the privatisation of state functions has shifted powers and responsibilities from governments to the market. Hence while – as a default rule – human rights are protected against public emanations of the state for the benefit of rights-holders physically located on the state's territory, creating a level playing field between states and globally operating business entities requires their extraterritorial protection in relation to private actors.

Secondly, and in transition from the state-based paradigm, the widening gap between globalised economies and state politics has given rise to alternative legal regimes to account for the human rights impacts of

---

[19] Understood in a broad sense of connoting the increased interdependency of states and private actors across national-territorial borders brought about by economic cooperation and competition; see e.g. the numerous United Nations communications on globalisation and human rights published over the past decade, most recently the Report of the Secretary General, 'Globalisation and its impact on the full enjoyment of all human rights' (26 July 2010) UN Doc A/65/171.

[20] See J Habermas (n 16).

[21] See further D Augenstein & D Kinley, 'Beyond the 100 Acre Wood: Navigating the Jurisdictional Jungle of Extraterritoriality, Multinational Corporations and Human Rights Violations' in S Deva & D Bilchitz (eds) *Human Rights Obligations of Business: Beyond the Corporate Responsibility to Respect?* (Cambridge University Press 2013) forthcoming.

multinational corporations which, in turn, further undermine the hegemony of the state and its (constitutional and international) human rights law. In a memorable lecture, Neil Walker has captured this tendential connection between the rise of the global and the fall of the state very well.[22] At one end of the national-international continuum, state law 'is increasingly rivalled by law otherwise spatially extended, including sub-state law, regional supranational law, transnational domain-specific private ordering, hybrid public-private ordering and, increasingly, new forms of global legal regime that neither claim universality nor obviously emanate from or respect the aggregative sovereign will'. At the other end of the continuum, the emergence of functionally differentiated transnational regimes and new forms of private and hybrid ordering threatens to undermine 'the idea of a shared "public" concern joining the various elements of international law'.[23] It may thus be that the complementary role of global law writ large is but a harbinger of its displacement of the Westphalian paradigm of human rights protection with, somewhat ironically, states becoming a driving force of their own marginalisation.

The third moment of crises I would like to draw attention to is perhaps the most critical from a human rights perspective. Whether or not one conceives – with Habermas[24] – of human rights as co-original with popular sovereignty, they certainly carry a significant part of the burden of transforming manifestations of state power into legitimate forms of political authority. The impact of economic globalisation on the statist distinction between constitutional human rights politics and international human rights policies gives rise to two as complementary as problematic developments. What we are arguably witnessing is an increasing bifurcation between territory-based forms of political authority that lose their regulatory grasp over global developments, and a de-territorialisation of legally unfettered state power in the coattails and service of the market.

For all the talk about the demise of state-based law, one should not underestimate the power that states still wield over the enjoyment of human rights in globalising economies. Examples abound:[25] states

---

22 N Walker, 'Out of Place and Out of Time: Law's Fading Co-ordinates' (2010) 14(1) Edinburgh Law Review 13.

23 ibid 36, 37.

24 See Habermas (n 16).

25 For a recent and instructive collection of concrete case-studies see F Coomans & R Künnemann (eds) *Cases and Concepts on Extraterritorial Obligations in the Area of Economic, Social and Cultural Rights* (Intersentia 2012).

authorizing, or not preventing, the operation of dangerous industrial and mining facilities by business entities that result in serious human rights violations; states delegating public functions to business entities in human rights sensitive areas such as the running of immigration and detention centres or the provision of security services; states' negligence of human rights impacts when contracting with business entities, such as in the context of investments by state-owned banks and pension funds in large-scale private construction projects; and states licensing or otherwise supporting the import or export of goods by business entities that have been produced, or will be used, in violation of international human rights standards.

3. The Transformations of Statehood in an Age of Globalisation

If the above analysis can lay some claim to empirical plausibility, one of the pressing questions for global law scholarship is how manifestations of institutionalised forms of power – whether public or private – can be re-channelled into legitimate forms of political authority. A related question from a human rights perspective is whether, in the absence of a global public good, all that can still mobilise individual empowerment towards collective self-restraint is a global *colère public* that validates human rights by means of scandalisation.[26] Arguably, and perhaps with a pinch of over-generalisation, many approaches to global law sketched out in section one can be read as attempting answers to these questions. While 'public' approaches to global human rights aim to counteract the hollowing out of the state by recovering the public and political nature of law at the global stage, 'private' global law without a state reinstates human rights as (self-) limitative constitutional norms of functionally differentiated global regimes that tame the destructive forces of their partial social rationalities.[27]

Instead of discussing the relative merits of these approaches, let me conclude my brief preliminaries to global law and human rights with a few words on my own research in this area that inquires the dissociation of the public and territorial nature of human rights from the Westphalian conception of statehood. In a nutshell, I am interested in transformations

[26] This position is attributed to N Luhmann, *Das Recht der Gesellschaft* (Suhrkamp 1993) ch 12.

[27] See especially Gunther Teubner's more recent work on global law and fundamental rights: G Teubner, 'Contextualising Polycontexturality' (2011) 20(2) Social & Legal Studies 210; and G Teubner, 'Transnational fundamental rights: horizontal effect?' (2011) 40(3) Rechtsfilosofie & Rechtstheorie 191.

of the public/private divide and the territoriality/extraterritoriality divide in globalising economies. As regards the former, the aim is to recover the political nature of the attribution of acts and actors to the public and the private that is concealed by the Westphalian re-interpretation of private human rights 'abuses' as violations of negative and positive state obligations. A good example is the discussion triggered in the United Kingdom some years back by an unduly restrictive judicial interpretation of section 6 of the Human Rights Act that imposes human rights obligations on private entities fulfilling public functions. The central political concern of the ensuing report of the UK Joint Committee on Human Rights is highlighted in its executive summary:

> As a result of the combined effects of a restrictive judicial interpretation of one particular subsection of the Act on the one hand, and the changing nature of private and voluntary sector involvement in public services on the other, a central provision of the Act has been compromised in a way which reduces the protection it was intended to give to people at some of the most vulnerable moments in their lives. The concern addressed by this report is that a narrow judicial view of the meaning of 'public authority' in section 6 of the Human Rights Act means that many private and voluntary sector providers of public services are considered to fall outside the scope of the Act, with no obligation to comply with the rights and freedoms it incorporated into domestic law.[28]

To conceptualise the territorial extension of political authority beyond the confines of the Westphalian state is a more intricate task, although the slogan of 'power entails responsibility' carried by both 'public' and 'private' approaches to human rights protection beyond the state[29] sums it up fairly well. A crucial element of this task is to disperse the epistemic bias against extraterritorial human rights obligations that is but the counter-part of the methodological nationalism of cruder versions of the doctrine of state sovereignty.[30] The common approach – that has also informed the work of the UN Special Representative on business and human rights[31] – is to

---

28 House of Lords & House of Commons Joint Committee on Human Rights, 'The Meaning of Public Authority under the Human Rights Act' (3 March 2004) Seventh Report of Session 2003-04, HL Paper 39 / HC 382.

29 See, respectively, R Lawson, 'Life after Banković: On the Extraterritorial Application of the European Convention on Human Rights' in F Coomans & M. T. Kamminga (eds) *Extraterritorial Application of Human Rights Treaties* (Intersentia 2004); and D Kinley & J Tadaki, 'From Talk to Walk: The Emergence of Human Rights Responsibilities for Corporations at International Law' (2004) 44(4) Virginia Journal of International Law 931.

30 I use methodological nationalism in Beck's sense here, see U Beck, 'Toward a New Critical Theory with a Cosmopolitan Extent' (2003) 10(4) Constellations 453.

31 See Report of the Special Representative of the Secretary-General on the issue of human rights and transnational corporations and other business enterprises, 'Guiding

assimilate extraterritorial human rights obligations to (prescriptive) extraterritorial jurisdiction under public international law, only to discard them as incompatible with the principles of sovereign equality and territorial integrity that reign over the international state community. However, while public international law is concerned with the legal competence of states to assert extraterritorial authority, extraterritorial human rights obligations are grounded in the facticity of the exercise of state power over individuals outside the state's territory.[32] This is paralleled by a distinction between an (state-territory based) 'all-or-nothing' approach and a (subject-based) 'gradual' approach to jurisdiction that determines the scope of the state's extraterritorial human rights obligations in proportionality to the level of control exercised over the person of the rights holder.[33]

The relationship between jurisdiction under public international law and international human rights treaties is admittedly more complex than that, yet it is worth pointing out that the traditional state-centred approach reifies the empirically less and less tenable distinction between 'internal' human rights politics and 'external' human rights policies by shifting the focus of debate from extraterritorial obligations imposed on states by virtue of human rights law to states' policy rationales to protect human rights in their foreign relations.

Let's just assume for a moment that there is some merit in what (among others) the UN Committee on Economic, Social and Cultural Rights has been preaching for over a decade now, namely that states are under an obligation to respect the human rights of individuals in third countries, and to prevent third parties from violating these rights in these countries by way of legal and political means in accordance with international law.[34] The question that arises on the eve of the Westphalian age is to whom such obligations would be owed. While an international lawyer may point to the

Principles on Business and Human Rights: Implementing the United Nations "Protect, Respect, Remedy" Framework' (21 March 2011) UN Doc A/HRC/17/31.

[32] For a review of the relevant case-law see Augenstein & Kinley (n 21); one of the clearest expressions of this principle is still the early dictum of the Human Rights Committee in *López Burgos*: what matters is 'not the place where the violation occurred, but rather (…) the relationship between the individual and the state in relation to a violation of any of the rights set forth in the Covenant, wherever they occurred', see HRC, *López Burgos v Uruguay*, Communication No. 52/1979 (29 July 1981) UN Doc CCPR/C/OP/1 para 12.1.

[33] See M Gondek, *The Reach of Human Rights in a Globalising World: Extraterritorial Application of Human Rights Treaties* (Intersentia 2009) for further references.

[34] See for all CESCR, 'General Comment 14: The right to the highest attainable standard of health' (11 August 2000) UN Doc E/C.12/2000/4 para 39.

other state, and a constitutional lawyer to the state's own people,[35] a global approach to human rights should press for the recognition that these obligations are owed to the individual subjected to the power of the state, anywhere and anywhen. Perhaps needless to add, the ensuing 'global' relationship between the state and the individual that rejoins power and authority beyond the national/international divide is bounded by the multiple sites of the state – and therefore does not constitute a unified global law of planetary extensions, either.

[35] I owe this insight to a discussion with Martin Loughlin.

The Global Legal Environment and its Future
Four Scenarios

Stavros Zouridis, Sam Muller, Laura Kistemaker & Morly Frishman
Members of The Hague Institute for the Internationalisation of Law
Tilburg University, The Netherlands
S.Zouridis@uvt.nl

Abstract
Both national and international law are created and upheld in a global legal environment that seems to be changing dramatically. Many lawyers and legal scholars have extensively signaled and analysed the internationalisation of law and the rise of private legal and governance regimes. In this article, these trends are used to explore the future of the global legal environment. The use of scenario techniques enables us to systematically scrutinise possible futures. In turn, the scenarios indicate major strategic challenges for both national legislators and international legal institutions.

Keywords
global legal environment; future scenarios; internationalization of law; private legal regimes

1. Predicting and Scanning the Future of Law

Legal futurism is not widespread among lawyers and legal scholars. Instead of writing legal science fiction novels, most lawyers and legal scholars prefer to meticulously scrutinise the law in order to establish what is legally valid. Since the future is too uncertain and anything may happen, why bother about it. The Law of the Future program we have set up attempts to break with this tradition.[1] Whereas predicting the future is impossible, the methodologies that have been developed by the future studies allow us to systematically scan possible futures. Instead of ignoring uncertainty, these methodologies embrace uncertainty by building theories on it. For example, scenario analysis enables us to imagine possible futures that are built

---

[1] Law of the Future Forum, 'How will law evolve in the next 20 years?' (2012) <www.lawofthefuture.org> accessed 31 July 2012.

on uncertain developments. In this article, we illustrate scenario analysis by applying it to the future of the global legal environment. A scenario refers to a story on what may happen.

All national legislators are confronted with a global legal environment in which authoritative rule making, rule enforcement, and processes of dispute resolution occur. Conceptually the global legal environment does not mean that global rules are made or that these rules are globally enforced. In our definition the global legal environment refers to a multi-layered phenomenon which includes all mechanisms of authoritative rule making, rule enforcement, and dispute resolution that transcend national borders. It emerges out of the actions of both public and private legal actors, the ideas and research of legal scholars, and the initiatives and actions of international institutions. Even though national legislators' behaviour affects the global legal environment, it emerges to a large extent without being directed.

A scenario analysis on the future of the global legal environment starts with mapping the major trends that occur now. These trends are presented in section two. The trends are then used to build future scenarios that picture possible futures of the global legal environment in section three. We conclude with a brief exploration of some implications of these scenarios for national legislators. The timeframe we have used for the scenarios extends to 2030. This timeframe is long enough to allow some imagination while it simultaneously prevents us from engaging in legal science fiction.

2. The Global Legal Environment: Major Trends

In order to map the trends in the global legal environment we have asked a number of legal scholars and lawyers from different disciplines and different parts of the world to write a paper on what they see happening in the global legal environment right now.[2] These papers indicate two major trends, which can be referred to as the internationalisation of law and the growth of private governance regimes. These trends are not new and have extensively been mapped in the literature. Both trends will be briefly explained.

First, a growing patchwork of international law, international institutions, and transnational cooperation is observed. Increasing international trade

[2] S Muller, S Zouridis, M Frishman, L Kistemaker, *The Law of the Future and the Future of Law* (TOAEP 2011).

goes along with the internationalisation of contract law, torts, business law, and intellectual property law. Since national laws are not harmonised, conflicts and gaps between national laws are increasingly revealed. These conflicts exert pressure on governments to harmonise their legislation and their legal systems. The internationalisation of law thus refers to growing interdependencies and interchange between national legal systems and the accommodation of national legal systems to these interdependencies and interchange. Internationalisation is a global trend but it is not happening in the same way, with the same depth, and in the same areas across the world. Two important clarifications must be made.

First, legal globalisation does not mean that a coherent corpus of global law is evolving. Legal globalisation is a patchwork both with regard to the legal areas involved and to the extent of internationalisation. For example, the legal globalisation of trade law is mainly located on the regional level. The EU is probably the most far-reaching instance. The patchwork pattern of internationalisation of the global legal environment also extends to the legal areas involved and the pace with which this development is unfolding. For example, the internationalisation of trade law seems to move faster than the internationalisation of criminal procedure. Second, legal globalisation does not imply voluntarism or a consciously built body of global law. Instead, incidents, crises, and the continuous manifestation of new problems are the primary drivers of the process. National legislators all over the world are confronted with political and legal problems that cannot be dealt with without the cooperation of other national legislators or international bodies. Migration, transnational criminal networks, terrorism, illicit trade, financial markets, and monetary crises compel national legislators to find solutions on a transnational level. There is no executive director.

The growth of private governance regimes for rule making, rule enforcement, and dispute resolution constitutes a second major trend. Both national and international law have firmly rested on public authority and state institutions. Nevertheless new private regimes seem to be booming. These private regimes appear in different shapes. A business sector, sometimes together with NGOs, can set standards, guidelines, or rules concerning governance or liabilities. For example, the Brewers of Europe have enacted the Responsible Commercial Communications Guidelines for the Brewing Industry.[3] The timber industry – with the Forest Stewardship

[3] The Brewers of Europe, 'Responsible Commercial Communications: Guidelines for the Brewing Industry' (2012) www.brewersofeurope.org/docs/publications/guidelines.pdf accessed 31 July 2012.

Council – produced standards on sustainable logging and the sale of timber.[4]

Sometimes an industry creates a standard contract or agreement. The Model Mine Development Agreement, developed in consultation with mining companies, governments, and civil society within the context of the International Bar Association, is a prime example.[5] Another facet of this trend is the growing use of alternative dispute resolution mechanisms instead of court systems. The eBay/PayPal resolution centre solves around 60 million disagreements between buyers and sellers every year.[6] In the EU, a Common Frame of Reference for European Private Law was drafted and freely made available on the web.[7] This was not a government initiative; instead it sprang forth from European legal scholars. It has now become a point of reference for legislators and courts in the EU.

The trend towards privatisation of law also requires some elaboration to prevent misunderstanding. First, the rise of private regimes does not mean that these are isolated from legal regimes created by public authorities. For example, sometimes the creation of transnational law starts as a private initiative and is later adopted by public authorities. Secondly, here too, we see wide diversity. Private regimes may refer to rules, standards or guidelines but these may also refer to authoritative mechanisms of dispute resolution. The term 'soft law' may be used, but in their actual effect, guidelines can sometimes be 'hard' as law. Private rule making may or may not include enforcement.

3. Key Uncertainties and Scenarios

There is no logical necessity to assume that these trends will continue in the same direction and at the same pace. These trends should therefore conceptually be regarded as key uncertainties or contingencies which may occur but which may also reverse. Will we witness continued

---

4 Forest Stewardship Council, 'Forest Management Standards' (2010) <www.fscus.org/standards_criteria/forest_management.php> accessed 31 July 2012.

5 'Model Mining Development Agreement Project' www.mmdaproject.org/ accessed 31 July 2012.

6 Innovating Justice Awards www.innovatingjusticeawards.com/View-Idea/165?idea=1265 accessed 31 July 2012.

7 'Principles, Definitions and Model Rules of European Private Law: Draft Common Frame of Reference' http://ec.europa.eu/justice/contract/files/european-private-law_en.pdf accessed 31 July 2012.

Table 1. Key Uncertainties and Scenarios

	Growth of private governance regimes	Reversed growth private governance regimes
Internationalisation of law	Legal Internet	Global Constitution
Reversed internationalisation of law	Legal tribes	Legal Borders

internationalisation of rules and institutions or will this trend reverse? Will private governance mechanisms and private legal regimes further expand and become predominant, or will state-connected institutions and legal regimes retain their position?

Taken together, these contingencies conceptually allow four different scenarios (see table 1).

We will briefly sketch these scenarios that picture possible global legal environments that emerge in 2030.[8] As said, scenarios are defined as stories on what may happen. These stories are both a product of imagination and a result of systematic analysis of the key uncertainties. The scenarios are meant to invite lawyers and legal scholars to picture what the global legal environment will look like if the trends described above either continue or reverse. The scenarios are presented from a future perspective in such a way as if they have already evolved. The scenarios also include the triggers and events that caused these future states of the global legal environment. Regarding the names we have given each of the scenarios, rather than take them for their literal meaning, one ought to bear in mind that they use metaphors meant to convey the central feature of each respective scenarios. Thus, *Global Constitution* does not imply there will actually be a single world constitution, but rather that in this scenario the global legal environment will increasingly resemble a constitutional order. In *Legal Internet*, the name does not mean that this scenario is about the Internet. It rather implies that the global legal environment in this world is characterized as a decentralized transnational network involving a big range of actors. Similarly, *Legal Tribes* does not denote a world that is composed of tribes, rather it hints to a reality whereby the global legal environment is composed of many relatively small 'communities' with relatively little contact and coordination and a weaker role for the state. Finally, *Legal Borders* does not imply that legal walls will be built between national legal systems, but

8 See also S Muller and others, *Law Scenarios to 2030* (Hiil 2012).

instead it emphasizes the increased importance or renaissance of national and regional sovereignty.

a) Global Constitution

In this scenario a global constitutional order has emerged in 2030, slowly but surely covering all major legal areas on a global scale – trade, environment, security, crime, finance, markets and competition, intellectual property, labour, taxation, and health – leaving only a few areas untouched by international rules and procedures. Global law has not been driven by a specific set of values or leading legal systems. Instead, the process of blending has to a large extent been eclectic. Whereas global competition law and contract law are primarily driven by free market ideals, global criminal law has been led by retaliation principles. It has therefore become more punitive and strict than European countries were used to.

In the Global Constitution scenario consumers are protected by a global system of consumer law that builds on the old European consumer law. Global consumer law is enforced – mainly via the internet – by a global regulatory agency with offices all over the world. Tort law is largely regulated through a global civil code that was adopted in 2028, which provides general parameters from which regional and national systems may not deviate. Constitutional and (global) administrative law have become hugely important fields. There are constant questions on areas of competence and jurisdiction. The principle of legality – all governments are bound by law – is the broadly accepted principle that underlies the global legal environment. The global constitutional order is not based on one document or charter, but rather on a series of charters and constitution-like documents, in which international regulators, adjudicators, and courts are defined and connected with each other. This multi-layered system is complex, and at times Byzantine.

The rules and institutions that make up this global legal environment are difficult to create and change once formalised. The enforcement of rules is public in nature, or a clear derivative thereof. The International Criminal Court (ICC) may have taken ten years to finally conclude its first case (Lubanga in 2012), but subsequent trials were concluded much more efficiently. The ICC's 'positive complementarity' approach proved successful in enhancing national capacity thus leading to limited ICC involvement. Technological developments have made it easier for enforcement bodies to share information. Criminal records, tax filings, debtor records, and in some instances, even things like employment records can be shared when needed.

How did the global legal environment evolve between 2012 and 2030? First, many challenges became apparent which revealed the global interdependencies. The financial crisis of 2008 is a prime example. Directed by the G-20, which slowly transformed into an effective economic and social global governing board, an impressive body of international regulation, aimed at building a more stable economic system was put in place. This body not only coordinated regulation in the financial area, but it was also able to build a more holistic definition of the notion of economy, which now includes the environment, social cohesion, and sustainability.

In 2016, the drug wars in Central America and Western Africa intensified and spread. This caused intolerable violence, social deprivation, migration, and problems for international shipping and aviation. These problems quickly jumped over to more stable and well-organised parts of the world. The Organisation of American States (OAS) and the African Union (AU) with Economic Community of West African States (ECOWAS) pushed the issue on the global agenda and a global approach was developed in 2018. The scarcity of water and food was also an important driver of change. It required global policies on water redistribution and agriculture. Here too the G-20 proved very effective; food security was placed on the agenda in 2016; water security followed in 2019. The Food and Agriculture Organisation was given a new life; it became a food security watchdog with direct lines to both the United Nations (UN) and regional Security Councils (in cases which involved war), and the Economic Council and its regional bodies.

b) Legal Borders

In this scenario national and regional legislation have become the primary source of rule making in 2030. Regional and sub-regional organisations have become the ultimate defence against what were widely perceived to be out-of-control international institutions and an international environment in which common values are scarce. The international level is for politics, not law. New global powers such as China, India, Indonesia, Brazil, Mexico, South Africa, Egypt, and the Gulf States fundamentally changed the nature of the debate in the global environment. There is lot less talk about universality than there once was. In fact, most would agree that there is no universality.

With regional legal pluralism, the rule of law has also been regionally pluralised. As a consequence context-specific regional and national interpretations of concepts such as fundamental human rights, separation of church and state, balance of powers, and the principle of legality have become predominant. The international institutions that had developed at the end of the 20th century have slowly eroded and lost their significance. In some instances states have withdrawn ratifications, in others they are being minimally interpreted at best, and otherwise completely ignored. International courts – insofar as they are given adequate funding – face strong pressure to reduce their footprint and the scope of their decisions.

New legal notions to determine whether something should be regionalized or not have been developed, requiring compatibility with 'inalienable national values' and 'core national legal principles'. They provide a key reference point for all constitutional lawyers, judges, and national lawmakers. The informal, flexible approach pioneered by the G-20 during the Great Crisis of 2008 – 2015 has become the norm and the UN has adapted to it. On global economic issues, the G-20 still runs the show. It is now linked to the R-5, a loose overarching framework built around the five regional groups that developed within the old UN. The previous decade, starting in 2020, witnessed a gradual and deliberate process of de-treatying; international negotiations replacing international regimes with political arrangements, if needed, or even terminating them. These processes sometimes worked out peacefully, but some of this legal disentanglement has ended with violence.

Yet many successful corporations have made their fortunes through legal tourism, taking advantage of the legal differences between states and regions. They are supported by international law firms, which have made huge investments in comparative legal knowledge and have specialized in legal tourism. Sometimes this race to the bottom yields dramatic results. In the environmental realm, it has led to poor states and regions that have become garbage dumps for strong transnational corporations using the legal regime. Enforcement is also a national affair. In some areas enforcement is loosely coordinated on a regional level to prevent natural disasters (e.g. environmental law).

Several trends and events between 2012 and 2030 triggered this scenario. It actually started with the 9/11 attacks. Initially led by the US, but soon followed by others, a common response was to toughen immigration restrictions, make more extensive use of criminal and administrative law to curb freedoms, and introduce restrictions on the movement of goods and capital. The financial crisis that started in 2008 also contributed significantly. It proved very difficult to resolve it internationally. The G-20 and its network seemed successful at first, but when after 2013 worldwide unemployment (especially for those under 30 years old) was still very high – up to 45% – states slowly abandoned the international law route. It also proved difficult to agree to effective international action regarding transnational crime, illicit trade, cross border fraud, and global terrorism. Legal and other borders gradually emerged. Immigration and the international flow of capital were curbed. Economic growth ended for many years, but security and stability were preferred above wealth.

c) *Legal Internet*

In this scenario, rules – in the sense of 'law' – in 2030 are a lot less important than they were in 2010. In the course of the first decade of the millennium the true potential of information technology and relationships supported by social media became apparent. Through cheap laptops, tablets and smartphones, connected by cloud technology and clever search engines, interaction across borders and access to useful and relevant information became accessible for most people around the world. By 2018, this had already radically changed the way people interact on a global scale. By 2030, it is engrained into the global legal environment. New generations became acquainted with new ways of rule making, law enforcement, and resolving disputes. Reputation, trust, transparency, mobilization of voice, and demonstrated effectiveness became the new mechanisms to secure a social and political order. Formal rules and procedures are now considered old-fashioned, too formal, ineffective, too uniform, and too inflexible.

Public rules have gradually been replaced or marginalised by standards developed by private actors. Monitoring and even enforcement are dealt with by private regimes and mechanisms created by the parties involved. Democracy or accountability is less a matter of working through parliaments and more a matter of working through interest groups and loosely organised structures that operate between interest groups. Self-regulation has become the prime source of legitimacy. The 2025 world summit that gathered in New York to celebrate the eightieth birthday of the United Nations was attended by the heads of 228 different states, the leaders of the 100 wealthiest companies, and 100 civil society leaders. Thanks to smart information technology it was possible to have a meaningful debate in the six months leading up to the final event. The leaders adopted the 2045 Good Governance Pact (GGP), which laid down 15 governance standards that the leaders consider fundamental for good governance, wherever it occurs.

Five years afterwards, a dozen measuring tools to assess implementation and compliance with the GGP were fully operational, keeping the leaders focused on the agreements that were made. Leaders, be they from government, business, or civil society, meet at regular intervals to discuss strategic directions on issues, and people and organisations at the operational level work things out and implement. If you have demonstrable added value, you can join the process. If not, you are no longer involved. The UN has largely been reduced to a web-based Internet forum, run by a relatively small secretariat, on which rule making initiatives are collected, published, and on which expert advice can be sought: the UN Rule and Process Forum (UNRPF). But even for this function it faces tough competition from private initiatives claiming to be faster and better facilitators.

Private rule making, enforcement, and dispute resolution mechanisms are usually flexible and efficient, whereas public regimes are more bureaucratic and rigid. The absence of clear, all-encompassing organising principles (like the principle of legality, the UN definition of the rule of law, or state sovereignty) makes the global legal environment complex, often confusing and most of the time unstable. The verb 'to regulate' is rarely used. The art is now known as R&O – Regulate & Organise. The pattern is usually the same: close to a problem or a challenge – be it local or international – a need for regulation emerges.

Actors confronted with a problem build a coalition to resolve it. Most enforcement takes place outside the scope of the state, or at the very least with the involvement of powerful private actors concerned. For example, global pharmaceutical corporations have not only adopted rules of conduct with regard to intellectual property, but they have also built an organisation that monitors counterfeit medicines and acts against the networks that make and distribute these medicines.

What chain of events triggered this scenario? The failure of formal intergovernmental organisations to prevent the financial crisis of 2008- 2015 and to quickly recover from it caused a tectonic shift in international governance. The networked G-20 system proved more effective in handling the crisis, but in general the loss of trust in state and state-based institutions had pushed corporations, NGOs and communities away from the state. The standards that were developed during the difficult years between 2008 and 2015 gained traction through civil society organisations and public private partnerships, and were helped by information technology. Most governments were caught by surprise. National courts could not handle the number or the complexity of transnational cases, national court decisions could not be enforced, and states or international legal institutions could not agree on norms. As a consequence private actors created their own regimes.

The substantial growth of powerful global private players after 2015 also played a role. Transnational corporations and civil society organisations continued to grow and became more powerful, both with regard to creating norms and with regard to enforcement. The legitimacy crisis in which many states found themselves after 2015 was also an important factor. Self-regulatory regimes were widely seen as more legitimate.

d) Legal Tribes

Whereas this scenario seemed least plausible in 2012, it has become a reality in 2030. The global legal environment witnessed a severe loss of relevance of the state combined with a loss of interest in internationalisation. In 2030, the global legal environment consists of a largely unconnected group of communities that govern themselves. In many ways states have become failed states. Global security is a serious issue and law has been completely abandoned as a way to achieve it. Local security, which is mainly self-organised, is the main basis for ordering. Besides, order is local and mainly privatised. It comes from small-scale networks of security corporations, communities and civil society organisations, and is supported, where possible and useful, by small public structures. The state and the international global legal environment have withered away, mainly as a result of the security and economic crises of the first two decades of the millennium. International organisations have lost their relevance and have closed due to lack of interest, funds, effectiveness, and legitimacy.

The scenario of Legal Tribes has not been too good to multinational companies either. Seen as remnants of failed internationalization, they had to change to survive. Many of them have broken into local or national entities. Very few have real global coverage; it is simply too risky economically, in terms of manageability, and even security. Wealth, effort, labour, profit are all generated at the local level and flow back to the local level. Security can really only be organised locally; at least then you know who you can trust. The dream of globalisation has been destroyed. Next to state borders, the global legal environment also witnesses religious borders, borders organised around economic activities, ethnic borders, and political borders. The old regional organisations have lost much of their economic *raison d'être*. The successful ones have transformed into security alliances: public-private regional fences within which smaller communities can conduct economic activity on a larger than local scale.

The main role of the public realm is to deal with the link between the huge variety of private self-regulatory regimes. But with a greatly reduced tax base, resources are limited. As a leading principle the rule of law has become an anachronistic concept. Enforcement is also a local and mostly private affair. In the most developed communities the public arena only plays an enforcement role in the area of crime, IT infrastructure, health, and linkages between private regulatory regimes. Again, local is good. In other communities, the public enforcement circle is even smaller. Social control, groups taking justice into their own hands, and militias maintaining order are predominant in many parts of the world, whereas religious or public authorities take up these tasks in other regions.

How did this all come about? First, states and international organisations did not prove to be effective in restoring stability and economic recovery after the 2008 crises. The severe budget cuts that were made from 2013 onwards by many governments around the world proved to be the beginning of the end of the state. It was a last 'win or lose' effort by states to deal with massive unemployment, debt levels, and inequalities, but it failed. As a result, trust in government and the international system diminished. Conflict was widespread. Health systems broke down. Food and water became scarce. In many parts of the world life expectancy decreased. States and businesses failed to deal with the global crisis and were also seen to be responsible for a number of other issues such as major failure to protect data and massive fraud on a global scale. This has given rise to great suspicion about all things global and international. The anti-globalisation movement attracted more supporters than ever before.

4. A Quest for Legal and Justice Strategies

After reading these scenarios many lawyers will wonder why this kind of legal science fiction is being practiced. The answer is quite easy. Systematically, building future scenarios on current trends help national legislators to improve their legal and justice strategies. The effectiveness of all national legal and justice strategies highly depends on which scenario will evolve. Since scenarios do not rule out uncertainty, national legislators have to take into account all scenarios. So how can national legislators use these scenarios? First, the scenarios indicate future challenges. Second, taken together the scenarios constitute a wind tunnel that enables each national legislator to test whether its legal and justice strategies are future proof.

Imagine a national legislator that pursues a rule of law strategy. Its legal order is based upon the principle of lawfulness that requires that all public authorities have to comply with law and which forbids arbitrariness. This imaginary national legislator has also adopted human rights. How future-proof are its legal strategies if confronted with the scenarios sketched above? This legislator first has to establish what happens if a specific scenario unfolds. If the Global Constitution scenario unfolds the main challenge in this scenario will be to institutionalise the rule of law in the evolving global constitutional order. Our imaginary national legislator is thus confronted with two strategic challenges.

First, how to institutionalise these principles in the evolving global constitutional order? This will certainly not be easy because of the complexity of the order the limited power of both national and international courts in this scenario, and the limited role that national and international parliaments play. Second, it certainly does not speak for itself that even in this scenario a global consensus will evolve with regard to rule of law principles. Instead, the global constitutional order will probably be a compromise. Our imaginary legislator therefore also has to develop a strategy on securing compliance to rule of law principles and a strategy on securing consensus on these principles.

In order to define its main future challenges, our imaginary national legislator should also explore an opposite scenario. If the Legal Internet scenario unfolds the major rule of law, the challenge in this scenario will be to institutionalise the rule of law in the evolving global self-regulatory frameworks. How to secure the principle of lawfulness, the universality of norms, democratic accountability, the separation of powers, and checks and balances in self-regulatory frameworks? In order to address this challenge, this national legislator first needs to find out how these self-regulatory frameworks actually work and how they deal with rule of law issues. Second, the national legislator has to connect with these frameworks in order to secure rule of law mechanisms. This will not be easy because of the diffuse nature of these frameworks. It remains to be seen whether these frameworks will actually allow regulation by international institutions and nation states simply do not have enough power to regulate these frameworks.

The imaginary national legislator should also explore the Legal Tribes and the Legal Borders scenarios in order to define its main challenges. This national legislator may also choose to use the scenarios as a wind tunnel to test whether a chosen legal strategy will survive different global legal environments. Using the scenarios as a wind tunnel teaches our imaginary national legislator at least two lessons. First, the scenarios demonstrate that national legislators should both be prepared for further internationalisation and renationalisation. At least two preparatory measures seem sound.

First, national legislators should think twice before giving up on national law and national constitutional principles. Adding international law is not a problem from the scenario point of view, but a substitution strategy may prove to be unwise. Second, national legislators should match their legal orders with evolving international or global legal principles. By removing inconsistencies and contradictions between the national legal order and the global legal order, national legislators will be better prepared in case of gradual or sudden further internationalisation.

Taken together, the scenarios also teach our imaginary national legislator that it is wise to preserve a complete legal order that at the same time allows self-regulatory frameworks. At least two preparatory measures seem sound. First, national legislators should not consider self-regulatory frameworks and standards as irrelevant from a legal point of view. Whenever possible, national legislators should connect self-regulatory frameworks and standards with formal state law. Second, the formal state legal order should allow self-regulation and create possibilities for self-regulatory frameworks. For example, the legal figure of an order declaring a collective agreement binding can be a suitable way of providing legal status for self-regulatory frameworks and at the same time securing the values embodied by the rule of law.

By using these scenarios national legislators can improve their legal strategies and prepare for a world in which global law becomes predominant. The real value of the scenarios though may be that they also force national legislators to consider a global legal environment in which global law will not evolve.

Global law will be Responsive Law, at least with regard to Cyberspace

Paul de Hert[a] & Eugenio Mantovani[b]
a) Professor of Law and Technology, Tilburg Institute for Law and Technology (TILT) and Faculty of Law and Criminology, Vrije Universiteit Brussel
paul.de.hert@vub.ac.be
b) PhD researcher, Research Group *Law Science Technology & Society*, Vrije Universiteit Brussel; seconded researcher, *Centre for Science, Society and Citizenship* (CSSC, Rome) – in the framework of the Marie Curie program VALUE AGEING
eugenio.mantovani@cssc.eu

Abstract
Multilevel global law is defying formal hierarchy in favour of a qualitative and responsive approach. As the cases of Solange and Kadi indicate, Courts may start giving priority to the legal order that better protects the values at stake. In law making, global law may be more and more responsive. Gone are the days of executives crafting ready-made treaties and bullying ratification back home; communities will react and force lawmakers to adjust and consult. The spectacular fiasco of Acta is a good example. The ACTA case, however, also instils the doubt whether this 'responsiveness' will be a general feature of global law or only of global information society law (cyberspace). Referring to the work of Andrew Murray on internet regulation and his discussion of failed enforcement against Wikileaks, one cannot but be prudent. The specific features of the internet make cyberspace another space than regular space. However, it is perhaps not to bold a pick to hold that the mechanism of responsiveness is, in due time and in some unexpected ways, to become a general characteristic of all law.

Keywords
global law; responsive law; ACTA; Murray; Cyberspace

1. Introduction

'There was private law and public law, national law and international law, each with its own domain (...)' could be the incipit of a class on global law

[1] Adapted from D Kennedy, 'The Mystery of Global Governance', Kormendy Lecture, Ohio Northern University, Pettit College of Law (2008). Available at: <http://www.watsoninstitute.org/blss/media/docs/kennedy.pdf> accessed 2 July 2012.

in the near future.[1] When no national system is completely autonomous, and no supranational system is completely autonomous either, political ordering is no longer something governed by a more or less precise, more or less stable hierarchy of domestic legal norms, but by multilevel systems of national and supranational norms. While there is no consensus of the notion of global law, just as there is no single definition, but several, a few would disagree that law making, but also law enforcement and jurisdiction, are steadfastly maturing into multilevel, non-hierarchical enmeshment of national, regional and international legal sources.

There is also little doubt about global law as a highly attractive field of knowledge and research for any lawyer. The peculiarity of this article is that it is written by a couple of lawyers and academics coming from the field of law and technology studies. What does developing global law have to share with the sizzling wires of the burgeoning information society? In our view, a common interest in regulatory theories.

Starting from a general definition of global law, the first part of the article discusses and, by using the opinions of legal authorities, underlines the relevance of the concept as both descriptive and normative representation of our times of global governance.

Based on this doctrinal introduction, the second part of the article illustrates global law in relation to two typical legal operations: jurisdiction and law making. In jurisprudence, we refer to two fundamental rights-centred Dworkinian 'hard cases': a national one (Solange, 1986) and a European one (Kadi, 2008). In law making, we describe the remarkable failure of ACTA, the Anti-Counterfeiting Trade Agreement, to show that, these days, individuals and communities, including parliamentary assemblies, no longer blindly trust, but defy and confront law making, especially when it comes as a package crafted far away from home.

The third and last part of the article is about cyberspace. In this section, we engage with Andrew Murray's regulatory theory of cyberspace which he derives from Actor Network Theory (ANT) and Social Network Theory (SNT).[2] Enabled or facilitated by the use of information and communication technologies, Murray argues that communities respond and react to regulatory command and control interventions forcing authorities to consult, to adjust and to change. In cyberspace at least, the object of the law, the good to be regulated, such as copyright, becomes an active subject.

---

2 Andrew D Murray, *The Regulation of Cyberspace* (Routledge-Cavendish 2007).

2. Global Law: Views from Legal Scholars

Talk of global law has been around for some years through the languages of unification, harmonisation, or convergence of law and legal systems. Though no agreement or common definition is found, the concept of global law can be safely taken to epitomise the demise of the hegemony of the Westphalian national state over the system of legal sources.

'Transplant' theorists suggest that global law could be the paradoxical outcome of the law's own success as 'the' mode of ordering, massively diffused throughout the world's legal systems, working in an almost semiautomatic way across the worlds through codes.[3] In this connection, James Gordley, a private law scholar, sees a turning point in the adoption, in 1911, of a Chinese civil code. Ever since, he claims, the basic structure and concepts and ideological assumptions of construct and more broadly private law, is globally shared. One can travel anywhere. He or she will know that larger legal concepts, like liability, are analysed much in the same way in Brussels and in Jakarta.[4]

The University of Sydney website nicely illustrates global law as 'encompass[ing] not just international law, but an approach to law that is transnational in scope, taking in the domestic laws of different countries, and integrating an understanding of domestic regimes within the broader context of international laws, instruments and institutions.'[5] This characterisation of global law as an approach to law that is transnational in scope tallies well with the views expressed by Sabino Cassese, international law scholar and constitutional judge.

Cassese describes global law as being based on agreements situated in a grey zone between global regulatory systems and national regulators,[6] in the field of arms control, food safety, financial instruments, internet governance, coffee and cocoa, fishing, forest, water, climate, to name but a very few.[7] Cassese and others[8] suggest the linchpin of global law should be

---

3 William Ewald, 'Comparative Jurisprudence (II): The Logic of Legal Transplants' (1995) 43 American Journal of Comparative Law 489.

4 James Gordley, *The Philosophical Foundations of Modern Contract Doctrine* (Oxford University Press, Oxford 1993).

5 See University of Sydney, 'Master of Global Law' (2012) Available at: <http://sydney.edu.au/law/fstudent/coursework/global-law.shtml> accessed 30 June 2012.

6 Sabino Cassese, 'Administrative Law without the State? The Challenge of Global Regulation' (2005) 37 Journal of International Law & Policy 663, 668.

7 ibid 673.

8 Sabino Cassese and others (eds), *Global Administrative Law: Cases, Materials, Issues* (2nd edn, Institute for International Law and Justice 2008); Benedict Kingsbury, Nico Krisch

guaranteeing the actual application, by global regulatory bodies and institutions, of principles and procedures of transparency, participation, and duty to give a reasoned decision.[9]

The principles-based, normative vision of Cassese is contrasted by scholars looking at the practice of the law. William Twining, for instance, warns against the dangers of generalisation and convergence, which, he writes, 'are only *prima facie* true in a superficial way.'[10] Convergence of law, be it contract or administrative law, tells very little about law in action in different countries and within different contexts within the same country. Convergence of global systems is a distinctly metropolitan perspective and suffers from the limitations of Hobbesian state centralism, he surmises.[11] At the same time, Twining does not doubt that 'there clearly are important general patterns and meaningful discourses about law in the world as a whole and in large parts of it'. The challenge is to identify which general patterns are meaningful and workable and to identify the important differences.

Neil Walker agrees with Twining's accent on pluralism and diversity between and within legal systems. In Walker's view, constitutional sites and processes are increasingly configured in a 'heterarchical rather than a hierarchical pattern.' This means that there are continuous overlaps between national legal systems, on the one hand, and international organisations, on the other hand. In his work, Walker seeks to understand whether these overlapping and contaminations foreshadow the emergence of a third, global constitutional configuration and he studies the legitimacy of such a development.[12]

---

and Richard B Stewart, 'The Emergence of Global Administrative Law' (2005) 68 Law and Contemporary Problems 15; Nico Krisch, Benedict Kingsbury, 'Introduction: Global Governance and Global Administrative Law in the International Legal Order' (2006) 17(1) European Journal of International Law 1. For a good overview on doctrine in this field, see Ming-Sung Kuo, 'Between Fragmentation and Unity: The Uneasy Relationship between Global Administrative Law and Global Constitutionalism' (2009) 10 San Diego International Law Journal 439; and Ming-Sung Kuo, 'The Concept of "Law" in Global Administrative Law: A Reply to Benedict Kingsbury' (2009) 20(4) European Journal of International Law 997.

[9] Kingsbury, 'The Emergence of Global Administrative Law' ibid.

[10] William Twining, *Administrative Law in Context: Enlarging a Discipline* (Oxford University Press, Oxford 1997); William Twining, *Globalisation and Legal Theory* (Butterworth 2000); William Twining, *The Great Juristic Bazaar* Aldershot 2002).

[11] William Twining, 'A Cosmopolitan Discipline? Some Implications of "globalisation" for Legal Education' (2001) 8(1) International Journal of the Legal Profession 1.

[12] Neil Walker, 'The Idea of Constitutional Pluralism' (2002) 65(3) Modern Law Review 317.

A more cynical voice, in starker contrast with Cassese's principles-based view, is that of Ugo Mattei. According to Mattei, global law resent from the encumbering legacies of Hobbessian and Lockian thinking on modern constitutionalism, with its embracement of state centralism *and* private individualism, property *and* sovereignty, private *and* public.[13] These two major legal and political institutions, private and public, carry on the dominant view of the world, he points out. On the one hand, 'private structures (corporation) concentrating their decision making and power of exclusion in the hands of one subject (the owner) or within a hierarchy (the CEO)'; on the other, public structures (bureaucracy) concentrating power at the top of a sovereign hierarchy.[14] In the *pars construens* of his radical critique, Mattei gives support to the vision of a legal system organised as an 'ecosystem'. In such an ecosystem, community of individuals or social groups are linked by a horizontal mutual connection to a network where power is dispersed, generally rejecting the idea of hierarchy in favour of a participatory and collaborative model, which prevents the concentration of power in one party or entity, and puts community interests at the centre.[15]

As we will underline below, Mattei's communities' activism is one of the constitutive features of Andrew Murray's architecture of responsive law in cyberspace. The point that Murray prompts is whether the communities' activisms and the responsiveness of the law that he sees at work in cyberspace can be generalised to become a general feature of global law, or whether this approach can only be developed to deal with information society issues.

3. Qualitative Turn and Responsive Law

Before entering Andrew Murray's notion of responsive law, this paragraph pushes a bit further the preliminary remarks on global law. The foregoing has shown that though several visions exist about what global law is, all

---

[13] Ugo Mattei, 'A Theory of Imperial Law: A Study on U.S. Hegemony and the Latin Resistance' (2003) 10(1) Indiana Journal of Global Legal Studies 383. Available at: <http://www.repository.law.indiana.edu/ijgls/vol10/iss1/14> accessed 01 June 2012; Ugo Mattei and Laura Nader, *Plunder: When the Rule of Law is Illegal* (Blackwell 2008).

[14] Ugo Mattei, 'The State, the Market, and some Preliminary Questions about the Commons (French and English Version)' (2011) Available at: <http://works.bepress.com/ugo_mattei/40> accessed 3 July 2012. See also Ugo Mattei, *Beni comuni: Un manifesto* (Bari 2012).

[15] ibid 11.

agree that the Westphalian model of nation state law does not exist any longer in an autonomous way. Less evident, but present in the analysis of Walker, is the observation that also international law suffers from this development: the hierarchical superiority of international law over regional and national law is quite changed, if not gone for good. When judges have to decide between international law norms and national law norms, no absolute priority seems to exist. Drawing from two court cases, we show that the decision, what legal norm will apply to a specific case, is not (any longer) taken on the basis of formal hierarchical criteria, but instead on what we call, for lack of better words, qualitative criteria.

When the case *Solange* II was debated, in 1986, the protection of fundamental rights at the European level had created a layer of fundamental rights that added to the national circles of fundamental rights. At stake was the coordination of European Community secondary law with basic rights grounded in the Federal German Constitution, or Basic Law. The question that arose in court was how these layers or circles were related to one another.[16] *Das Bundesverfassungsgericht*, the German Constitutional Court, accepted the new status quo, acknowledging both the validity of the higher European, supranational source of law (abiding by a consolidated case law on the supremacy of EU law developed in Costa/ Enel[17] and Van Gend en Loos[18]), and a division of competence between itself and the European Court of Justice (ECJ).

As Adams and Witteveen underline,[19] at the same time, the German court stated that the validity of that higher source of law was not given

---

[16] For a detailed discussion see E R. Lanier, 'Solange, Farewell: The Federal German Constitutional Court and the Recognition of the Court of Justice of the European Communities as Lawful Judge' [1988] 11 Boston College International and Comparative Law Review 1 Available at: <http://lawdigitalcommons.bc.edu/iclr/vol11/iss1/2> accessed 01 June 2012; August Reinisch (ed), *Challenging Acts of International Organizations Before National Courts* (Oxford University Press 2010). Compare the Bosphorus case, decided in 2005, which allowed European Court of Human Rights to clarify the relationship between the EU's and the Council of Europe's human rights regimes. Paul de Hert and Fisnik Korenica, 'The Doctrine of Equivalent Protection: Its Life and Legitimacy Before and After the European Union's Accession to the European Convention on Human Rights' (2012) 13 German Law Journal 874 Available at: <http://www.germanlawjournal.com/index.php?pageID=11&artID=1445> accessed on 01 June 2012.

[17] Case C-6/64 *Costa v ENEL* [1964] ECR 585.

[18] Case C-26/62 *Van Gend en Loos v Nederlandse Administratie der Belastingen* [1963] ECR I.

[19] Maurice Adams and Willem Witteveen, 'Gedaantewisselingen van het recht' [2011] 86-9 Nederlands Juristenblad 540; Maurice Adams and Willem Witteveen, 'Gedaantewisselingen van het recht' [2011] Rechtskundig Weekblad 1120.

solely by its formal hierarchical position. Its validity had to be measured according to qualitative criteria. Thus, '"as long" as Community law did not contain comparably adequate fundamental rights protection (the *Bundesverfassunsgericht* upheld the admissibility of its human rights scrutiny of Community acts)',[20] and, '"as long as" equivalent human rights protection was guaranteed by the ECJ (the German judiciary will dismiss competence of German judiciary over acts of community organs).'[21] Adams and Witteveen would probably subscribe to Davor Jancic's expression 'Solange democracy'.[22] Jancic uses it to underline that, further to Solange, parliamentary involvement in EU affairs has significantly been refurbished. Solange jurisprudence had indeed the effect of enhancing the legal position of the German Parliament vis-à-vis the Federal Government and the international policy agreements contracted by it, Jancic points out.

The *Kadi* case is another example of a court decision where formal hierarchy plays second fiddle to search for qualitative judgement. This time the 'struggle between legal systems' is between the European Union's and the United Nations (UN).

The Kadi judgment of 3 September 2008[23] concerned the annulment of an EU Council regulation giving effect within the EU area to a number of UN Security Council (UNSC) resolutions specifically aimed at the freezing of funds belonging to certain persons and entities associated with Osama Bin Laden and the Taliban movement. One of the targeted natural persons, Mr Kadi and others brought an action of annulment in relation to regulation EC no. 881/2002 in so much as that act related to them, alleging a breach of their fundamental rights.

In a first hearing, the Court of First Instance dismissed the actions brought against the Council Regulation.[24] The dismissal was appealed in front of the European Court of Justice. In what has rightly become a landmark case, the ECJ found that the Court of First Instance had erred by dismissing the lawsuit. The dismissal infringed upon the principle of judicial review in that neither decision nor regulation, even one implementing Security

---

20 *Internationale Handelsgesellschaft "Solange I"* [1974] 2 C.M.L.R. 540 (Solange I).

21 Re Wünsche Handelsgesellschaft "Solange *II*" [1987] 3 C.M.L.R. 225 (Solange II).

22 Davor Jancic, 'Caveats from Karlsruhe and Berlin: Whither Democracy after Lisbon?' (2010) 16(3) Columbia Journal of European Law 337.

23 Joined cases C-402/05 P and C-415/05 P *Yassin Abdullah Kadi and Al Barakaat International Foundation v Council of the European Union and Commission of the European Communities* [2008] ECR 11-3533.

24 Case T-315/01 *Yassin Abdullah Kadi v Council of the European Union and Commission of the European Communities*, ECR II-3649.

Council resolutions, can escape judicial review.[25] The court reminded that respect for human rights is a condition of the lawfulness of Community acts and that measures incompatible with respect for human rights are not acceptable in the Community.[26] It concluded that international agreements cannot prejudice the community constitutional order and fundamental rights, including the right to be heard, the right to an effective judicial review and the right to property.[27]

Some international law doctrine criticised *Kadi* for the 'constitutionalist–dualist posture' taken by the court.[28] Others, like Adams and Witteveen, mentioned above, instead argue that this is exactly what is expected from a qualitative approach, not to be afraid of shaking the coherence of the international legal system. In *Kadi*, the European Court of Justice performed as an interpretative community: confronted with a concrete case of global governance impinging on fundamental values, but still accepting the disciplining rules of the law to restrain thinking and decision.[29]

4. ACTA, Andrew Murray, and Responsive Law

Will the qualitative turn create more unpredictability in courts' decision-making? Maybe yes, maybe not, the answer to the question depending largely on the case by case assessment and by the way Courts of Justice will interpret the law and take decisions. If, vis-à-vis courts, talk of unpredictability commands prudence, it is not as impudent for the claim to be made about unpredictability with regards to treaty law making.

As the ACTA case (discussed below) suggests, the Pandora's box of global law is opened on the face of the legislator and pushes it to adopt a new way of engaging with performing international cooperation. Echoing the question asked above at the end of paragraph 1: is this new approach to (global) law making something that is becoming a dominant feature in all spheres

---

25 Joined cases C-402/05 P and C-415/05 P para 281, referring to Case 294/83 *Les Verts v Parliament* [1986] ECR 1339, para 23.

26 Joined cases C-402/05 P and C-415/05 P, ibid para 284.

27 Joined cases C-402/05 P and C-415/05 P (n 25) para 316.

28 Andrea Gattini , 'Case Comment' (2009) 46 Common Market Law Review 213.

29 Owen M Fiss, 'Objectivity and Interpretation' (1982) 34 Stanford Law Review 739. Joined cases C-402/05 P and C-415/05 P (n 27) paras 287-288. While annulling the contested regulation and putting conditions on it, the ECJ made clear that its decision did not challenge the primacy of the UN SC resolution under international law.

of law making, or is it a prerogative of law making in the information society or cyberspace?

The Anti-Counterfeiting Trade Agreement (ACTA) is a draft trade agreement that addresses commercial-scale counterfeiting and online piracy by coordinating global enforcement of existing copyright (violation) laws.[30] It was drafted through 11 rounds of negotiations involving 37 countries, which opened in June 2008 and came to an end in November 2010. As for its scope, the agreement addresses issues that go beyond 'counterfeiting' – such as fake designer clothes – to encompass, knowledge transfer about, e.g., basic medicines, car parts, technology, software, etc. notably through tighter digital IP enforcement efforts.[31] The agreement was designed to curb the flow of counterfeit goods across the globe requiring States and information society actors to conform to and/or adopt relevant policing, law enforcement, and liability norms.

As with all international mixed agreements, the European Commission, acting on a mandate from the Council, was the negotiator on behalf of the European Union, while the Member States were represented by the rotating presidencies. Before the agreement could become binding on EU countries, consent from the European Parliament had to be obtained.[32] After four contrary votes in four committees,[33] in the 2-5 July 2012 plenary session, the European Parliament withheld its consent, rejecting ACTA. The draft text, the outcome of lengthy negotiations between dozens of domestic and international offices and experts and lobbies, came to naught.

One of the reasons of the 'no' was arguably the ambiguity of many provisions. Content users did not like the undetermined notion of 'commercial-scale'[34] Privacy advocates did not appreciate the provisions

---

[30] On copyright and legal aspects of enforcement see Augustì Cerillo and others (co-ordinators), *Challenges and Opportunities of Online Entertainment: Proceedings of the 8th International Conference on Internet, Law & Politics,* Universitat Oberta de Catalunya. Barcelona, 9-10 July 2012 Available at: <http://edcp.uoc.edu/symposia/IDP_2012.pdf> accessed 29 July 2012.

[31] EDRI, *Cooperative Efforts in ACTA's Digital Chapter,* Issue 05 number 27 Available at: <http://www.edri.org/files/2012EDRiPapers/Article27.pdf> accessed 29 July 2012. Axel Metzger and Rita Matulionyte (coordinators), *Opinion of European Academics on ACTA,* 3 December 2010, open for signatures until February 7, 2011. Available at: <http://www.iri.uni-hannover.de/tl_files/pdf/ACTA_opinion_110211_DH2.pdf> accessed 3 July 2012.

[32] As well as ratification by individual Member States.

[33] EP Press Release, ACTA now rejected by four EP committees, 6 May 2012.

[34] Article 23 ACTA defines acts carried out on a 'commercial scale' as 'commercial activities for direct or indirect economic or commercial advantage.' Will someone who mixes music be criminally prosecutable?

on the disclosure of personal data, ACTA imposing a duty to disclose data of network subscribers both of infringing and non-infringing intermediaries.[35] Digital rights activists criticised the ambiguity on the role of a key player, or node, internet providers or intermediaries.[36] Economists saw ACTA provisions on border control as imposing on specific copyright controls potentially of *any* goods traded covered by IP rights, including, e.g., goods of humanitarian importance such as generic drugs. Consumer associations saw in it the viaticum to not-so-subtle coercive tactics against alleged copyright infringers, e.g., charging large sums of 'settlement' payments to avoid court appearances.[37]

Another important reason for ACTA to be rejected concerned the secret nature of the negotiations of the agreement phase, which excluded the general public. In conclusion, the ACTA was not convincing. 'Given the vagueness of certain aspects of the text and the uncertainty over its interpretation, the European Parliament could not guarantee adequate protection for citizens' rights in the future under ACTA', concluded David Martin, one of the European Parliament rapporteurs.[38]

Are the days of parliamentary rubber-stamping, (when the executive went away to an international forum and signed a draft, returned home and the national parliament ratified – no questions asked), gone? We will answer this question using Andrew Murray's theory of responsive regulation, which, *prima facie* seems to sit quite comfortably, almost to demonstrate *ex post*, ACTA law making fiasco.

Andrew D. Murray would most probably say yes, indeed, those days are gone: at least when the regulator touches information society issues. As mentioned in the introduction, Andrew Murray derives his theory on regulation of cyberspace from studies on Actor Network Theory (ANT) and Social Network Theory (SNT).[39] According to Murray, communities or, in

---

35 Article 27.3 ACTA.

36 EDRI, 'What makes ACTA so controversial (and why MEPs should care)' Available at: <http://www.edri.org/files/acta-bklt-p2s.pdf> accessed 3 July 2012.

37 EDRI, ibid.

38 David Martin, MEP, (Rapporteur), Committee on International Trade, European Parliament, 24 April 2012, 2011/0167(NLE).

39 On Murray's work: Eugenio Mantovani and Paul de Hert, 'Review of The Regulation of Cyberspace by Andrew Murray' (2008) 2(1) Studies in Ethics, Law, and Technology 1; Andrew D Murray, 'Nodes and Gravity in Virtual Space' (2011) 5(2) Legisprudence 195; Andrew D Murray, 'Internet Regulation' in David Levi-Faur (ed), *Handbook on Regulation* (Edward Elgar 2011); Andrew D Murray, 'Uses and Abuses of Cyberspace: Coming to Grips with the Present Dangers' in Antonio Cassese (ed), *Realizing Utopia: The Future of International Law* (Oxford University Press 2012).

social network theory language, *nodes*, are elements of a network that act and relate to each other - whether they are diplomatic bureaus of the state, organizations, trade unions, interest groups, small groups, or individuals. The individual is considered an opinion maker, not alone, but as a member of a community of other individuals.[40] Communities are central because they give signals to, e.g. markets, and regulators, they give or remove legitimacy. The presence of these reactive communities/nodes in cyberspace characterise regulation as being torn by the ability to control and effectiveness and legitimacy of control mechanisms.[41] This distinction is for Murray normative.

According to the British scholar, law operators should come to terms with the dynamic characteristics of the environment they seek to regulate. In order to be effective, it is advisable, that the regulatory model 'harnesses, as best as possible, (i.e. chaos theory permitting), the relationships already in place between the actors.'[42] In order to be legitimate, traditional command and control intervention should be tempered by techniques which 'afford all participants in the regulatory matrix an opportunity to shape the evolutionary development of *their* environment'.[43]

This hybrid regulator ought, thus, to measure his intervention in a two-stage process: first, map the environment (the 'communications that naturally occur between regulatory actors') and, secondly, 'predict what feedback will occur after intervention is made'. This gives rise to a regulatory 'hybrid' system where law must be open to the regulatory web or matrix and to be able to negotiate with it.[44]

ACTA is an illustrative case of responsive law in which communities, other than those traditionally devoted to shape the law, reclaim opportunities to shape the evolutionary development of *their* environment. In this sense, Murray's 'symbiotic regulation' shares some features with those international law scholars, mentioned in paragraph one, who insist on the plurality and diversity of law in action (Twining), constitutional enmeshment (Walker) and, in particular, Ugo Mattei's vision of an ecosystem, 'generally rejecting the public/private dichotomy and its idea of hierarchy, in favour of a participatory and collaborative model, which prevents the

---

[40] Murray 'Nodes and Gravity in Virtual Space' ibid, 204.

[41] Andrew D Murray, *Regulation of Cyberspace: Control in the Online Environment* (Routledge-Cavendish 2007).

[42] ibid 244.

[43] ibid 243.

[44] ibid 229.

concentration of power in one party or entity, and puts community interests at the centre'.[45]

5. Cyberspace is Different

Are we precipitating the conclusions that the responsiveness of the law in ACTA is or, following Mattei, should be, illustrative for all law, and not only information society law? Although the parallelism arouses the interest of the author, Murray opines that responsiveness of the law concerns primarily cyberspace. Murray reaches this conclusion after putting his theory to the test in the Wikileaks case.[46]

Facts of this case are well known. In November 2010 a web site named Wikileaks began to reveal confidential and even secret US government diplomatic cables both via its website and international media. According to Murray, the revelation of confidential cables had seriously violated the right to privacy of state officials. Notwithstanding the blatant violation of a fundamental right, Murray observes that, as a matter of fact, the law could not be enforced and Wikileaks could not be brought to justice.

Indeed, a bank had brought a lawsuit against Wikileaks for revealing confidential information about it. Lodged in the United States, the lawsuit sought to obtain an order of injunction against Wikileaks' domain name registrar 'Dynadot' to halt access to the web address.[47]

The questions arose as of whom to sue. Indeed, as UK newspaper *The Guardian* reported 'people behind Wikileaks include Tibetan, Chinese, and Thai political campaigners, an Australian hacking author, and (...) a mathematician living in West London.' A person representing Wikileaks never showed up in court.[48] The relevant forum and applicable law were difficult to establish. Personal data were gathered in the United States and leaked via servers in Sweden and other countries globally, including in the United States. Outraged cyber activists and free speech groups, such as American

45 Mattei, 'The State, the Market, and some Preliminary Questions' (n 16) 2.

46 Murray, 'Uses and Abuses of Cyberspace' (n 41) 3.

47 *Bank Julius Baer & Co. Ltd. and Julius Baer Bank and Trust Co. LTD v. Wikileaks, Wikileaks. Org and Dynadot LLC* California Northern District Court, filed in on February 6, 2008 Case Number: 3:2008cv00824.

48 David.Leigh and Jonathan. Franklin 'Whistle while you work', *The Guardian* (London, 23 February 2008) Available at: <http://www.guardian.co.uk/theguardian/2008/feb/23/internet.usa/print> accessed 30 June 2012.

Civil Liberties Union (ACLU),[49] defended Wikileaks in court as *amici curiae*, using the First Amendment and *Reno* jurisprudence.[50] The case pending, Wikileaks site had remained online through the support of web users globally, while groups of online activists carried out Distributed Denial of Service Attacks (DDOS) on a number of sites that had attempted to suffocate Wikileaks, including Amazon, PayPal and MasterCard. The injunction, initially granted, was lifted and the applicant bank, voluntarily dropped charges against Wikileaks.

For Murray, the Wikileaks case shows a specificity about legal cooperation in cyberspace that does not apply to real space. Online content cannot be stopped using principles of jurisdiction, domicile and enforcement of rights and duties bordered by one's physical location in space. The ultimate reason may be, he suggests, that cyberspace is essentially a cyberlibertarian terrain. 'Content may just be beyond the direct control of the international legal community, as predicted by the cyberlibertarians, after all', he says.[51]

6. Conclusion

In conclusion, it may not always be possible for lawyers to get their hands on the map. Legal documents do not suffice to organise global legal cooperation in cyberspace because the field is ridden with many communities who react, granting or removing legitimacy and effectiveness. One understands the frustration of the lawyer who, in the Wikileaks case for instance, has to give up because his or her toolbox operates not. One wonders, however, whether frustration is justified at all. There are other regulatory practices than the law, aren't there?

If we understand Murray correctly, responsive law encourages respect for other practices, giving a chance to their unexpected creativity, other than the law's, to come to grips with new events or new needs.[52] Responsiveness of the law is what Murray suggests for cyberspace regulation, at least.

---

49 Application to Appear as Pros Intervenors or Amici Curiae <http://www.aclu.org/files/images/asset_upload_file63_34218.pdf> accessed 31 July 2012.

50 *Reno v. ACLU* [1997] 521 US 844 concerning the trading of forbidden material on the Internet.

51 Murray, 'Uses and Abuses of Cyberspace' (n 41) 3.

52 Serge Gutwirth, Paul de Hert and Laurent de Sutter, 'The trouble with technology regulation from a legal perspective: Why Lessig's 'Optimal Mix' will not work' in Roger Brownsword and Karen Yeung (eds), *Regulating Technologies. Legal Futures, Regulatory Frames and Technological Fixes* (Hart Publishers 2008) 193.

It is probably too bold a pick to hold that the same mechanism of responsiveness will become a general characteristic of global law. We are quite optimistic, but the optimism should be backed by more research. Responsiveness can be triggered by many instruments and practices.

Patrick Goold, in a recent analysis of copyright law, notes that legal scholarship in this more classical area of law is changing.[53] Legal scholars start doing just more than providing normative advice about the law. Because judges and legislators do not listen to academic opinions, academics express themselves, not only through law reviews or similar traditional academic outlets, but through publicly oriented books and social media.

Rather than aim normative advice to lawmakers, scholars give their advice to the public generally. The public then holds the lawmakers accountable for enacting bad laws.

In this way, academics are retaining their position as normative advice givers. Again, we see a crucial role in this development for technology, but the example shows that the impact of it (and responsiveness as a possible result) goes beyond the scope of cyberspace law and touches upon other domains of law.

---

[53] 55 Patrick R Goold, 'The Evolution of Normative Legal Scholarship: An Example from Copyright Discourse (2012) Available at SSRN: <http://ssrn.com/abstract=2077417> or <http://dx.doi.org/10.2139/ssrn.2077417> Accessed 30 July 2012.

The Impact of the Financial Crisis on EU Economic Governance: A Struggle between Hard and Soft Law and Expansion of the EU Competences?

Sonja Bekker[a] & Ivana Palinkas[b]
a) Senior Researcher at Reflect Tilburg University
s.bekker@tilburguniversity.edu
b) PhD candidate at Reflect Tilburg University
i.palinkas@tilburguniversity.edu

Abstract
The EU's crisis response of introducing stricter economic governance has broadened its scope of interference in national policies significantly. This triggers questions on the effectiveness and legitimacy of hard and soft governance in a multi-level setting. Based on two examples the article illustrates the changing role of law in a globalised world and the consequential tensions. It thus provides input to further explore the concept of global law.

Keywords
EU governance; industrial relations; economic governance

The EU is an example of supranational coordination using both hard and soft law methods to steer the coordination of employment and social policies of its member states. However, following the global economic crisis, the EU introduced a stricter regime of policy coordination, by introducing more hard law measures. The new measures are also increasingly mingling with matters of national competences. These new tendencies raise new questions not only about effective and legitimate coordination of economic and social policies, but also about issues of overlapping competences of the authorities within a multilevel system.

This article illustrates two domains of the new expanding tendencies: employment policies being increasingly affected with hard law by the Macroeconomic Imbalances Procedure and collective bargaining traditions becoming affected by the Euro Plus Pact, on the example of Slovakia. It shows how the EU's stricter economic governance creates an awkward balancing-act between uniform supranational ideas and diversified local practices and demands. By explaining these two examples the article aims at allocating possible tension areas within the EU and gives an input for further development of the concept of global law.

1. A Theoretical and Historical Perspective on Soft Law Governance

The emergence of various forms of new governance such as soft law have been analysed as a shift from traditional hierarchical command-and-control regulations.[1] From a sociological point of view, such a shift is necessary to meet the challenges of strongly diversified societies and growing interdependence of actors, which consequently requires more 'horizontal' and 'cooperative' regulations instead of uniform rules.[2] Soft law coordination meets the new demands of dealing with complex issues in complex societies, as it allows for setting joint targets while leaving the precise policy formation to the national level, thus also minding the autonomy of member states in areas such as employment and social policy. The effectiveness of soft law is often explained by mechanisms such as naming & shaming, diffusion through discourse, deliberation between actors, learning, sharing best practices and networking.[3]

The past decades show that global challenges were more than once a reason to seek the improvement of governance structures. In the 1980s, the structurally high unemployment rates across member states eventually

---

[1] J. Lenoble, 'Open Method of Coordination and Theory of Reflexive Governance' in O. De Schutter and S. Deakin, *Social Rights and Market Forces: Is the Open Coordination of Employment and Social Policies the Future of Social Europe?* (Bruylant 2005).

[2] ibid.

[3] For overview of these mechanisms and scholar debate on the nature of soft law policy coordination see: D.M. Trubek and L.G. Trubek, 'The OMC and the debate over "hard" and "soft" law' in J. Zeitlin, P. Pochet and L. Magnussen (eds.), *The Open Method of Co-ordination in Action: The European Employment Strategy and Social Inclusion Strategies* (P.I.E.-Peter Lang 2005); D.M Trubek, P.Cottrell and M. Nance, '"Soft Law," "Hard Law," and European Integration: Toward a Theory of Hybridity' (2005) *University of Wisconsin Legal Studies Research Paper* No. 1002; S. Smismans, 'From hamonization to co-ordination? EU law in the Lisbon governance architecture' (2011) 18 *Journal of European Public Policy* 504-524; J. Zeitlin, P. Pochet and L. Magnussen, *The Open Method of Coordination in Action: The European Employment and Social Inclusions Strategies* (PIE-Peter Lang 2005).

resulted in the development of the European Employment Strategy (EES), which used soft law coordination to steer national employment policies. In the late 1990s, globalisation, fast technological development and the ageing of society, further underlined the need for joint action in important employment and social policy dossiers. The so-called Lisbon Strategy was launched, aiming to convert the EU into the most competitive knowledge economy in the world by 2010.

Although in the end, the Lisbon Strategy failed to reach most of its goals, the EU implemented a follow-up strategy called Europe 2020. The development of the new strategy coincided with the outbreak of the world-wide economic and financial crisis, the severity of which was again a large reason for the EU to seek for joint answers to joint challenges. The EU saw its unemployment rate growing from 7.1% in 2008 to 9.7% in 2011 and youth unemployment exploded in some countries, for instance reaching almost 50% in Spain.[4] Also, the struggle with depths and deficits in some member states impacted the EU's economy as a whole, especially where it concerned Eurozone countries such as Greece and Spain.

2. Response to the Crisis: Stricter Economic Governance

This time around the EU wanted to improve the governance structures by both improving the soft law structure and by introducing more hard law elements. One example is the introduction of the macroeconomic imbalances surveillance in 2011, as part of the Six-Pack legislation. The macroeconomic imbalances surveillance aims at preventing and correcting macroeconomic imbalances in its member states,[5] and accordingly introduces preventive and corrective measures, to make sure that member states keep or regain a sound economic climate. This in the first place involves a scoreboard of indicators acting as an alert system in case of perceived imbalances.

After a scoreboard alert, an independent and in-depth country review will be undertaken. The country review may include employment issues,

---

[4] European Commission, Eurostat data, 'Unemployment statistics until June 2012', at <http://epp.eurostat.ec.europa.eu/statistics_explained/index.php/Unemployment_statistics.> accessed 03 August 2012.

[5] Europa, 'EU Economic governance: a major step forwards' MEMO/11/364, 31 May 2011. Regulation (EU) 1176/2011 of the European Parliament and of the Council on the prevention and correction of macroeconomic imbalances (2011) OJ L306/25.

for instance, taking account of the employment recommendations issued in the scope of the EES (Art. 148 TFEU). The in-depth review may lead to more precise country-specific recommendations, for instance addressing corrective action to counter the excessive imbalance and giving deadlines.

By entering this stage, the member state is in the excessive imbalances procedure (EIP). The member state has to make a plan of action to correct the imbalances. This corrective action plan should also include the economic and social impact of the policy actions.[6] Should the Council approve of the corrective action plan of the member state, it will list recommendations of specific actions and deadlines; otherwise, it can ask the member state to submit a new plan. When assessing the progress of the member states, the Council may adopt a decision establishing non-compliance in combination with recommendations and new deadlines for corrective actions.

For Eurozone countries, the EIP is accompanied with an enforcement mechanism consisting of an interest-bearing deposit,[7] which can be imposed after a member state has failed once to comply with the recommended corrective action. If the member state fails to take corrective action a second time, this interest-bearing deposit can be converted into a fine of up to 0.1% of GDP. Moreover, a sanction can be issued for twice failing to submit a sufficient corrective action plan.

The example shows that stricter economic governance procedures may include employment issues, which by the virtue of EIP become increasingly affected by hard law. The Council seems to be aware of the potential sensitivity of having influence in issues of national sovereignty. It therefore states that while taking preventative actions, it shall fully observe the autonomy of the social partners and their right to collective bargaining and action as anchored in Art. 152 TFEU and Art. 28 of the Charter of Fundamental Rights of the EU. It thus states that it will not affect the right to negotiate, conclude collective agreements or to take collective action.[8]

ETUC nevertheless fears that the Commission seeks new ways to intervene in areas such as collective bargaining and labour market institutions.[9]

---

6 ibid, Regulation (EU) 1176/2011, Article 8.

7 Regulation (EU) 1174/2011 of the European Parliament and of the Council on enforcement measures to correct excessive macroeconomic imbalances in the euro area (2011) OJ L306/8, Article 3.

8 See Regulation 1176/2011, Article 1 and Article 5 (n 5).

9 European Trade Union Confederation, 'Resolution on Economic and Social Governance' Brussels, 13-14 October 2010, at <http://www.etuc.org/a/7769> accessed 03 August 2012.

The EU however explains and justifies the need for integration of policy fields as follows:

> Better EU employment governance and coordination has become essential for at least two reasons. First, labour market participation, unemployment and labour cost play a role in macroeconomic stability, and are taken into consideration in the new regulation on the prevention and correction of macroeconomic imbalances. Second, the crisis has further revealed the interdependence of EU economies and labour markets, underscoring the need to accompany the new economic governance with strengthened coordination of employment and social policies in line with the European Employment Strategy provided for by the Treaty.[10]

It thus seems that hard law coordination has started entering the soft law governance cycle of employment and social policies. This begs important questions concerning the legitimacy of the EU in doing so. The next section develops the second example of the tension between the new EU initiatives and local implementation by exploring the collective bargaining traditions in Slovakia.

3. Decentralisation Pressures and the Case of Slovakia

After the crisis, reaction of world-wide stock exchanges and the budget deficit problems, some EU countries signed the Euro Plus Pact. This Pact, which uses soft law coordination, introduced measures which may have implications for the national systems of collective bargaining, by openly advocating decentralisation of industrial relations,[11] i.e. putting the emphasis of collective bargaining to lower, company level. While the economic rationale for decentralisation is justified by the needs of the companies to cope with economic difficulties more easily, several non-economic arguments raise doubts.

Firstly, from a general perspective, the interference of the EU with the national collective bargaining matters is problematic, since these matters have always been decided upon at the national level and the national social partners are protected by the principle of autonomy. Secondly, the EU does not explain and define in more substantive terms the notion

---

[10] European Commission, 'Communication from the Commission - Towards a job-rich recovery' COM (2012) 173 final, 18 April 2012; 20.

[11] European Council, 'Conclusions of European Council 24/25 March 2011' EUCO 10/1/11, Brussels, 20 April 2011.

of decentralisation, leaving its interpretation unclear. The interpretation is difficult given the variety of degrees, modes and legal regulation of decentralisation in all 27 member states.

In addition, it is also questionable whether further decentralisation is eventually possible for the countries which have already fairly decentralised collective bargaining. Putting the emphasis to lower bargaining levels is a particular issue for those countries which do not have strong structures at higher levels (sectoral or cross-sectoral), as it is the case in the majority of the countries in Central and Eastern Europe. Namely, from the legal point of view, the collective bargaining at the higher levels represents an important safeguard against uncontrolled decentralisation because of setting the rules and points of departure for further negotiations at lower levels. Also, the decentralisation which is not controlled by the virtue of sectoral or cross-sectoral collective agreements provides trade unions with fewer powers to control the state of the labour rights.

An example of the country where, for instance, further decentralisation of collective bargaining would not be possible, without hampering the state of labour rights, is Slovakia. In this country, collective bargaining takes place predominantly at the company level and not all sectors have collective agreements. The organisation of social partners is the weakest at the company level, where the trade union presence is weak, especially in small companies with smaller number of employees.

Slovakia is one of the acceding countries, in which the European Commission has been promoting capacity-building of social partners in the past decade. However, during the period of the economic crisis, the several labour law amendments which were introduced in Slovakia further deteriorated the bargaining position of trade unions. To illustrate, the representation of workers in companies has been made legally difficult by imposing the stricter rules on representativeness. Also, no sectoral agreement has been extended to cover employees in the entire sector since 2009, which is a legal possibility otherwise regularly practiced in the majority of EU-27. The reason for the absence of the extensions is the modification of the legal rules which set the conditions hardly applicable in practice.

These developments implicate that further decentralisation of collective bargaining, without simultaneous increase of trade unions' capacities at all bargaining levels, could deteriorate the state of labour standards in Slovakia. Unfortunately, this concern was not perceived by the EU when prescribing decentralisation, which may have negative consequences for the workers' standards in the countries with similar collective bargaining issues as this country.

4. Conclusion

The EU's soft law governance methods fit the theoretical assumption that the most effective governance method should set EU level targets in response to joint actions while leaving ample room for member states to work out tailor-made policies. The effectiveness of soft law methods of governance is nevertheless coloured by various tensions, as it, for instance, does not always obtain the desired result. As a response to the global crisis, the EU developed stricter economic governance with more hard law aspects. The two examples in this article illustrate that these initiatives partly act in contradiction with the theoretical notions of soft law steering, as they may prescribe to member states how to act in too much detail.

Via the backdoor of economic governance the EU moreover enters domains of national sovereignty, such as unemployment, labour cost and wage bargaining. The EU pressure for collective bargaining decentralisation for instance triggers the re-definition of the relationship between national and EU-sphere of competences. This raises questions concerning legitimacy and effectiveness of these new EU initiatives. Can the EU indeed impose employment policies on member states? And is this the most effective way of intervention? Or does the EU need to take better into account the specific situation in member states, as the Slovakian example shows?

www.ingramcontent.com/pod-product-compliance
Lightning Source LLC
Chambersburg PA
CBHW070909230926
51613CB00013B/151